SPEAKING THE GOSPEL THROUGH THE AGES

SPEAKING THE GOSPEL THROUGH THE AGES

A History
of Evangelism

Milton L. Rudnick

Publishing House
St. Louis

Copyright © 1984—Concordia Publishing House
3558 South Jefferson Avenue, St. Louis, MO 63118
Manufactured in the United States of America

Library of Congress Cataloging in Publication Data

Rudnick, Milton L.
    Speaking the Gospel through the ages.

    1. Evangelistic work—History. I. Title.
BV3770.R83 1984   269'.2'09   83-15157
ISBN 0-570-04204-6

---

1 2 3 4 5 6 7 8 9 10 PP 93 92 91 90 89 88 87 86 85 84

To Rich

Contents

Preface

From the very beginning in various ways Christians have tried to make Christians of others, often with remarkable success. In many cases their goal was the personal conversion of the non-Christian, his vital incorporation into the worshiping and serving community, and the transformation of his conduct according to Christian standards.

However, in other cases Christians were satisfied, at least initially, to relate others only externally to Christ and the church. Frequently this latter approach was followed, sooner or later, by efforts to bring such nominal Christians to authentic faith and obedience.

The term "evangelism" in this study is used in a rather broad sense to refer to these numerous and diverse processes by which people have tried to Christianize others.

Closely related in form and spirit to these efforts to reach outsiders are recurring movements to revitalize and redirect negligent Christians. Recruitment for renewal was often pursued as intensively as recruitment for affiliation and conversion. The attitudes of the recruiter, the methodologies employed and the experiences of those approached in these efforts are strikingly similar to those in the evangelism of non-Christians. In fact, the same movements frequently address candidates for renewal as well as candidates for conversion. Consequently, as the term is used in this study, evangelism also refers to these efforts to lead Christians to a more earnest and active response.

The subject of this book may be distinguished from two related topics. This history of evangelism differs from a history of missions in that it does not cover the worldwide expansion of Christianity. Rather, it concentrates on representative processes of Christianization employed at various times and places. Furthermore, it also differs from the history of Christian nurture. The evangelism for renewal considered here is that which seeks a rather dramatic and radical change. Christian nurture, on the other hand, may be understood as the ordinary preaching and teaching of the church designed to change Christians gradually, or even merely to sustain them against the impact of affliction and temptation.

This book is an examination of the recurring impulse of Christians to share their perception of Jesus Christ with other people so that they too might belong to Him or respond to Him more appropriately. It examines their motives, the content of their message, their strategy and methodology, as well as the consequences of their work. In addition, it attempts to discern the extent to which evangelism has been shaped by the cultural context in which it has taken place. The scope of the study is broad, covering the entire Christian era. The focus is relatively narrow, concentrating specifically on the evangelistic impulse, its expression and results. Limitations of time and space have made it necessary to treat the subject briefly and selectively. In no sense is this a comprehensive or definitive work. It attempts to bring together from the best available sources what historians have learned about the evangelistic experience of Christians down through the ages.

The purpose of this historical review and analysis of Christian evangelism is, first of all, to provide historical perspective. In order to understand and appreciate contemporary evangelistic efforts and ideas, it is essential to be acquainted with their roots and earlier counterparts. Second, the history of evangelism can provide the basis for both inspiration and caution. Like all history, that of evangelism is a combination of the beautiful and the ugly, truth and error. We need to come to terms with both aspects. From the positive side of the record we can find encouragement to meet the evangelistic challenges of our day. From the negative we can be alerted to mistakes and abuses that can easily creep into our own evangelistic efforts.

As is so often the case, this book has grown out of teaching experiences. For several years I have been teaching a course on the history of evangelism to students preparing for professional evangelism ministry. In connection with that assignment I learned to my dismay that there is no survey of the history of evangelism in print. Michael Green has produced an excellent work which covers the first three centuries, *Evangelism in the Early Church*. Paulus Scharppf's *The History of Evangelism* has been out of print for some time.

There are a number of useful studies of revivalism and revivalists. There are histories of Christian expansion, of which Kenneth Scott Latourette's five-volume work, *A History of the Expansion of Christianity*, is the most notable, while Stephen Neill's *A History of Christian Missions*, is one of the more distinguished one-volume surveys. But no one, to my knowledge, has done something comparable with the history of evangelism. This modest work is an attempt to begin to fill this gap in the literature.

At the time of this writing there is a clear resurgence of evangelistic interest and activity in many parts of the Christian world. It is too early to assess the potential or even the direction in which this wave is moving. There are serious disagreements among Christians about what the evangelistic task is—especially the relationship between proclamation and social involvement.

Of the powerful forces in the world opposing or competing with Christianity, secularism and communism are among the most obvious. What appears to be the beginning of a new era of Christian outreach, growth, and renewal may turn out to be one of stagnation or decline. But, if the history of Christianity in general and of evangelism in particular teaches anything, it is that the expansive and revitalizing forces within Christendom are remarkably strong and stubborn. More than once the impulse to share Christ has recurred, persisted and even exploded despite persecution, controversy, or widespread apathy and apostasy.

Hopefully, better acquaintance with the Christian past through a study such as this will contribute in some small way to a mounting awareness of and commitment to the evangelistic commission of the church as well as more effective fulfillment of that commission.

The reader is entitled to know the author's basic beliefs and opinions as they relate to the subject under consideration. I believe that apart from faith in Christ people are lost and under the wrath of God. I believe that saving faith itself is the gift and work of God, that the Holy Spirit creates this faith through the Gospel, whether in the form of proclamation or Holy Baptism (in the case of infants). Furthermore, I believe that authentic renewal is also a work of God. The Gospel is the offer of God's love, forgiveness, and newness of life through the redemptive life, death, and resurrection of His divine-human Son, Jesus Christ. Acts of Christian love and social responsibility are essential results of faith in the Gospel. In addition, they prepare for the Gospel—they help to make people receptive to the Gospel; however, they are not the Gospel itself. The Gospel is always and only the message of what God has done to rescue condemned sinners from His wrath and to make new persons out of them. From this it is evident that in the debate about the relative importance of proclamation and social involvement I stand with those who give priority to proclamation. I reject universalism and synergism.

However important it is for a historian to reveal his bias, it is even more important that he attempt to control that bias as he gathers his information, and as he organizes, analyzes, and interprets it. My goal in this book is to deal fairly with individuals and movements at all points of the evangelistic spectrum. Strength and weakness, faithfulness and neglect, wisdom and foolishness are recorded and evaluated regardless of my personal affinity to the parties involved.

Evangelism to me is more than an academic interest. Ten years of my pastoral ministry were spent in congregations that were responding with vigor and success to awesome evangelistic challenges. More recently I have been coordinating a professional program at the college level that prepares people for full-time evangelism ministry. In connection with this assignment I am in daily contact with a remarkable group of students whose evangelistic gifts, commitments, and experiences keep me very close to the action. In addition, I have contact with congregations throughout the North American continent where exciting evangelism is happening. Furthermore, I have the privilege of associating with ecclesiastical and academic evangelism leaders of various faiths.

My ongoing interest and involvement in evangelism is combined with a deep love for church history. This was my major field of graduate study. Among the scholars with whom I worked most closely were Jaroslav Pelikan and Carl S. Meyer. For the past 18 years I have been teaching primarily in the field of church history. It is especially interesting and gratifying to me to be able to bring evangelism and church history together in this present work.

I have had the benefit of much encouragement and support. Administrators, colleagues, and students at Concordia College, St. Paul, Minnesota have been most considerate. Karen Barnes, who typed and revised the manuscript on the word processor, was exceptionally accommodating. Members of my family were patient and loving. Financial assistance enabling me to be relieved of some teaching responsibilities was generously provided by Mr. Andrew Duda Jr. and the members of the Duda family of Oneida, Florida. I am sincerely grateful to all.

Milton L. Rudnick
Saint Paul, Minnesota

1/Evangelism Under Pressure: The Early Period
(to A.D. 500)

During the first five centuries of its existence the Christian church experienced spectacular growth. Numerically it increased from about 4,000 followers after Jesus' resurrection to 43.4 million nominal adherents representing 22.4 percent of the world population early in the sixth century. Geographically it extended from its starting point in Palestine to all parts of the Roman Empire and beyond.[1]

Although there were factors in the situation that favored growth, there was also formidable resistance. Religious, cultural, and political opposition culminated in episodes of devastating persecution. Doctrinal controversies and jurisdictional disputes were disruptive within the Christian community and confusing to those without. Enervating apathy and worldliness periodically set in.

Nevertheless, growth continued. Despite pressures and setbacks Christians continued to reach out and expand. In a variety of ways and out of diverse motives they managed to attract people to Jesus Christ. In this chapter we examine the amazing progress of early Christian evangelism as it was carried out under pressure.

External Factors Aiding Evangelism

Roman Peace

A number of external factors facilitated the spread and acceptance of this new faith. For the first (and only) time in history the entire Mediterranean basin was under the control of one government—that of Rome—and it was an effective government. People complained about Roman rule. It was costly and could be very severe. However, it maintained order and peace at unprecedented levels, built and policed a marvelous system of roads throughout the empire, and guarded the sea lanes against pirates. Consequently, people could travel freely throughout that vast region, exchanging merchandise and ideas.

Graeco-Roman Culture

As a result, alongside of or overarching the distinctive cultures of each nation and people within the empire, there was a significant and growing culture that many held in common, usually designated as Graeco-Roman. It consisted of the art, literature, philosophy, and religion of the ancient Greeks as appropriated and modified by their Roman conquerors.

Greek Language

One aspect of this culture that greatly aided the growth of Christianity was the widespread use of the Greek language. A measure of the Romans' admiration of Greek culture was their adoption of the Greek language throughout much of the empire as a medium, not only of learning, but also of business. This meant that in any major urban center of the empire people of different nations and tongues could communicate in Greek. Christian evangelists during this early period had a great advantage over many of their later counterparts in that they did not have to contend with a serious language barrier.

Rational Moralistic Monotheism

The direction in which Graeco-Roman culture was moving was favorable to the spread of Christianity. By the dawn of the Christian era the religious and philosophical thought of that civilization had for centuries been shifting toward a rational and moralistic monotheism. Ancient pagan polytheistic religions with their capricious and malicious deities were losing credibility under the impact of rationalistic Greek philosophy. From a variety of sources a consensus was forming that there is one controlling element or principle of the universe rather than many, that it is rational rather than arbitrary and erratic, and that it is moral, devoted to the good, rather than predatory and vindictive. In these respects, at least, the God of the Christians conformed to the notions and expectations of many first-century people.

Logos

One widely used philosophical term expressive of this trend is "*logos*," the Greek term meaning either "reason" or one of reason's chief products—"word." *Logos* was closely identified with God both by Aristotle and the Stoics. The latter understood it as the divine element through which all things were created and controlled and which is part of every human being. This concept became a bridge between Greek philosophy and Christianity. The Johannine literature of the New Testament, as well as some early Christian fathers, used *Logos* to refer to Jesus Christ.

Mystery Religions

Other religious developments in the Roman world also engendered openness to the Christian message. The eastern mystery religions became widespread and well established during the second and third centuries. They were diverse in origin and content—Cybele from Asia Minor; Dionysus from Greece; Isis, Osiris and Serapis from Egypt; Mithras from Persia. However, they were similar in that all were mythical personifications of the cycles of nature; all featured dying, rising gods; all included rites comparable to Baptism and the Lord's Supper; all offered cleansing from sin and immortality through union with gods. To people familiar with these religions the crucified and risen Savior of the Christians did not seem as strange as He otherwise might have.

Judaism of the Dispersion

Judaism of the dispersion was undoubtedly the most significant religious development which opened doors for the Christian message. By the first century, Jews were a sizable and conspicuous minority throughout the empire. They had been scattered far and wide from Palestine during the pre-Christian era both as prisoners of war and in connection with business ventures. Estimates vary, but they probably constituted seven to 10 percent of the population—not much less than the black minority in the United States in the latter part of the 20th century. Wherever they went Jews established synagogues and to these synagogues many Gentiles were drawn. Judaism of the dispersion (outside Palestine) was less separatistic and ritualistic and was more eager to win converts than that of the homeland. Worship was conducted in Greek. It centered in the reading and discussion of the Jewish Scriptures in Greek translation. Compared with pagan religions and philosophies, the lofty moralistic monotheism of the Jews was very impressive. Some Gentiles were fully integrated into Judaism by way of circumcision and acceptance of the dietary and ceremonial obligations which in modified forms also were part of dispersion Judaism. Many more Gentiles, without going that far, accepted the doctrine and moral standards of Judaism, worshipped in the synagogues, and were informally attached to those religious communities. It was these God-fearing Gentiles who responded most readily to the preaching of Paul and other early evangelists. Judaism became an avenue through which large numbers of Gentiles moved into Christianity.

Legalization and Favor

Surprisingly, early in the fourth century Christianity was granted legal status as a result of Emperor Constantine's conversion (312). Before long Christianity was favored above all other religions in the empire. By the end of the century it was the only legal religion—both paganism and heresy were being repressed. This change in status brought in a great flood of converts. Fear of persecution, which had discouraged all but the most earnest inquirers, was gone. It was now safe, even advantageous, to be a Christian.

Pressures Opposing Early Evangelism

Even more striking than the factors that facilitated the spread of Christianity were the awesome forces standing in its way. Evangelism, during most of this early period, was done under great pressure, not only from Judaism, the parent religion of Christianity, but also from certain elements in Graeco-Roman culture and, above all, from the Roman government itself. For two and a half centuries the Roman colossus tried with increasing intensity to repress and even to crush the Christian movement.

Jewish Antagonism

From the very outset Christian evangelism was threatened and impeded by the Jewish religious establishment. Shortly after Pentecost the same authorities who had conspired against Jesus had Peter and John arrested for proclaiming Jesus and the resurrection. For this first offense the apostles were only warned and released (Acts 4:1-18). However, later clashes with Jewish authorities proved to be more painful and costly. Not long afterward, Peter and the apostles were imprisoned, only to be miraculously released (Acts 5:12-21). Stephen, one of the seven men chosen to assist with the distribution of food, became active in evangelism and was executed as a result (Acts 6 and 7). Under the leadership of Saul of Tarsus a great persecution was carried out against Christians in Jerusalem, causing many to flee to more remote areas of Judea and Samaria (Acts 8:1-3). With the support of the hierarchy in Jerusalem, Saul was determined to extend the persecution all the way to Damascus in Syria

(Acts 9:1-2). To please the Jews, Herod Agrippa beheaded James, the brother of John, and also seized Peter (Acts 12:1-4).

After Saul was converted and began his evangelistic tours, he encountered recurring and severe opposition from some elements of the Jewish religious community. Paul (Saul's Roman name) customarily began his evangelistic work in the Jewish synagogue. As a Jew thoroughly trained in Scripture, he was often invited to comment on the Scripture reading. In his commentary he would proclaim Jesus as the promised Savior, who by His death and resurrection provided pardon from sin and liberation from the tyranny of the Law. In city after city, after an initial welcome, Paul was rejected by most Jewish leaders and their congregations and hounded out of their cities. This happened not only in Galatia and Asia but also in Macedonia and Achaia (Acts 13—14, 17—19). When Paul returned to Jerusalem he encountered a particularly violent reaction from the Jews. He was taken into protective custody by Roman authorities and kept there for several years, during which time there were several assassination plots against him (Acts 20:17; 25:5).

Jewish antagonism against Christianity remained aggressive for a century and a half after Paul. They are said to have incited Nero against the Christians at Rome in A.D. 64. In what is now called Asia Minor, at the end of the first century during the persecution related to emperor worship, some Jews apparently accused Christians before the Roman authorities (Rev. 2:9; 3:9). On the occasion of Polycarp's martyrdom (ca. 165) the Jews gathered wood for his burning. During the Severan persecution in Rome (A.D. 202), Jews united with pagans in committing atrocities against Christians. Both Tertullian and Origen, writing in the early third century, complain about the relentless enmity of the Jews.[2]

It is not difficult to understand why Jews were antagonistic against Christianity. Christians claimed that Jesus, whom Jewish authorities had crucified, was the Messiah. If this was true, these authorities and the whole religious establishment was guilty of a horrible mistake and was thoroughly discredited. Furthermore, a large and rapidly growing segment of the population of Jerusalem—20,000 or more—had joined the Christian movement within a few short years after Pentecost.

Still more threatening were the fundamental claims of the Christians over against Judaism. They, the Christians, were the new Israel. All Jewish history and institutions were fulfilled in Jesus. Through Him and His followers God's revelatory and redemptive work was to be offered to all nations. All who believed in Jesus were incorporated into the new people of God, the new Israel. Whoever rejected Jesus, including Jews, were condemned. No longer did Jews have a favored status. By faith in Jesus, Gentiles were fully acceptable to God.

The implications of this for Jewish religious life were staggering. Judaism had been transcended. Its traditions, its culture, its leadership, its very identity could easily be swept away by the size and the claims of the swelling Christian movement. Fear and outrage at such prospects exacerbated Jewish antagonism.

Other key elements of the Christian message were also deeply offensive to Jews. The concept of plurality within the Godhead, which followed inevitably from belief in Jesus' deity, violated the radical monotheism of Judaism. The teaching of salvation by grace alone ran counter to the essentially works-oriented theology of Judaism and appeared to discourage moral effort. That God would join the human race and submit Himself to punishment and death seemed, to Jews, to be unworthy of Him and inconsistent with His majesty. Since Christianity began as a movement within Judaism, it was only natural that it be evaluated by Jewish criteria. When it was judged by the authorities to be false and dangerous, antagonism and even persecution were inevitable.

Greek Skepticism

Although some elements in Greek culture seemed to pave the way for the Christian Gospel, others offered resistance. For one thing, Greeks thought of truth in terms of universals. Plato and those who followed his thought saw reality in terms of eternal and universal ideas or patterns, of which particular material objects are poor and dim replicas. Christianity, on the other hand, located ultimate truth and wisdom in one specific historical person, Jesus Christ, and particular events in His life and experience. In addition, Greeks were repelled by the newness of Christianity. To them only that which was ancient could be true. Furthermore, the cross as the supreme expression of religious truth was regarded as absurd because it was a death without honor and dignity. In general, Greek intellectuals were contemptuous of the cultural inferiority of most Christians. Why should they take seriously the truth claims of people who, for the most part, were unsophisticated and unlettered?

Besides intellectual objections of this kind, people immersed in Graeco-Roman culture were put off by some of Christianity's religious and ethical demands. The exclusiveness of Christianity was particularly galling. Other religions of the empire, except for Judaism, recognized one another's validity and approved of simultaneous adherence to several or many religions. Christianity, on the other hand, demanded exclusive and undivided religious loyalty. To make matters worse, Christianity denounced all other religions as false. This seemed incredibly arrogant and intolerant to the Greek mind. Not as offensive but, nevertheless, discouraging were the strict moral demands that Christianity made upon converts. Again, except for Judaism, this was virtually unknown in the Graeco-Roman world. Some philosophies, notably Stoicism, were concerned about morality at least in theory, but religions, generally, did not make stringent moral demands upon their adherents.

Finally, Christian social withdrawal was a problem for many. On religious and ethical grounds Christians refused to participate in certain social and recreational activities that were extremely popular. They would not attend the theaters or the games because the performances were often indecent and brutal. They would not serve as magistrates or in the military because this required the taking of human life. Non-Christians recognized this withdrawal as an indictment of their institutions and behaviors and naturally resented this. People who otherwise might have been drawn to Christianity hesitated to give up exciting and socially important activities or government service, which would incur the resentment of their fellow citizens.

Roman Persecution

Certainly the greatest deterrent to evangelism in the early period (although it also provided marvelous opportunities) was the persecution of Christianity by the Roman state. For almost 250 years Christians lived and witnessed under the threat of severe government sanctions or mob violence on account of their faith. Most persecutions were local and sporadic. However, there were two general and sustained efforts to stamp out the Christian movement.

In some cases it was primarily their relation to Judaism that got Christians into trouble. Christianity was from the outset a movement within Judaism, and it made its initial growth outside Palestine through the synagogues of dispersion Judaism. Even the first Gentile converts were people who first of all had been attracted to the God and the faith of the Jews and were related formally or informally to the Jewish religious community. In the minds of most people in the Roman world the earliest Christians were a Jewish sect.

There were definite advantages to this. As an ancient and established religion, the official religion of a people incorporated into the empire, Judaism had legal status. That is to say, adherents of this religion were permitted to practice it, not only in their own land, but throughout the empire, provided that their rites were not offensive to the

Roman people or their gods. They were even permitted to proselytize. However, they were not to make converts of Roman citizens. This did not constitute a serious obstacle, since only a relatively small percentage of Roman subjects possessed citizenship until late in the second century, and the law against proselytizing citizens was not consistently enforced. Until the 60s of the first century, when the break with Judaism became final, Christianity enjoyed the privileges and protections granted to its parent religion. This included exemption from the requirement of worshiping the traditional Roman gods and even the emperor. In a remarkable show of tolerance, Romans respected Jewish objections to these practices and allowed them instead to pray for the emperor and his realm to their own God and in their own way.

However, there were more than a few instances in which association with the Jews became the primary cause for Christian persecution. Anti-Semitism intensified in the eastern Mediterranean world after the Maccabean revolution (167—142 B.C.). This conflict, as religious as it was political, increased hostility toward Jews and marked the Jews as a fanatical minority whose fierce commitment to independence posed a threat to the general welfare. Recurring Jewish revolts after Rome became dominant spread anti-Semitism to the west and led not only to counterrevolutionary measures but to persecutions of Jews. Because they were regarded as a sect of Judaism, Christians were sometimes caught in these persecutions. When confronted with outbreaks of violent anti-Semitism, Jews would sometimes divert the hostility to the despised Christian element, which Gentiles still regarded in some sense as part of Judaism. This appears to have been the case in the Neronian, Domitian and Severan persecutions, as well as those in Lyons and Vienne. What began as pogroms against the Jews ended as Christian persecution.[3]

The association with Judaism was not the only cause of Roman persecution. Although the evidence is not altogether conclusive, it seems clear that Rome opposed Christianity as a threat to the state. A fundamental and enduring conviction of the Romans was that the remarkable growth and success of their empire was the result of faithfulness to their traditional gods. The converse was also widely believed: neglect of the Roman gods or offense of the gods would lead to ruin and failure of the state. What the gods required was not love or trust or moral earnestness, but outward respect and worship. By the end of the first century, worship of the traditional gods was augmented by the cult of emperor worship. The emperor was regarded as the embodiment of all that made Rome great. Not as a rival to the gods but as their underlord, he, his genius, and his image were to be worshiped. To the average subject this was more like patriotism than religion, but it was encouraged and, ultimately, required.

Christians could not, in clear conscience, worship the Roman gods or the emperor. As the Christian movement grew, this meant that an ever larger segment of the population was no longer giving the required recognition of or veneration to the gods. Consequently, the gods were certain to retaliate. From the Roman point of view, this could be seen in the foreign powers that were a growing threat to imperial security as well as in the grave social, economic, and political problems developing within the empire. As the Christian era progressed, conditions grew worse and the collapse of the empire appeared imminent. Critics of Christianity charged it with responsibility for these problems. Not only did Christians personally abstain from the practice of Roman religion, they also encouraged others to do the same. What was worse, they denounced the Roman gods as nonexistent or even as demons and held that only their God is God. Also ominous to the Romans was the development of an empire-wide network of Christian congregations, a large and powerful institution whose purposes could be regarded as nothing less than subversive.

Lacking legal status because of their break with Judaism and regarded as irreligious in a way that endangered the Roman state, Christians were vulnerable to arrest and prosecution by the government. This could happen to Christians anytime and anywhere. However, for the first two centuries of Christian history the government took such action only occasionally and in certain places.

Most early persecutions were initiated, not by the government, but by hostile mobs. Anti-Christian sentiment among the populace was fed not only by the factors mentioned above but also by false suspicions of gross misconduct on the part of Christians. A misunderstanding of the Lord's Supper led to accusations of cannibalism. Christian meetings held secretly late at night—including participants of both sexes—led to charges of sexual immorality. Christians had condemned the cruelty and immorality of much public entertainment in their society. Others were eager to accuse them of clandestine offenses even more reprehensible.

In various parts of the empire antipathy against Christians would erupt periodically as mob violence and as accusation before the authorities. Before A.D. 250 the authorities did not often go out after the Christians, but if they were reported by enemies and if they refused to renounce their faith, the Christians were punished, usually with death.

There were two decades of intensive and extensive persecution. Imperial edicts enforced throughout the empire were designed to stamp out Christianity or at least effectively to suppress it. The first of these (250—259) was initiated by Emperor Decius and continued with some interruption by his successors. Christian leaders were arrested and church properties confiscated. All free inhabitants of the empire, including women and children, were required to sacrifice to the Roman deities, pour a libation to them and eat some sacrificial meat. Those who refused were put to death. The purpose of the decree was not only to identify and persecute Christians but to unite all subjects in the worship of the Roman gods. This was part of the emperor's broader program to unify his people against the internal and external threats to the state. The impact upon Christianity was devastating. Large numbers apostatized. However, enough were faithful even in the face of torture and death to insure survival of the movement and even, by their steadfastness, to attract new converts.

There was a respite of 44 years between the end of the Decian persecution and the beginning of the last great persecution, that initiated by Emperor Diocletian and continued intermittently by his successors (303—311). The purpose was to restore the greatness and glory of the Roman people under the Roman gods. In order to do this, the emperor began by eliminating Christians from the armed forces and government service. This was followed by the burning of Christian churches and their Scriptures, and the arrest of Christian leaders who were forced either to sacrifice to the Roman gods or face imprisonment. Initially, the death penalty was not employed. Ultimately, under Diocletian's successors all citizens were compelled either to sacrifice or to suffer torture, death, or a life sentence of forced labor in the mines.

Once again, many Christians defected under the pressure of persecution. However, far more courage and constancy were apparent at this time than during the Decian persecution. Thousands died horribly rather than deny their Lord, and others continued to confess Christ despite extreme torture. In several instances Christian groups were militantly defiant. Although fear of persecution doubtless discouraged many prospective converts, others were so deeply impressed by the steadfastness of Christian martyrs and confessors that they accepted the faith themselves. Conversions were stimulated by the persecution that was designed to crush Christianity. The persecution came to an end in 311 when ailing Emperor Galerius issued an edict granting amnesty to Christians; in return, Christians were asked to pray for his recovery. Following the conversion of Emperor Constantine in 312 Christianity was granted legal toleration and moved from there, during the course of the fourth century, to a position of favor and dominance.

Doctrinal Controversies

Quite a different kind of obstacle to early Christian evangelism was the series of controversies that disturbed and divided the church during this era. It is beyond the scope of this study to discuss these controversies in any detail. Rather, the purpose here is to indicate the manner in which they may have exercised an inhibiting effect upon some who otherwise might have responded to Christian outreach. According to Jesus, the unity among His followers would commend Him and His faith to the world (John 17:21). Disputes and divisions among Christians would understandably have the opposite effect. Porphyry, for example, writing late in the third century, claimed that disagreement between Peter and Paul proved that their message was not from heaven.[4] The anonymous author of 2 *Clement*, writing in the mid-second century, denounced his fellow Christians for their loveless bickering and noted the disenchanting effect that this had upon some who initially had been drawn to Christianity by its beautiful message of love.[5] Celsus reveals his disdain for the discord among Christians and the resulting divisions.[6]

The list of major Christian doctrinal controversies during the first five centuries is long. Among the groups regarded as dangerously false were: Judaizers, Docetists, Gnostics, Marcionists, Montanists, Monarchians, Novatianists, Donatists, Arians, Nestorians, and Monophysites. Among the issues disputed were the necessity of observing Jewish traditions, the humanity of Christ, the deity of Christ, continuing revelation, the relation of God to the material universe, the relation of the divine and the human in the person of Christ, recovery from serious sin and the validity of sacraments administered by unworthy clergy. In addition, there were disruptive disagreements over the date of Easter, during which the bishop of Rome excommunicated several eastern bishops. Without exception these controversies were conducted with a considerable amount of bitterness and vindictiveness. Ecclesiastical and imperial politics figured prominently. Arrogance and personal ambition reared their ugly heads frequently. In all of this critics and enemies of Christianity found ample material for their attacks. Even those who found Christianity appealing in other respects were at times alienated by the chronic contentiousness of Christians.

It is impossible to measure the negative impact of these controversies. In all likelihood it was considerable. Not only did they tend to discredit the church in the eyes of the world, but they also resulted in painful and debilitating divisions.

However, there were also some very positive consequences. The challenge of dissent and heresy forced Christians to rethink their faith and to research Scripture intensively on the controverted issues. As a result they were able to understand and articulate the Christian message with greater clarity, consistency, and accuracy than before. The church emerged from the controversies with renewed confidence in the correctness of its teachings, which is a vital aspect of the evangelistic spirit.

The Expansive Character of Early Evangelism

Christianity is not the only evangelistic religion. As mentioned above, Judaism of the first century was remarkably zealous in its outreach. Jesus commented that the scribes and Pharisees would traverse sea and land to make a single proselyte (Matt. 23:15). Judaism of the dispersion was even more active in this respect than the Palestinian Judaism to which Jesus referred.[7] Gnostics and Manichaeans, early rivals of Christianity, were also eager to share their faith. Islam, beginning early in the seventh century, has also displayed the urge to win converts from time to time. However, the inclination of the early Christians to reach out with their faith, their desire to share with others what God had done for them in Jesus Christ, was qualitatively and quantitatively different from anything with which it might be compared.

The Impulse to Share

From the very beginning people who encountered Jesus were moved to tell others about Him. The shepherds on Christmas eve, after visiting the child's manger-bed, joyfully and spontaneously shared with others what the angel had told them about Him and, presumably, also what they had seen out in the field and in the stable (Luke 2:8-19). Forty days later, the elderly prophetess, Anna, after recognizing Jesus at His presentation ceremony in the temple, "spoke of Him to all who were looking for the redemption of Jerusalem" (Luke 2:38).

When Jesus was about to launch His public ministry, John the Baptist, informed by divine revelation, bore witness to Him as the Lamb of God. In response to this, two of John's disciples began to follow Jesus. One of them, Andrew, immediately found his brother, Simon Peter, and brought him to Jesus. The very next day, after Jesus personally recruited Philip, that new disciple found his friend Nathaniel and told him about Jesus (John 1:35-51). The woman of Samaria who came to know Jesus at the well of Sychar went back into the city and told her fellow townspeople about Him and His messianic deeds (John 4:28-30). Levi, the tax-collector, upon his conversion, made a great feast for Jesus creating an occasion in which he could introduce Jesus to a large group of his fellow sinners (Luke 5:29).

After Jesus healed the man with an unclean spirit during synagogue worship, His fame spread everywhere throughout the surrounding region (Mark 1:28). The leper whom Jesus healed disregarded the command not to say anything about the miracle and instead began to talk freely about it (Mark 1:44-45).

The invalid whom Jesus healed at the pool of Bethsaida told the Jews what Jesus had done (John 5:15). All of Judea was talking about Jesus' raising the young man of Nain (Luke 7:17). The Gerasene demoniac, after his miraculous cure, began to proclaim how much Jesus had done for him (Mark 5:20). Those who witnessed the raising of Jairus' daughter sent the report of that amazing event through the district (Matt. 9:26). The two blind men whose eyes Jesus opened spread His fame far and wide (Mark 7:32-37). Spectators to Jesus' healing of the deaf-mute insisted on publicizing this act despite Jesus' prohibition (Mark 7:36). The crowd that was present when Jesus raised Lazarus from the dead bore witness to Him, thus swelling the multitude at the Palm Sunday procession (John 12:17-18).

Especially notable is that the testimonies relating to these events were unsolicited and even irrepressible. Some people were so impressed by Jesus personally, what He was like, what He said and did, that they could not resist telling others about Him. That His miracles would evoke this reaction is not surprising. However, His presence and His words had the same affect upon people, as the first group of references given above make clear. To come into contact with Jesus and to gain even a partial awareness of who He was and what He could do was to feel the impulse to share Him with other people.

The impulse to share the Good News of Jesus was reinforced by the command to share. John the Baptist, even before his conception, was designated as the one who, by his witness, would prepare the way for Jesus (Luke 1:17). On the day of his circumcision this divinely assigned role was reaffirmed (Luke 3:15-18; John 1:19-35). The command to share is also implied in Jesus' words to Simon Peter when He called him to discipleship after the great catch of fish: "Henceforth you will be catching men" (Luke 5:10).

As His ministry progressed Jesus appointed 12 of His followers to go out and preach and cast out demons (Mark 3:13-19a). Sometime later He actually dispatched them on a brief tour of duty (Matt. 10:5-15). In His parting instructions He warned them of the hostility they would meet, and He assured them that the Holy Spirit would aid them in difficult witness situations. The importance of sharing the Gospel even in the face of persecution and the danger of their apostatizing was explained in no uncertain terms: "So everyone who acknowledges Me before men, I also will acknowledge before My Father who is in heaven; but whoever denies Me before men, I also will deny before My Father who is in heaven" (Matt. 10:16-33).

On another occasion Jesus appointed and sent out 70 followers to proclaim the kingdom and heal the sick. From the context it is clear that the agent of the kingdom is Christ Himself; He is the divine King come into the world to restore God's saving and transforming rule in the hearts of people (Luke 10:1-24). In connection with His discourse on the signs of the close of the age, spoken days before His death, Jesus reiterated His warning that for His sake they would be dragged before hostile authorities. This should be recognized as an opportunity for witness, He told them, and He Himself would supply the words (Luke 21:12-15).

The closer He came to the cross, the more explicitly He referred to their responsibility and resources for sharing the Gospel. In the upper room He promised that the Holy Spirit would help them to remember and communicate His Word (John 14:25-26; 16:7-11), and He reminded them that they were to be His witnesses (John 15:27). In Jesus' high priestly prayer to the Father on that same occasion, He said that He had given His people God's Word and sent them into the world. Through their sharing of the Word others would believe in Him (John 17:6-20). On Easter evening He stated directly, "As the Father has sent Me, even so I send you" (John 20:21).

However, it was after the resurrection that the command to tell was expressed most emphatically. The angel told the women at the empty tomb to tell the disciples that Jesus had risen from the dead (Matt. 28:7). On Easter evening Jesus told the startled assembly that repentance and forgiveness of sins should be preached in His name to all nations beginning from Jerusalem. "You are witnesses of these things" (Luke 24:46-48). From the mountain in Galilee He gave the Great Commission, "Go therefore and make disciples of all nations, baptizing them in the name of the Father and of the Son and of the Holy Spirit, teaching them to observe all that I have commanded you; and, lo, I am with you always, to the close of the age" (Matt. 28:16-20). Finally, at the ascension, the command was repeated yet another time, "You shall be my witnesses in Jerusalem and in all Judea and Samaria and to the end of the earth" (Acts 1:8).

Pentecost triggered marvelous expressions of the impulse to share. All 120 believers who were filled with the Holy Spirit on that day began to speak to the assembled multitude about the mighty works of God in Christ (Acts 2:1-12). Peter and John, shortly thereafter, preached Jesus

Christ not only in the temple (Acts 3), but also before the very council that had condemned Him. When that council forbade them to speak or teach in Jesus' name, they replied, "We can not but speak of what we have seen and heard" (Acts 4:20). Further arrests and punishments by the authorities were also completely unsuccessful in squelching their proclamation (Acts 5). During the persecution that followed Stephen's martyrdom, the believers were scattered throughout Judea, Samaria, Phonecia, Cyprus and Antioch. Wherever they went they preached the Word (Acts 8:4; 11:19). Cornelius the centurion called his kinsmen and close friends together to hear the preaching of Peter (Acts 10:24). Similarly, the Philippian jailer gathered his household to hear the preaching of Paul (Acts 16:31-33). Whether by proclamation or by invitation, these early believers expressed their inclination to bring the Gospel to others.

The apostles transmitted not only the Gospel itself, but also the impulse and command to share it. Paul wrote to the Ephesians that they should speak the truth (of the Gospel) in love and devote their conversation to that which edifies and imparts grace (Eph. 4:15, 29). His reference to those in Rome who spoke the Word of God boldly implies that his Philippian readers should do the same (Phil. 1:14; 2:16). The Colossians are urged to utter gracious speech that will answer the questions about Christ raised in the minds of unbelievers by their distinctively Christian conduct (Col. 4:6). Timothy is ordered to guard the truth and entrust it to faithful men who will be able to teach others (2 Tim. 1:13; 2:2). Peter reminds his readers that they are a royal priesthood who are privileged to declare God's wonderful redemptive deeds (1 Peter 2:9). He goes on to tell them to be in constant readiness to give account of their Christian hope (1 Peter 3:15). John alerts his readers to their responsibility of confessing the Son (1 John 2:23). The author of the Epistle to the Hebrews urges his readers to hold fast the confession of their faith without wavering (Heb. 10:23)

The impulse to share the Gospel remained alive and strong in Christians well beyond the New Testament age, as later sections of this chapter will indicate. What surprises the modern observer is how little is said in the post-New Testament literature to encourage this sharing. Many authors address themselves to other responsibilities of the Christian life. Very detailed instruction is offered about the attitudes and behaviors that the Christian should seek to cultivate in self and others. However, virtually nothing is said about how Christians ought to tell other people about Jesus. They were, of course, urged to confess Christ in the face of persecution, rather than to apostatize. But they were not frequently reminded to converse informally about Him with family and friends or to approach strangers with a Gospel presentation. This is extremely interesting and significant.

The near silence of post-New Testament literature on this kind of encouragement could be interpreted in several ways. It might indicate either that the impulse to share the Gospel was regarded as unimportant, or that it was already so strong and active that no encouragement was necessary.

The latter is unquestionably the case. During these early centuries Christianity grew so rapidly that the chief agents of growth were, not the leaders of the church nor professional evangelists, but rather ordinary believers who shared the Gospel in the roles and relationships of their daily lives. Without the benefit of evangelism programs or materials, without even any special encouragement, these people talked to others about the help and the hope they had found in Christ. It was an informal and spontaneous type of sharing, natural rather than forced. People talk quite readily and enthusiastically about things that matter a great deal to them, especially when these things have been recently discovered and are not widely known. So, in their homes and shops, in the course of their travels and while relaxing, as they conducted business and worked at their jobs, early Christian lay people were impelled to share the Gospel to all who seemed open to it.[8]

An important aspect of the impulse to share was the preoccupation with moral behavior so prominent especially among second- and third-century Christians. Confessing Christ with a godly life was regarded as important as verbal witness. Christians knew that they were being watched carefully and critically by the pagan world, and that their conduct would bring either glory or disgrace to the name of Jesus. In fact, they seemed to regard their conduct as their chief and most effective testimony to Christ, that which more than anything else might win others to the faith.[9]

Motivation—Accent on Privilege

Few subjects are more complex and elusive than motivation. Why people do what they do is extremely difficult to determine even for the agents themselves. Stated motivations in many cases are obviously very different from what is really moving people to act. Identifying and analyzing motives of people from the early period of Christian history is infinitely more difficult even than exploring one's own motives or those of one's contemporaries. However, no consideration of early Christian evangelism would be complete without at least some exploration of this dimension.

As observed above, the early Christians were characterized by a compelling desire to offer others the incomparable blessing they had received through faith in Jesus Christ. What they had was simply too good to keep quiet about, too good to keep to themselves. Certainly part of their motivation in sharing the Gospel was simply the natural delight related to bringing any kind of good news to others. It is rewarding to put smiles on people's faces and joy into people's hearts. The Good News of Christ, when believed, had that effect.

The most prominent and compelling aspect of their motivation to evangelize was a high sense of privilege about this activity. The element of duty was certainly also there, but the accent was clearly on privilege. These were not guilt-driven or works-righteous witnesses (for the most part), but rather joyful and eager messengers of the Word. Paul exemplifies this very vividly in his defense before King Herod Agrippa II (Acts 26). What began as a rather conventional reply to accusations that had been leveled against him by the Jews soon shifted into a pointed testimony to Christ aimed at the king himself. When Agrippa realized what had happened, he replied in astonishment, "In a short time you think to make me a Christian!" Paul replied that this was exactly what he had in mind. "I would to God that not only you but also all who hear me this day might become such as I am—except for these chains" (vv. 27-29). He felt so privileged to know and trust Christ that he simply could not resist trying to share this faith with others, even on such an apparently inappropriate occasion.

In his correspondence Paul repeatedly expresses this sense of privilege with regard to sharing the Gospel. The assignment to proclaim Christ was itself a gift of grace. He was proud of his work as "a minister of Christ Jesus to the Gentiles in the priestly service of the gospel" (Rom. 15:16, 17). His ministry was the delightful task of spreading the fragrance of the knowledge of Christ everywhere (2 Cor. 2:14). He was an ambassador of the most high God (2 Cor. 5:20). He distributed the unsearchable riches of Christ to the Gentiles and revealed mysteries hidden for ages (Eph. 3:8-9). He never ceased to be amazed that he, the chief of sinners, had been given the opportunity, not only to be saved by the Gospel, but also to transmit it to others (1 Tim. 2:12-17).

Peter emphasizes that this same high privilege belongs to all of God's people, as well as to their apostolic leaders: "But you are a chosen race, a royal priesthood, a holy nation, God's own people, that you may declare the wonderful deeds of Him who called you out of darkness into His marvelous light" (1 Peter 2:9). Ordinary and less than ordinary people were exhilarated by the realization that they could be God's instruments by communicating His saving message to others, that they could actually bring divine light to people who were still in darkness. Having been granted this amazing privilege, the early Christians were eager to exercise it.

In the post-New Testament era, too, we encounter striking examples of Christians who regarded it as a great privilege to bring Christ to others. As Ignatius of Antioch was en route to martyrdom in chains because of his witness to Christ, he referred to these bonds as "spiritual pearls" (*Ephesians* 11:2). Polycarp, while tied to the stake awaiting death by fire for the sake of Christ, praised God for the honor of bearing witness in this way (*Martyrdom of Polycarp* 14:2). An anonymous second-century preacher, reflecting on the salvation and sonship obtained for us by the suffering of Christ, wonders how we might praise and repay Him for all this. The answer, he concludes, is by acknowledging Him with lips, heart, mind and life (*2 Clement* 1:3-5; 3:1-5). Justin Martyr, at the conclusion of a long discussion with an unbelieving Jew, expresses an attitude of privilege reminiscent of Paul's statement to Agrippa, "I can wish no better thing for you...[than that] you may be of the same opinion as ourselves and believe that Jesus is the Christ of God."[10] Origen obviously feels greatly honored to be able to lead men to the worship and fellowship of the God of the universe, and into a state of spiritual and moral healing (*Against Celsus*, Book III, Ch. I, LIV. LXI).

The root of this sense of privilege about evangelizing was love—love for God and for the lost, based on His seeking and saving love for all. It was recognition of, and identification with, the universal mission of Jesus Christ. A disturbing conviction behind the impulse to share Christ was that without the benefit of faith in Him people are condemned eternally. Clear New Testament statements to this effect (John 3:36; Acts 4:12, 2 Thess. 1:8-9) are also echoed in the early fathers (Justin, *Second Apology* 15; Tertullian, *To Scapula* 1; Clement of Alexandria, *Exhortation to the Heathen*, 9). This sobering assumption added urgency to the evangelistic efforts of the early Christians.

An additional motivating factor was fear of judgment and even eternal punishment for failure to evangelize and especially for failure to confess at a time of persecution. Jesus' warnings (Matt. 10:33; Rev. 3:11) were the basis of that fear and the teaching of Paul about accountability at the judgment reinforced it (1 Cor. 3:10-15; 2 Cor. 5:10). Christians urged to deny Christ in order to avoid persecution remembered these warnings. To the proconsul, who with the threat of death by fire tried to convince aged Polycarp to apostatize, the bishop replied that he was far more afraid of the everlasting fire in store for those who renounced their

Lord (*Martyrdom of Polycarp* 11:2; 2:4).

The positive counterpart of the fear motivation was the hope of reward. Paul praises the Christians at Philippi for their partnership in the Gospel and holds before them the prospect of fulfillment and recognition on the day of Christ (Phil. 1:3-11). In the Apocalypse "those who conquer" are those who confess Christ even in the face of terrifying opposition. They are told that they may look forward to "the crown of life" (Rev. 2:10), white garments of victory (Rev. 3:5), a place and part of the heavenly temple (Rev. 3:12), and even the privilege of sharing the throne of Christ (Rev. 3:21). Again and again the joy and comfort of the life to come are held before Christians as an incentive to faithful witness, even under pressure (Rev. 7,19,20,21). The *Letter of Barnabas* urges Christians to keep the day of judgment in mind night and day, and in view of that to be busy saving souls by speaking the Word (19:10). Presumably, the prospect of commendation on that day was the positive motivation in that statement, while the possibility of condemnation was the negative. A later reference in this work similarly alludes to the prospect of reward as reason for steadfastness in word and deed (21:6). In a more general way, Polycarp reminds his readers that the glory of the world to come is awaiting those who please God (*Letter to the Philippians* 5:2). Although evangelizing is not specifically mentioned in this passage, it may be implied.

If the materials referred to above are typical and have been interpreted adequately, it appears that the overriding motive for evangelism in the early church was a sense of privilege. The evangelizers felt deeply honored by the opportunity to communicate the Good News, even under difficult and threatening circumstances. Awed by the magnitude of God's love, overwhelmed by His sacrificial work in Christ and the grand scope of His plan of salvation, they eagerly and readily participated in extending these blessings to those who were still without them. Not to do so would have marked them as ungrateful, unfaithful and vulnerable to judgment themselves.[11]

Content—The Message They Shared[12]

In this brief section no attempt is made to analyze comprehensively the content of early Christians' communication about their faith. Rather, the discussion that follows seeks to capture in brief summaries the central thrust of that message in the New Testament and then to note some variations in expression and emphasis during the remaining centuries of this early period.

In a word, the content of the message that the New Testament believers announced as the best news of all times (*euaggelizesthai*), which they proclaimed (*kerussein*) and to which they bore witness (*marturein*), was *Jesus*. Not merely a set of doctrines or a moral code (although these, too, were essential elements), but a historic person was the focus of their evangelistic remarks. Furthermore, this person was not just someone who had once lived and done some remarkable things, but One who still lived and who was available, even eager, to relate personally to all who would have Him. What Jesus did and endured as well as what He said was the heart of the message. Its relevance to the hearers was that the meaning and benefits of Jesus' work were the solution to their worst problems and the key to a grand new life for them now and hereafter. In short, New Testament witnesses and evangelists were not speaking in abstractions, but introducing people to a person, a unique and helping person, one who could make all the difference in the world to them.

That Jesus Himself is the central theme and substance of the New Testament message is supported abundantly by virtually all the documents. In Acts not only the evangelistic preaching of the apostles but also the witness of ordinary believers was the presentation of Jesus. To Cornelius Peter preaches "the good news of peace by Jesus Christ" who is Lord of all (10:36). To the Samaritans ordinary believers from Jerusalem scattered by persecution proclaimed Christ (8:5). Paul characterizes his preaching as preoccupation with Jesus Christ and Him crucified (1 Cor. 2:2), which, of course, included the offer of divine pardon through His death, as well as victory through His resurrection (1 Cor. 15:3-4). Peter summarizes the Christian Good News as deliverance from sin for glory through the suffering and rising of Jesus Christ (1 Peter 1). The author of the Epistle to the Hebrews introduces Jesus to his readers as the divine Son of God through whom God delivers His ultimate communication and through whose incarnation and sacrifice He provides purification for sin and empathy and support in temptation (Heb. 1—2). The gospels are nothing more or less than the portrayal of and testimony to Jesus with heavy emphasis on His suffering, death, and resurrection as atonement for human sin, the dynamic for Christian obedience and the basis of Christian hope.

With rich variety the gospels describe Jesus. He is the divine King come into the world on a mission of rescue in fulfillment of God's Old Testament promises (Matthew). He is the one by whose mighty deeds the dark powers are routed and God's kingdom is established (Mark). He is the divine-human Savior who reached out with compassion and gentleness to all who were in need (Luke). He is the Word of God, who is

God, the source of divine life and light; the Lamb of God who takes away the sin of the world; the Son of God; the Son of Man; the King of Israel; the Bread of Life; the Good Shepherd; the Way, the Truth and the Life; the source of the Spirit, the true Vine (John).

The specific form of the Gospel was determined by the background and situation of the hearers. To Jews, for example, Jesus was introduced as the Messiah promised to their fathers (Acts 13:16-41) and the heavenly High Priest foreshadowed in the Old Testament history and cultus (Heb. 7—10). To Gentiles He was presented as Lord of all (Acts 10:36), the unknown God, creator and judge, whom they worshiped without realizing who He was (Acts 17:22-31), the image of the invisible God, who by His blood reconciled all things to God whether on earth or in heaven (Col. 1:15-23), the King of kings and Lord of lords (Rev. 19:16).

As we turn from the New Testament evangel to that confessed in the centuries immediately following, we are struck both by the continuity with and deviation from the New Testament message about Jesus. On the one hand, most of the major Christian writers from the second through the fourth century contain clear and reasonably adequate testimonies to the revelatory and redemptive work of the divine-human Christ.[13] Of these, none presents Christ and His work more eloquently, winsomely, and biblically than the author of the *Letter to Diognetus* (second or third century). No brief excerpts or paraphrase can do justice to this marvelous Gospel statement. The reader is urged to examine it in its totality.[14] Christian truth, this author explains, was not discovered by men but rather was disclosed by the most high God. He made this disclosure through no one less than His divine Son, through whom all things were made and are ordered. Not with coercion, but with gentle persuasion this Son came, as one of us, to help us know His attitudes toward us and His plan for us. Since we are totally incapable of delivering ourselves from the grip and consequences of sin and thus are unable to make ourselves eligible for God's fellowship and kingdom, God provided this for us through the innocent and substitutionary sacrifice of His Son. In a mysterious and marvelous transaction, He accepts our guilt and punishment and we receive His righteousness (chs. 7—9).

On the other hand, throughout the Christian literature of this period we also encounter numerous and serious distortions of the Gospel. The *Didache* and the *Shepherd of Hermas* are legalistic and works-righteous in the extreme. Even Ignatius of Antioch, who in some places reflects the New Testament evangel adequately, in others lapses into language and concepts that contradict or bend basic elements of the evangel. Similarly, leading thinkers and writers of later generations, such as

Irenaeus, Tertullian, Origen, and even Athanasius, despite their monumental theological contributions in other areas, were weak and incorrect at times in their testimony to the work of Christ.

For example, although Ignatius affirms that Jesus saved us by His suffering and death, he also made it clear that only the sacrifice of martyrdom makes discipleship and freedom in Christ complete (*Romans* 4:2-4). Reconciliation with God was accomplished by Christ, according to Irenaeus, primarily by His life and obedience rather than specifically by His suffering and death (*Against Heresies* Book V, 17:1). Tertullian teaches atonement by incarnation (*Concerning the Flesh of Christ* 17) and also describes satisfaction for sin as something that the sinner accomplishes by penitence and good works (*Concerning Penitence* 3, 5, 9, 13). Origen speculates that the sacrifice of Christ may be supplemented by the blood of the martyrs (*Homily on Numbers* X, 2). This is not the place to undertake an extensive and intensive analysis of the Gospel according to the early fathers. From these and many other similar examples that could be cited, it is clear that the quality and clarity of the Christian Gospel suffered after the end of the New Testament era. Not only do the writers locate the center of God's saving work elsewhere than on the cross, but they also, in some cases, view the sinner's efforts as contributing to the process of salvation.

What about the ordinary Christians? What was the content of their witness? As was already observed, most conversions during this expansive early period were the result, not of the testimony of renowned Christian leaders or writers, but rather of that of countless and, for the most part, nameless Christians of no prominence or distinction, who in simple, quiet ways made others aware of Jesus Christ. How did they express themselves so as to awaken interest and faith in others?

Often their most effective testimony or, at least, that which opened the hearts of others to that testimony, was simply their lives. The suspicion and hostility of an unbelieving world often crumbled before the purity, compassion, generosity, and piety of their Christian neighbors and relatives. St. Peter tells Christian women that their unbelieving husbands may be won without a word by their reverent and chaste behavior (1 Peter 3:1-2). In his *Apology* Aristides in the mid-second century describes how he was converted by reading the Christian writings. However, what he goes on to describe at length is not so much what he read in their literature but what he had observed in their behavior—their glad obedience to God's commandments, their amazing love for one another and helpfulness to those in need, their constant praise of God, and the unostentatious way in which they did all this (15, 16). Obviously, these qualities of Christian behavior underscored and made credible to Aristides what he had read in Christian literature. The determination of Christians to witness by their lives has already been documented above (see note 9).

No conduct of the early Christians did more to draw others to Christ than their incredible steadfastness in the face of persecution. Their verbal witness in these situations was often minimal. Faced with the option of denying Christ by an act of pagan worship or experiencing hideous torture and death, they refused the former and chose the latter by stating with eloquent simplicity, "I am a Christian." This simple confession, followed by heroic and even joyful endurance of the consequences caused many unbelievers to wonder about the source of their courage, to inquire and ultimately believe. With scorn Tertullian explains to Roman officialdom that the persecutions were counterproductive. The more savagely Christians are punished for their faith, he says, the more attractive that faith becomes to others. The more Christians they cut down, the more new ones rise up to take their place. The blood of Christian martyrs is seed from which more converts spring up. Those who observe the staunch faithfulness of Christians are led to faith and, ultimately to martyrdom themselves (*Apology* 50:13, 15). *The Acts of the Martyrs* report that those assisting the executioners were themselves sometimes converted.[15]

From the very beginning Christian testimony to Jesus was combined with a polemic against idolatry. At Lystra, Ephesus, and Athens, Paul denounced the false deities to which the people were devoted. In 1 Corinthians Paul says on the one hand that an idol has no existence (8:4), and, on the other hand, that what is offered to an idol is offered to demons (10:19, 20). The apparent inconsistency in these comments is resolved if belief in idols is recognized as a demonic delusion. The Revelation of St. John condemns the cult of emperor worship as the work of Satan (13). The apologists of the second and third century vigorously, sometimes mercilessly, expose and ridicule the beliefs and practices of pagan idolators. Clement of Alexandria, in his *Exhortation to the Heathen*, devotes most of this treatise to describing and discrediting the religions and philosophies of the Graeco-Roman world. Before anyone could say an authentic "yes" to Jesus Christ, he would have to say "no" to idols. Unlike most of its rivals, Christianity was intolerant of syncretism.

After Christianity "triumphed" in the Roman Empire, paganism by no means disappeared. It was deeply rooted and pervasive, especially in the west and most especially in the rural areas. Well beyond the early period and into the middle ages, Christian evangelists and missionaries began their efforts to convert or more fully to Christianize the populace with direct assaults upon the idolatrous views and practices to which so many were still attached. These verbal attacks were combined with legal sanctions against paganism imposed by Christian rulers and even by the destruction of idols and places of worship.

Strategy and Methodology

The broad assignment which Jesus gave to His 11 closest followers was to make disciples of all nations. The means by which they were to accomplish this were baptizing and teaching (Matt. 28:19-20). In other words, they were to reach out to all people everywhere in such a way as to make them aware of Jesus Christ and, furthermore, to draw them into the same trusting and obedient relationship with Jesus which the Eleven themselves enjoyed. Elsewhere Jesus explained that they were His witnesses, those who had observed and experienced personally who He is and what He had done (Luke 24:48; John 15:27). At the ascension He charged them to report what they had witnessed in Jerusalem and in all Judea and Samaria and to the ends of the earth (Acts. 1:8).

There is no evidence that the Eleven or any subsequent group of early Christian leaders sat down and developed a comprehensive plan of action by which to accomplish this mission. In a way, the evangelizing of the Roman world just happened as Christians shared their faith wherever they happened to be.

However, as we examine the evangelistic activities and ventures reported in Acts, we do observe certain consistent patterns: (1) They concentrated their efforts on major centers of influence, the great cities of the empire (Antioch, Ephesus, Corinth, Alexandria, and Rome, for example). (2) In virtually every location they began their outreach with those who were likely best to be prepared for their message—the Jewish religious community and those Gentiles who were drawn to Judaism. Apparently they expected the faith to spread from these centers to the outlying areas by means of the established channels of transportation and communication. (3) They gave immediate ownership and responsibility to the new believers, expecting them to keep the faith going and growing in their midst under their own leadership. (4) The evangelists kept in touch with their new churches by means of letters, messengers, and personal visits and put these churches in touch with one another. The purpose of these contacts was to supply encouragement, nurture, guidance, and correction as needed, as well as to maintain a sense of the whole body of Christ.

Certainly the most important method of evangelizing in the early church was simply personal conversation. This grows out of the widely accepted conclusion mentioned above that most people gained for Christ during this era were reached through their relatives, friends, and acquaintances, who found opportunities to speak of Jesus or in some other way to direct them to Him. Examples of this in the New Testament have already been given. From the second century we have Justin's record of his encounter on the beach near Ephesus with an elderly Christian philosopher. This man struck up a conversation with Justin, drew out his philosophical views, and then gently but effectively challenged his assumptions and conclusions and offered Christ to him as a superior alternative on the basis of Old Testament prophetic testimony. This one conversation with an earnest and informed Christian witness drew Justin to Christ and other Christians, led to his conversion, and ultimately to his martyrdom (*Dialog with Trypho* 3-8).

A third-century reference is the disparaging comment of Celsus, quoted by Origen, which describes the eager conversational witness of simple Christian craftsmen. While at work in private homes they would share, especially with the women and children, something of their Christian faith and seek further opportunities to inform them more fully. What disgusted the pagan Celsus is that these uneducated Christians would presume to know better than the head of the house the truth about God and life (*Against Celsus*, Book III: LV). For our purposes the important point is that not only the learned but the unlearned communicated Christ to others through personal conversation.

The experience of Augustine of Hippo in the fifth century reveals numerous instances in which his mother and other Christian individuals tried to talk to him about Christ—for a long time quite unsuccessfully. Following his conversion, Augustine himself reached out to others conversationally with earnest Christian testimony (*Confessions*, I:11; III:11; V:13; VII:2; IX:3).

Public preaching was also a standard and effective evangelism method during the early period. The ancient world afforded many opportunities for the open proclamation of the Gospel. Jesus and the apostles addressed the Jewish community in their synagogues and temple. Paul inevitably began his evangelistic work in a synagogue, if one was available. As Paul and others penetrated the Gentile world, they took advantage of the popular practice of addressing crowds in outdoor public meeting places (Acts 16 and 17). Jesus, of course, often preached out of doors—at the lake shore, on a hillside or wherever people would gather. Irenaeus, late in the second century, did so much evangelistic preaching to the Celts of his diocese in their own language that he lost some of his fluency in Greek (*Against Heresies*, Book I, Preface). Gregory the Wonder Worker, third-century bishop of Pontus in the east, is said to have applied himself so diligently to evangelism, probably by public preaching, that while there were only 17 Christians in his city when he began his ministry, 30 years later there were only 17 pagans left.[16] In the same century Origen writes about traveling Christian preachers who went to cities, villages, and country houses in order to make converts to God (*Against Celsus*, Book III, IX). A century later Martin of Tours preached and healed so powerfully in a pagan village that the entire population was converted (*Dialog II of Sulpitius Severus*, Ch. III).

In addition to the public preaching of an evangelistic nature described above, prospective Christians were permitted to attend at least portions of Christian worship services and to hear the Gospel in that way. The great preachers such as Ambrose, John Chrysostom, and Augustine succeeded in attracting significant numbers of non-Christians to their services, and not a few were gained for Christ and the church through their preaching.

Early Christian preachers were clearly aware of their evangelistic opportunities and responsibilities, and they utilized this form of communication very effectively. They went out into the midst of unbelieving communities and preached Christ with the goal of making converts. In addition, they spoke to the hearts of inquirers who were attracted to their worship gatherings, and, to use the language of the Book of Acts, "the word of the Lord grew" (19:2).

According to the Great Commission (Matt. 28:19-20), Baptism and teaching were the basic means by which new Christians (disciples) were to be made. Throughout the early period of Christian history both were utilized. However, their meaning and relationship as well as the practices associated with them varied considerably from time to time and from place to place. An important point to be noted in this connection is that the basic content of the Commission is to *make disciples*. Jesus did not simply command the 11 to proclaim the Gospel or even to bring people to the point of conversion through that Gospel. Rather, He commanded discipling, bringing people to faith and obedience, incorporating them as functioning members of His body through the proclamation of the Gospel. The discipling task, then, is a unified operation involving both outreach and nurture, both initiation and education. It is interesting and significant that evangelism in the early church developed in a manner which conformed to the Great Commission. It was, in fact, a discipling process emphasizing both Baptism and teaching as the means to that end.

Originally, Baptism was administered immediately after conversion had taken place through evangelistic preaching or personal witness (Acts 2:41; 10:48; 16:33). The method of Baptism appears to have been immersion in most cases, although some New Testament references seem to imply sprinkling or washing (Heb. 10:22; Titus 3:5); and an early second-century source specifically allows pouring (*Didache* 7:3). Infant baptism is not mentioned explicitly in the New Testament. However, the Baptism of whole households (Acts 10:48; 16:15, 33), involving not only a husband, wife, and their children, but also slaves, servants, and their families, as well as the inclusiveness of the Great Commission ("all nations") and the precedent of Jesus' blessing of infants (Luke 18:15-16), constitute compelling evidence that this was New Testament practice. Tertullian acknowledged the widespread practice of infant baptism, but opposed it (*Baptism*, 18), while his third-century contemporary, Origen, endorsed it as an apostolic custom (*Comm. on Romans*, 5). By A.D. 500 it was universally practiced.

In the New Testament, the discipling process continued after Baptism with teaching in the context of the Christian community (Acts 2:42). Numerous early witnesses indicate that they were lifelong Christians to whom the faith was transmitted by parents.[17] Infant baptism followed by Christian instruction in the home was apparently the pattern followed in these cases. The significance of Baptism was cleansing from sin, incorporation into the church, and newness of life through union with the redemptive death and resurrection of Jesus (Rom. 6:1-4; 1 Cor. 12:13; Titus 3:5).

A shift in baptismal practice occurred early in the second century when a period of instruction and probation was introduced for adult converts. Later in that century—and in the next when large numbers were seeking admission to the church—this was formalized into the cate-chumenate. The procedure eventually developed that the serious inquirer, after learning enough about Christianity to decide that he would like to join, would be admitted into tentative and limited membership as a catechumen. For a period of time varying from 40 days to three years, the catechumen would undergo education and evaluation. If judged sufficiently informed, sincere, and morally earnest, he would be received into full membership by Baptism, usually on Easter eve. Prior to Baptism the catechumen could not be present at the celebration of the Eucharist and did not even receive instruction about that sacrament. Although the catechumen was regarded in some sense as a Christian even before Baptism, not until he had been thoroughly taught and tested and then baptized was the discipling process regarded as complete. This shift away from the New Testament practice of immediate baptism may or may not have been an improvement, but it does reflect a high regard for teaching as a vital element of the discipling process.

Evangelistic teaching directed more specifically to outsiders was utilized already by Paul in Ephesus, where he hired a hall and over a two-year period taught and debated the Christian message with all who would come (Acts 19:9-10). Justin, who had been a teacher of philosophy before his conversion, continued in that vocation, but with a Christian emphasis (Martyrdom of Justin, 3). The most highly developed agency of this type was the catechetical school of Alexandria founded by Pantaenus, a converted Stoic philosopher, whose work was continued by his student, Clement, and developed even more extensively by the brilliant and energetic Origen. This school was not only an institution for the instruction of catechumens, as the name implies, but a center of Christian higher education. Curious or interested pagans would come to hear the great Christian teachers expound, not only on Christian doctrine, but also on various philosophical and scientific topics from a Christian perspective. By his teaching, which was undergirded by an exceptionally pious life, Origen was instrumental in converting many, some of whom sealed their faith with martyrdom.[18]

Finally, literature was used extensively by the early Christians for evangelistic purposes. The New Testament documents are, of course, the primary example. These inspired testimonies to the person, words, and works of Jesus Christ were widely recommended to and shared with unbelievers with the aim of converting them, although their chief use was for the nurture of those who already believed. Mark and Luke appear to reflect a special awareness of outsiders. However, nowhere is an evangelistic objective more clearly stated than in the Fourth Gospel, ". . .these are written that you may believe that Jesus is the Christ, the Son of God, and that believing you might have life in His name" (John 20:31).

Much early Christian literature besides the New Testament also presented Jesus Christ to those who still did not know or trust Him. The great apologists of the second and third centuries—Justin, the unknown author of the Letter to Diognetus, Athenagorus, Tertullian, Origen, etc.—were interested not only in defending Christianity but in commending it. Clement of Alexandria's Exhortation to the Heathen is really nothing but an evangelistic tract that exposes and discredits contemporary religions and philosophies and pleads with his readers to accept

Christ as a superior alternative. Augustine's *Confessions* are a testimony to the incredible grace of God which he had experienced in his own life. The list of examples that might be cited is very long. Not only with their lives and with their lips, but also with their pens many early Christians, some of considerable ability, expressed their witness to Jesus to the reader who still did not belong to Him.

So it was that early Christians spread the Gospel of Jesus Christ throughout the Roman world, and by the year 500 had gained the vast majority of that population, as well as millions more outside the empire—at least nominally—for His faith and fold. Certain factors in the political, cultural, and religious situation facilitated their evangelistic outreach. The Roman peace made travel relatively safe and easy. Graeco-Roman culture, widely spread in that empire, provided important commonalities, and the Greek language virtually removed communication barriers. Religious and philosophical trends anticipated some of the key elements of Christianity and appeared to some degree to dispose people favorably toward it. Judaism of the dispersion provided invaluable entrees into the Gentile population through the many Gentile converts or near converts to Judaism that the Jewish religious communities had attracted. Finally, early in the fourth century when Christianity was legalized, favored by the state, and even had become the established Roman religion, vast numbers abandoned paganism and flooded into the church.

However, these favorable factors were more than offset by the powerful pressures that resisted Christian outreach and growth. For several centuries elements in the Jewish religious establishment repeatedly tried to squelch the new movement by force. To the Greek mind Christian theology was absurd and its claims arrogant. Most dangerous and devastating, however, was the growing determination of the Roman state to stamp out Christianity by means of persecution. The prospects for growth or even survival of the Christian church appeared extremely dim.

Yet the movement flourished and expanded. The impulse to share Jesus Christ did not succumb to these pressures. Regardless of the danger, even in the face of torture and death early Christians felt privileged and honored to confess their Lord. Clear and compelling witness to Jesus in the post-New Testament era is found alongside some serious distortions of the Gospel. Confronted with the Savior's commission to make disciples of all nations, early Christian evangelists like Paul concentrated on the major urban centers and let Christian influence spread from there. In addition, the new churches they founded were indigenous from the outset—self-governing, self-supporting and self-perpetuating. The chief evangelistic methods utilized during this period of unprecedented expansion were personal conversation, preaching, teaching, and literature.

An important dimension of evangelism already in this early period has not been discussed in this chapter—outreach for renewal. As indicated in the Preface, evangelism also includes efforts to lead those who have already been converted into more earnest and active discipleship. The role of teaching in the initial discipling process has been considered above. In contrast with that, outreach for renewal is directed toward the negligent Christian or one whose commitment appears to be weak or whose life grossly contradicts his profession. Throughout the early period and, indeed, throughout all Christian history, the need for renewal has been evident. There have always been lax and wavering members of the Christian community for whom other more earnest Christians have felt a special concern and to whom they have reached out with an evangelical invitation and challenge. A variety of movements devoted to this purpose appear already during the first five centuries. However, since their development and significance were greatest in the medieval period, that discussion has been reserved for the next chapter.

II/Christianization by Conformity and Coercion: The Middle Ages
(500—1500)

During the course of the fifth century the newly Christianized Roman Empire in western Europe underwent traumatic and pervasive change. Germanic peoples from the north, who for centuries had been infiltrating and even forcedly penetrating the borders on a limited scale, now broke through in great numbers and with devastating effects. They defeated the Roman military machine, overthrew the government, formed six kingdoms of their own out of what had once been the western Roman Empire, and at the local level seized whatever they wanted of the land and other wealth. Although their intention was not to destroy the Roman Empire, but rather to join and dominate it, the former was, in fact, what happened. Not only the military and the state but also the economy and culture largely collapsed under the impact of these invasions.

Christianity, too, was threatened and deeply disturbed by all of this. However, it did not collapse. The church was the one major Roman institution to survive the Germanic conquests. By the year 800 most of the descendants of the pagan invaders had been Christianized, and those of Arian background had become Catholics. Furthermore, from Christianity came much of the vision and the energy to develop a new civilization in western Europe, one which was to be permeated significantly by Christian values and influenced profoundly by church leaders. During the middle ages western Europe became the stronghold of Christianity.

Outside western Europe, Christianity faced far more serious threats and suffered major setbacks during the millennium under consideration in this chapter. The southern and much of the eastern part of the Mediterranean basin fell to non-Christian powers, most of whom were Muslims. In this repressive and often hostile environment Christianity languished and declined. A diminishing remnant of the old Roman Empire survived among Greek and Slavic-speaking people of the Balkan peninsula until 1453, when it and eventually all of eastern Europe fell to a new Muslim power—the Ottoman Turks. While it endured this, the Byzantine Empire, as it was called, remained a vital source of Christian influence and outreach. From there Christianity spread to many northeastern European peoples, the most important of whom were Russians, as well as to some parts of the Orient.

Many new peoples and areas became Christian during this challenging era, nearly offsetting the tremendous losses which were sustained.[1] Our purpose in this chapter is to examine the processes by which Christianization took place. At this point we see a series of mass movements into Christianity, strikingly different from the evangelism of the early period. Whole tribes, communities and nations were baptized and declared Christian, usually without regard for their personal feelings and even under coercion. Frequently the process of Christianization was closely related to the acquisition, consolidation, or expansion of political power.[2] The other side of the picture is that there were also strong and extensive efforts to win the hearts of those who had been only superficially Christianized. In addition, numerous renewal movements arose to summon lax and negligent Christians to a more earnest and obedient response to God.

The story of medieval evangelism is largely the story of monasticism. This institution consisted of individuals and communities dedicated to what were regarded as the highest standards of Christian obedience. By their example as well as by their teaching and preaching, medieval monks were instrumental in the conversion and renewal of unnumbered multitudes.

The Call for Renewal

Already in the early period the call for renewal sounded frequently and emphatically within the church. Then as now Christians struggled against their residual sinfulness, and many capitulated shamelessly. Indifference toward God and conformity to the corrupt influences of the world were all too evident. Instead of the total dedication to God and His will required by Christ and the apostles, many who bore the Christian name responded with a low level of commitment and obedience. When it was safe or even advantageous to be a Christian, a change of heart did not always accompany the change of religion. Second and third generation Christians often lacked the ardor and rigor of their ancestors.

Virtually every New Testament document addresses this problem in some way. Jesus' Sermon on the Mount (Matt. 5—7), for example, attacks spiritual and moral compromise of various kinds and challenges His followers to live by the highest ethical and religious standards imaginable. Paul warns against conformity to a corrupt world and calls for renewal of mind and transformation of life (Rom. 12:1-2). The Epistle of James exposes all kinds of weakness and worldliness in the Christian community and advocates return to a fervent, living faith productive of good works. The letters to the seven churches of Asia Minor (Rev. 2) in almost every case denounce some type of worldliness and urgently appeal for repentance and reform.

The theme of Christian renewal echoed throughout the early and medieval periods and has, in fact, been heard in every age. It has been expressed in literature, preaching, personal admonition, and, especially, personal example. It has been embodied in movements and institutions. There have always been some Christians who have been impelled to take their Christian faith and life with the utmost seriousness. Convinced that if Christianity is worth anything it is worth everything, they have tried to live out the implications of this. In many cases they have also attempted to influence others to do the same. Our purpose in this section is to explore the phenomena of Christian renewal, especially its contagion. This is to say, we will examine and try to understand how some Christians influenced others to turn sharply and dramatically away from what was regarded as a worldly and impious life toward one of exemplary devotion and service.

The call for renewal is being considered in this history of evangelism because it was an attempt more fully to Christianize people. Those who issued the call often did so with the kind of zeal and urgency characteristic of those who evangelized for conversion. In fact, the term "conversion" was frequently applied to those who responded positively to a call for renewal. The reason for this is that those considered in need of renewal were regarded as persons in grave danger. If not already apart from Christ and headed for judgment, they were thought to be perilously close to this dreadful state. A number of institutions and movements worked both for conversion and renewal.

On the other hand, many efforts to promote Christian renewal do not, strictly speaking, belong in the category of evangelism for the simple reason that they actually ignored or undercut the Gospel, the evangel. In the New Testament, sanctified renewal is a response to the Gospel. Christians are urged to improve spiritually and morally because they are already pardoned and reconciled to God through the redemptive work of Christ, and because the transforming power of the Spirit is at work in them (Eph. 1:3—2:10). Many who later called for renewal presented it as a substitute for the Gospel, thus confusing justification with sanctification. They claimed that until and unless we transform our hearts and lives we cannot be forgiven. Renewal is presented as a means by which we make ourselves right with God and earn His blessing, rather than as a result, a loving response to the pardon and eternal relationship with God that He has given us graciously in Christ. Specific examples of this will be given in the discussion below.

Early Literature

Much early Christian literature in the post-apostolic age focuses on dramatic and even drastic renewal. The anonymous second-century sermon entitled *2 Clement* is a strong plea to Christians to repent of their continuing sinfulness and to honor God with loving obedience. Apostasy, immorality, and lovelessness bring a person under judgment. Grateful faith and conscientious conformity to God's will bring the reward of eternal life. The dual motivation utilized is (a) the suffering and saving love of Christ and (b) rewards and punishments. Although not presented with great clarity and power, the Gospel is expressed in *2 Clement*. Another extremely important work from the same century, *The Shepherd of Hermas,* is an earnest admonition to weak and worldly Christians to cleanse themselves by sincere and humble penitence and to secure salvation by observing all God's commands (parable 8, ch. 11). Their initial cleansing from sin was through the work of Christ (parable 5, ch. 7). However, they are responsible for removing subsequent defilement and for remaining pure with the help of the Spirit (parable 10, ch. 3). Reference to the saving and transforming work of Christ is exceedingly sparse and vague in the *Shepherd.*

An interesting and important aspect of both writings is that they portray the ideal Christian life in a manner largely consistent with the New Testament. To please and honor God, they tell us, we must simply obey His commandments and reflect the virtues He describes and prescribes in the Bible. The asceticism advocated so ardently in the third century and thereafter is not yet evident in these works. Furthermore, both were widely read and highly respected, regarded by some as being worthy even of Scriptural status.

The Ascetic Way

Asceticism is that way of life which stresses self-denial and deprivation. It has appeared in various forms in most major religions, including Judaism. Already in the second century it began to surface in Christianity, and it became a prominent element in several groups rejected as heretical. During the third century ascetic views and practices were increasingly tolerated in mainstream Christianity. By the year 500 and for a thousand years thereafter asceticism was regarded by many as the highest form of Christian response. For them the call for renewal was the call to asceticism. To be a sincere and serious Christian, they believed, was to adopt the ascetic life. Anything short of this was thought to be catering to corruption and a disappointment to God.

The earliest Christian ascetics concentrated on the repression of their sexual and acquisitive inclinations. They chose to live in celibacy and poverty. Some never married and refrained from all sexual activity. Others, although married and living with their spouses, discontinued sexual intercourse. Still others became celibate after the death of their spouses. All gave their wealth and property to the poor, except what was required to meet their barest needs. They did not wear distinctive garb, and until well into the third century they did not live communally.

The purpose of the ascetic way was multifaceted. It was meant to be a way of giving oneself completely to God, of removing distractions, of avoiding temptation, of enabling the person to devote more time and attention to the worship of God and His work, of exercising control over one's body and life, of compensating for sins and of earning an eternal reward.

The ascetic was reacting both to corruption in the world and to worldliness in the church. Asceticism flourished during periods of moral and spiritual decline. When society was abandoning itself to lust and materialism and many Christians were also being drawn into these evils, the ascetic, by his example, was protesting all of this. Ascetic individuals and groups were conspicuous at Christian gatherings and in society. The conscience of even the most worldly person could be stabbed by an encounter with those who had renounced some of their most urgent human desires in order more closely to follow Christ. By the end of the second century and the early part of the third, leading Christian writers such as Tertullian and Cyprian were advocating aspects of asceticism. However, more eloquent and compelling than any words were the lives of many Christian ascetics.

One source of the ascetic way was the dualist philosophies and religions of Greece and the Orient. Their fundamental and controlling principle was that matter and everything associated with it is evil, and that only spirit and mind are good. Salvation consists of liberation from the tyranny of one's physicality and the allurement of the material universe, which God, as pure Spirit, abhors. Some religions, such as Gnosticism and Manichaeism, taught that matter, including the human body, is the creation of beings hostile to God. Plato and those philosophers and theologians who followed him taught that ideas are the most real elements in the universe, and that material objects are at best dim and imperfect expressions of ideas. Early and medieval theology and practice absorbed some of these dualistic notions.

The New Testament in certain places seems to support these dualistic, self-denying ideas. Jesus called upon people to deny themselves, forsake all and follow Him (Matt. 16:24-25; 19:16-22; Luke 14:25-33). Jesus also refers with apparent approval to those who made themselves eunuchs for the kingdom of heaven (Matt. 19:12). This, together with His own example and that of John the Baptist and of Paul, suggested celibacy as a lofty Christian goal. Furthermore, Paul specifically encouraged celibacy for those who had the gift, in the interest of unfettered service in view of the imminence of Christ's return (1 Cor. 7). In addition, there is a reference in Revelation 14:4 to the 144,000 in heaven who have not defiled themselves with women, but who, because they are virgins, are privileged to follow the Lamb wherever He goes. Paul speaks about pommeling and subduing his body (1 Cor. 9:26). It is not difficult to understand how Christians living in a culture already saturated with dualistic views would find in these Scriptures the directive to renounce property, sexuality, physical comforts and pleasures of all kinds, and even family ties in order more effectively to worship and work for their Lord.[3]

What Christian ascetics tended to overlook was that the general thrust of Scripture explicitly affirms the physical and the material as God's good creation.[4] Paul, for example, describes the Christian life as embracing marriage, family life, and the world of work (Eph. 5-6; 1 Tim. 3). While he denounced immoderation and immorality (1 Cor. 5:9-11; 6:9-10; Eph. 5:3-17), the apostle also endorsed the grateful use of food and drink (1 Tim. 4:1-5). To regard the deprivation of basic human drives and needs as the ideal route to sanctity is contrary to these Scriptural teachings.

Inevitably, asceticism led to elitism. The essence of asceticism was renunciation. This was closely related to obedience and service. The ascetic renounced much or all in order to be unencumbered for total involvement in God's will, worship, and work. The goal was perfect compliance with all of God's commandments and more. According to the ascetic ideal, it is possible to conform to everything that God requires and then to assume additional burdens as well, which, although not required, are highly valued by God. These burdens were celibacy and poverty.

The same forms of renunciation that freed the ascetic for spiritual and moral excellence also constituted an over and above sacrifice which gained him special divine recognition and rewards. Not every Christian could or would give up or do that much. He could meet only the requirements, at best. The ascetic, on the other hand, did all that was expected and more. He was the super-Christian. Not only the ascetic example, mentioned above, but also the appeal and challenge of excellence and even of perfection drew increasing numbers of Christians down the ascetic way during the early centuries.[5]

In addition to the theological inadequacies of this position, it had the regrettable effect of disparaging the efforts of the ordinary Christian who tried to honor and serve God in the normal roles and relationships of life. Nevertheless, there was also something admirable and inspiring, especially when spiritual and moral laxity were rife, about people who cared enough about God to give Him their all.

Monasticism[6]

Late in the third and early in the fourth century asceticism evolved into monasticism. What had been a rather personal and informal arrangement developed into a vast and growing movement, complete with institutions, traditions, programs, and a distinctive literature. In some respects, monasticism was the most important element of medieval Christianity. Usually it was a reliable gauge of the health of the church. When monasticism was flourishing, so was the church. When it was floundering, so, generally, was the church. By the high middle ages (13th century) monastic orders were proliferating, and into their ranks were flooding some of the most able, energetic, and spiritually sensitive men and women in Christendom.

Monasticism had its ups and downs. Until the 14th century, however, the overall pattern of growth and vitality was upward. In the pre-Reformation centuries decay set in and much criticism was leveled at monasticism. However, in the mind of the average person, monasticism was the way to go if you wanted to be a first-class Christian, and if you wanted to be certain of eternal life.

Several elements were added to asceticism in order to transform it into monasticism. One was withdrawal, both from the world and from the church. The monastic was convinced that the world was hopelessly corrupt, full of seductive and offensive evils. Furthermore, he believed that the church was incorrigibly worldly, populated by many who were insincere, uncommitted, disobedient, and quite indistinguishable from the people of the world. During times when persecution ceased and especially after the conversion of Constantine (A.D. 312), large numbers of people flocked into the church, often without knowing or caring what Christianity was all about. Many continued in pagan behavior patterns and even pagan religious practices.

How could a serious Christian survive and grow in this environment? Only with great difficulty, if at all, it was believed. A clear and logical solution was withdrawal. By isolating one's self from the corrupt world and the worldly church, the Christian who was truly committed to perfection now and to glory hereafter could escape temptation, distraction, and contamination and more successfully attain his objectives.

Another aspect of monastic withdrawal was the sacrifice it entailed. To become a monastic means literally "to stand alone." The earliest form of monasticism, which began late in the third century, was eremitical or solitary. That is, it consisted of the individual becoming a hermit, fleeing alone into the wilderness or being enclosed in a cell or a cave out of contact with other human beings, or in an arrangement that kept such contact to a minimum. The early ascetics sacrificed sex and property. The monastic, in addition, sacrificed family ties and human companionship. Some hermits lived in close proximity to one another for protection. Older monks revered for their wisdom and sanctity served as teachers to those who were considering or entering monastic life. However, even in these cases interaction between eremitical monks was limited.

Many who attempted the eremitical approach to monasticism found it to be destructive. They were mentally or physically broken by the extreme isolation. An alternative introduced early in the fourth century by Pachomius was cenobite or communal monasticism. Like-minded people formed a community, usually in a remote location. Together under strong leadership and a strict set of rules, they would aid each other in a life of self-denial, worship, and work. Although the individual member had contact with other members of the community, this was functional rather than social. The purpose was to promote one another's sanctity rather than to enjoy one another's company. Furthermore, members of the monastic communities were ordinarily required to sever ties with family and friends, as well as with church and world or, at least, to restrict contact severely. The renunciation of human relationships was regarded as part of the high cost of true discipleship, which liberated the individual to concentrate almost exclusively on the relationship with God.

Monastic isolation was not usually as complete as the above discussion might suggest. Hermits accepted students and often attracted sizable numbers of admiring spectators. They visited with one another and even made brief returns to society. In the monasteries a strong sense of community was often cultivated. Although isolated from the world, the cenobite monks did often experience Christian closeness with one another.

In the case of communal monasticism there was also the sacrifice of one's self-determination, one's will. To the vows of celibacy and poverty was added the vow of obedience. Those who became members of a monastic community forfeited their right to make personal decisions and agreed to obey their superior in all things, to accept his correction and discipline without question or complaint. The renunciation of personal freedom and autonomy was for many the most difficult part of monastic life.[7]

Another aspect of monasticism which distinguished it from earlier asceticism was institutionalization. As the middle ages progressed, monasteries were linked together into cooperating networks, and a variety of new religious orders came into being, each with a distinctive emphasis or purpose. The contemplative focus of early monasticism was maintained in orders that emerged in the middle ages, for example, the Cluny monasteries and the Cistercians.

Others developed traditions of humanitarian service—the eastern monasteries which followed the Rule of Basil and especially the Franciscans. As will be noted later, evangelism and missions were major concerns of Roman and English monks as well as Franciscans and Dominicans. The latter two also got deeply involved in education. The point here is that as monasticism became increasingly institutionalized it added a variety of objectives and functions that were not originally part of it.

In this study we are particularly interested in the processes by which people were drawn into monastic life, how they were "converted" from what was regarded as nominal or lax Christianity to radical renewal, to a life of impressive rigor and devotion. The numerical growth and geographic spread of monasticism was swift and substantial despite a considerable amount of initial opposition. How did this happen?

Certainly a major factor was the magnetic power of example. Hermits, especially those renown for sanctity, wisdom, or extreme asceticism, drew crowds of curious and almost worshipful spectators. Similarly, monasteries attracted attention even when planted in the wilderness of pagan territories. People came to them to find out what they were up to and why. The piety, order, and kindliness of the monks often evoked respect for them as well as interest in their message. Many monks apparently made no effort to recruit others for renewal through the monastic life. It happened quite naturally and incidentally as they pursued their goal of Christian perfection. Perhaps the most striking example of this is Francis of Assisi, who, early in the 13th century after a rather frivolous youth, gave himself wholly to Christlikeness. Although he had no intention of founding an order, disciples soon gathered around him, and the formal development of a new and different monastic organization soon followed.

On the other hand, deliberate recruitment for monastic life also took place. When people came to hermits either individually or in groups seeking instruction and advice, they often heard strong appeals to flee the world and follow Christ in radical obedience and sacrifice. Also extremely influential were the *Lives* (biographies) of monastic heroes— that of Anthony reputedly written by Athanasius and of Martin of Tours by Sulpicius were especially important in the fourth and fifth centuries. Readers of these works encountered dazzling models of Christian earnestness and dedication that challenged them to follow suit. Augustine of Hippo (A.D. 354—430), who eventually was to become a monastic model himself, describes in his *Confessions* the transforming effect of the *Life of Anthony* on several of his friends, as well as the impact it had upon him personally (Book VIII). Other monastic literature, especially the *Rule of Basil* (fourth century) and the *Rule of Benedict* (sixth century), not only described monastic life and prescribed for it, but also commended monastic life to the serious reader.

Personal recruitment for monastic life was also very common. Jerome (A.D. 342—420) was active in Rome enlisting aristocratic Christian women for various types of ascetic and monastic life. His letters contain urgent appeals to friends and acquaintances to adopt or maintain the monastic life (e.g. #14, 24, 54, 66, 107). Certainly a most effective recruiter for monasticism was Bernard of Clairvaux (1090—1153). When he became a monk at age 22 he brought 30 friends and relatives into the order along with him. He was so persuasive that when he was coming to an area many mothers are said to have hid their sons from him and wives their husbands, so as not to lose them to monastic life.

The call to renewal that came forth from monasticism was not only recruitment for monastic life. The Franciscans of the 13th century traveled far and wide preaching a message of repentance and newness of life and demonstrating that newness by their own joyousness and love. Not only in the rapidly growing cities of that era, but also in the village and rural areas, they called upon weak and wayward Christians to turn from their sins, to seek God's mercy, and to commit themselves to His service and obedience. At a time when many parish clergy and even bishops were caught up in worldliness or were neglectful of their duties, these colorful, passionate preachers of repentance were able to get through to the rank and file of the church and to ignite in them the fires of renewal. The goal of Franciscan preaching was not primarily to recruit more Franciscans, although that, indeed, happened on a large scale. Rather, their chief goal was to call people to a more serious commitment to Christ and a more Christlike life.

Later in this chapter we will return to monasticism and its evangelistic work among non-Christians or those only nominally Christian. At this point we have emphasized monasticism as a powerful force for Christian renewal during the middle ages. The defects and limitations of monasticism have been noted. It was a works-righteous approach that virtually obscured the Gospel and was also elitist. It was permeated by an unscriptural fear and even hatred of the physical. However, on the positive side, at its best it was also a needed critique of social corruption and ecclesiastical worldliness and an inspiring attempt at total Christian consecration.

Mysticism

The subject of mysticism is exceedingly broad and complex. No attempt will be made here to describe and analyze it in full, even in its Christian forms. In keeping with the limits of this study and specifically those of this section, we will briefly examine medieval Christian mysticism only as it became a significant source of Christian renewal. This happened especially in the 14th and 15th centuries, when mystical influences broke out of the confines of monasticism (where they had been prominent since the beginning) and found their way into popular religious life.

Mysticism is that approach to religion that above all else values and pursues an inner, personal experience of union with God, one in which the soul is confronted directly and consciously with God's presence and is caught up into the fullness of His love. Techniques for fostering this experience vary widely among the different branches of mysticism, as do the anticipated results in the life of the individual mystic. However, virtually all forms of mysticism contend that the essence of religion is deeply personal and experiential. They emphasize the subjective rather than the objective. Nearly all focus on divine love. Mystics minimize or even disparage the value of external supports to the God-relationship, such as sacraments and clergy. Frequently mysticism is a reaction against what is regarded as an excessive preoccupation with the intellectual side of religion and strives for a knowledge of God that transcends reason.[8]

Mysticism and monasticism were closely related, and many mystics were monastics. But there was also a difference. Monasticism was often crassly works-righteous, directing the sinner to strive to repair his broken relationship with God and to attain perfection by means of the deprivations he endured and the extraordinary works of piety he performed. The mystic, on the other hand, attempted to contact and experience the God of love who was already present in his own soul. This too required effort—seeking, waiting, emptying the soul of everything else, meditating, exerting oneself spiritually and even physically.

Rather than being regarded as compensation for sin and the acquisition of merit, mystic exertion was viewed primarily as preparation for and cultivation of the experience of oneness with God. The human contribution to the process of getting together with God was interpreted differently in mysticism than in monasticism. Man had to pursue or discover God, rather than appease Him, as in monasticism. It was a different kind of contribution, and yet a vital one. Unless man made his mystical move he would not connect with God, at least not in the most meaningful way possible. Thus, mysticism likewise compromised divine monergism.[9]

Prominent in much mysticism after the 12th century was preoccupation with God's suffering and saving love in Jesus Christ. For example, the Christ which Bernard invites people to contemplate and to follow is the man of sorrows. In his wounds alone are peace and security to be found. These wounds are God's testimony that He has reconciled the world to Himself. Meditation on the passion of Christ causes joy mixed with sorrow, according to Thomas Aquinas—joy because it reveals God's love, and sorrow because it reveals our sins which caused Him so to suffer. Francis of Assisi instilled devotion to the crucified Christ in his followers and was so absorbed in it himself that he is said miraculously to have received the wounds of Christ in his own body.

Contemplation of Christ's wounds gains the mystic entry into the heart of Christ, intensifies his love and leads ultimately to union with the Savior, according to Bonaventure. Henry Suso emphasizes the growing

conformity of the mystic to the suffering of Christ. The devotion of
Catherine of Siena to the blood of Jesus approached morbidity.[10] Jan Van
Ruysbroeck affirms that meditation on the passion of Christ liberates
from evil and stirs to greater devotion. That despised and crucified Servant not only reveals divine truth but also, through Baptism, adorns us
with merit.[11] Examples such as these demonstrate that elements of the
Scriptural Gospel were preserved and transmitted in medieval mysticism. It was not stressed nearly as much as was human mystical initiative, and it was not exalted as the only source of pardon, moral
transformation, and eternal hope. Even so, the Gospel element in mysticism was a factor in the spiritual renewal of many.

Late in the middle ages mysticism was spread with evangelistic zeal
among the rank and file of Christendom, especially in northern Europe.
Popular preachers and writers such as Meister Eckhart (1260—1328),
John Tauler (1300—61), and Jan Van Ruysbroeck (1293—1381) cultivated in ordinary clergy and laity an appreciation for the mystical
approach to God, which until this time had been largely restricted to
monastics and some intellectuals. In southern Europe Catherine of Siena
(1347—80) by both word and work was a missionary for Christian mysticism.

The "Friends of God" were conspicuous particularly in the Rhine
Valley. They were a rather loosely organized but active movement consisting of monks (primarily Dominicans), nuns, and priests, but primarily lay people who sustained mystical piety in one another and also
commended it to others. Groups were formed in various communities
for the nurture of the mystical life, and these groups were in contact
with one another. Letters were exchanged between individuals in which
they shared experiences and instruction. The pastoral work of many parish priests expressed and fostered mystical ideals. The Friends of God
were a large movement. Their piety centered in the belief that God
wanted them to be His friends and to progress toward perfection, that is,
toward Christlikeness. The process by which this occurred involved
withdrawal from things to the integration of the self. As the soul thus
grows, they believed, it attains the state in which, being possessed fully
by God, it has and loves all things. In the midst of political and ecclesiastical turmoil and a series of natural catastrophes (the most devastating
being the Black Death, which took one-fourth of the population of
Europe), these people found strength and serenity in their mystical
approach to Christianity and in their fellowship with one another.[12]

From the Friends of God, late in the 14th century, there arose
something of a spiritual revival called the *Devotio Moderna*, the New

Devotion. It combined personal, mystical piety with service and social involvement. Gerard Groote (1340—84), who was associated with the Friends of God, became an itinerant preacher. In response to his earnest message of sin and salvation many converts—both clergy and laity— formed groups or fellowships for study and service to others. In Deventer, Netherlands, one such group organized into a community devoted to religious life of a mystical type. The members shared income and expenses, took no vows except those of obedience to superiors and rules, and busied themselves with the care of the sick and the education of the young, as well as the cultivation of the inner life.

Both male and female communities were founded under the name "Brothers (or Sisters) of the Common Life." By 1500 there were many such centers not only in the Netherlands and the Rhine Valley, but as far east as Magdeburg. A treatise called *Spiritual Ascensions*, prepared as a guide for the inner growth of the members, was also widely used by people outside the brotherhood. The specific purpose of the Brothers and Sisters of the Common Life was the reformation of the laity by combining a renewed inner life with a balanced and directed outer life. Their influence was substantial and lasting. Some of the most important Christian leaders of the 15th and 16th centuries, including Calvin and Luther, were connected with their schools. Unlike certain other mystical and reform-minded movements of that age, this one remained within the Roman Catholic fold.

A monastic counterpart of the Brothers and Sisters of the Common Life was organized in 1386 at Windesheim. Eventually dozens of similar monasteries were formed under the leadership of the Windesheim congregation. The Windesheim monasteries and the brotherhood were kindred spirits, except that the former was devoted to the mystical renewal of monasticism. A devotional classic, entitled *The Imitation of Christ*, probably authored by a Windesheim monk, Thomas a Kempis, communicated the spiritual and mystical goals of the *Devotio Moderna*. It was widely circulated and read and became a devotional classic.[13]

This brief sketch of a few aspects of late medieval mysticism is an attempt to highlight some important efforts to evangelize for Christian renewal. Earnest and able Christians who themselves had been drawn into a closer and more meaningful relationship with Jesus Christ reached out eagerly to one another for mutual support. They also were eager to involve others in a renewal experience that would result eventually in their spiritual and moral transformation. Mysticism was plagued with theological error and with extremism, but it also restored some neglected dimensions of the Christian life. In addition, mysticism produced some inspiring Christian personalities, some stimulating literature, and some effective methods of calling people to more earnest and active discipleship.

Impact of Political Change

The previous section dealt with the efforts of some Christians to deepen and vitalize other Christians spiritually. The call to renewal was aimed at those already inside the church, however questionable their status or weak their response may have been. In this and the concluding section of the chapter we examine outreach to non-Christians by words and deeds designed either to convert them or, at least, to secure their outward conformity to Christianity.

No factor during the middle ages or even during the last two centuries of the early period did more to bring people into the Christian community than political change. As was noted in Chapter I, when the Roman government legalized Christianity and even began to favor it above all other religions, great masses of people came into the church. Some of these had been deterred from joining earlier by fear of persecution. Others were eager to gain the advantages which this change of government policy seemed to imply.

The process of Christianization was accelerated by campaigns of church and state forcedly to stamp out paganism within the empire. When Christian powers conquered and annexed pagan tribes and nations, the victors often insisted on religious and ecclesiastical as well as political submission. In other cases Christian influence flowed in the opposite direction. Conquerers absorbed Christianity from people whom they had subjugated. Of supreme importance in a number of nations was the encouragement and even insistence of their converted rulers who required their subjects to follow them into the faith.

Mass Christianization by coercion and conformity seems inappropriate and immoral to most modern observers. It also differs markedly from the methods of individual conversion usually employed during the early period, although even then entire households and whole communities at times were brought to Christ and into the church in ways that were at least subtly coercive. The chief objections to Christianizing people by means of political and social pressures include violation of personal religious freedom, encouragement of superficial and hypercritical involvement, and disavowal of divine monergism. But the modern observer must remember that in the middle ages the ideal of religious freedom had not yet taken hold among the peoples who were being

Christianized. Religion, for them, was part of social behavior and under the authority of the ruler. It was a corporate rather than a personal matter. Furthermore, the religions out of which these people came did not require personal conviction or commitment, but merely external conformity. In view of these factors it is not surprising that many people during this era were initially processed into Christianity *en masse* without the benefit of conversion.

This does not mean, however, that conversion and nurture were deemed unimportant. Sooner or later efforts were also made in those directions. The rationale was that for the benefit of the individuals involved, as well as for the state, it was important to bring them into the Christian fold. Even if they were largely unaware of the meaning of Christianity, they could be transferred by Baptism into the dominion of the saved. Then, later, as conditions permitted, they could be instructed and inspired. Ultimately some, at least, could be expected to become ardent and conscientious followers of Christ.

Suppressing Paganism

After Constantine every Roman emperor except one was a professing Christian, and most made attempts to counteract paganism and to promote acceptance of Christianity. Although pagans were not persecuted as persistently and violently as the Christians had been, they were forbidden to worship their gods and were commanded to receive Christian instruction and Baptism. For refusal to accept Baptism they could be punished with exile or the loss of their property. In addition, there were periodic mob assaults against pagan temples which were frequently led by monks. These repressive measures during the fourth century succeeded in turning most of the Roman urban aristocracy away from paganism and toward Christianity. However, in rural areas and among the lower classes paganism persisted for centuries.

During the fifth century there was a fresh intrusion of paganism into western Europe in the form of migrating and conquering Germans.[14] In the east as well as the west pockets of paganism survived well into the sixth century. Athens remained a center of pagan philosophical thought. Because significant numbers of Christian youth were attracted to these schools and subsequently many lost their faith, the schools were closed in A.D. 529 by Emperor Justinian, who also instituted other more severe anti-pagan measures.[15] Later in the middle ages among the Norwegians, Saxons, Wends and Prussians, paganism was ultimately destroyed by political and military power. As will be seen, there were also instances during this era in which paganism crumbled because people recognized Christianity as superior. However, what has just been referred to is the smashing of paganism by the iron fist of Christian rulers. Usually, church leaders approved of this repression. A heartening exception is Alcuin, adviser to Charlemagne, who deplored the coercive measures employed against paganism and advocated instead winsome preaching and exemplary Christian piety.[16]

Why did Christians suppress paganism? Why did they feel that it was necessary to destroy pagan idols and places of worship and to forbid participation in pagan rites and the propagation of pagan views? Divine commandments and historical precedents in the Old Testament era suggested it. God's honor and glory seemed to require it. Recollection of pagan persecution of Christians certainly stimulated it. The desire to protect Christians against relapse into paganism was an important motivation. Finally, the desire to do what was best for the pagans themselves prompted it. Convinced as they were that paganism was not only erroneous but fatal, Christians believed that anything they could do to discourage adherents from practicing it was in the best interests of the pagans themselves. If they were deprived of the outward symbols and supports of their religion, they might ultimately become more responsive to Christianity. As it turned out, in many instances this did happen.

Christianizing the Conquered

Medieval Christians used force, not only to combat paganism, but also to compel outward acceptance of Christianity. This was done in connection with wars of conquest with pagan peoples. The price of defeat was not only political submission but also Christian baptism and submission to the spiritual authority of the church.

Charlemagne's conquest and conversion of the Saxons (772—97) is a prime example of this approach. Charlemagne was the great Christian ruler of the Franks, one of the Germanic peoples that had invaded and conquered part of the old Roman Empire in the west during the fifth century. He had consolidated and extended his realm substantially, but was frustrated by the stubborn resistance of the still pagan Saxons on his northern border. They would have no part of his plan to incorporate them into his kingdom. Nor were they receptive to the missionaries who had been sent to them. Furthermore, they continued to ravage and raid Frankish lands and people near the border.

Therefore, with the prayerful support of his clergy and the approval of his political officials Charlemagne undertook a military solution. He invaded Saxon territory, overthrew their idols, and took hostages to ensure the safety of missionaries who accompanied the expedition. Initial successes were reversed in a revolt led by Widukind. Repeated campaigns were required to suppress the uprising. Refusing Baptism or showing disrespect to Christianity were made capital crimes. For a full quarter of a century only by the most severe and persistent measures were the Saxons kept within the Frankish realm and the Christian fold. In 785 Widukind finally surrendered and was baptized at his own request. Hostilities finally ceased in 797, after which coercion was relaxed, good relations were established between the warring peoples, and Christian evangelism continued among the Saxons in an atmosphere of comparative freedom.

Charlemagne's motives for forcing conformity to Christianity were not entirely imperialistic and defensive. As an ambitious ruler he did want to subdue and annex the Saxons. However, he was also a devout Christian and, undoubtedly, was moved in part by a sincere concern for their spiritual and eternal well-being. They needed to be saved whether they realized it or not, and, from his point of view, conversion could be authentic even under duress. If they refused to be converted, they were doomed anyway, so killing them was no real loss. Although this is not an adequate rationale either theologically or ethically, it does reflect the good intentions on the part of the Christian warrior king.[17]

Far more bitter and prolonged were the efforts of the Germans to conquer and convert the Wends—Slavic people who inhabited the region between the Elbe and Oder rivers along the southern Baltic shore. During the period from 930 to 1162, warfare, reprisals, and finally the relocation of the Wendish people and the mass introduction of German immigrants succeeded in subjugating and Christianizing the area. The mutual hatred of the Germans and the Wends, the highly developed religion of the Wends, the obvious subservience of the church to the expansionist goals of the German nation, and the preoccupation of the clergy with land and tithes rather than evangelism all help to explain the stubborn resistance of the Wends to Christian outreach. In the end few were actually converted. They were either exterminated or expelled from their land and replaced by German Christians.[18]

In Charlemagne's conquest and conversion of the Saxons, political and missionary considerations were somewhat in balance. But in the German campaigns against the Wends political objectives far overshadowed evangelistic concerns. Another example of Christianizing by conquest is the conversion of the Pomeranians in the 12th century. In this case military and political power were used with restraint, and the process of Christianization was characterized by persuasion, patience, and diplomacy. The key figure in this venture was Otto, bishop of Bamberg, who at age 60 was summoned from his comfortable and prestigious position by Duke Boleslav III of Poland to undertake an awesome missionary challenge.

In a series of brutal conflicts, Boleslav had succeeded in conquering western Pomerania, where the Oder River empties into the Baltic Sea, as well as some territory to the east. When the Pomeranians surrendered, their duke, Wartislav, agreed that they would accept Christianity as well as Polish rule. At this point Boleslav recruited Otto, having failed in his attempts to enlist missionaries from his own nation. Otto's approach was to visit strategic Pomeranian cities with an impressive retinue of clergy, political dignitaries, and a modest military force. Although he represented a hated foreign invader, Otto's task was aided by the previous conversion of some of the Pomeranian ruling class and the erosion of confidence in the traditional Pomeranian gods. In his presentations to public assemblies he reminded the Pomeranians that their duke had agreed to their conversion, that he, Otto, was there only to promote their salvation and not to take away their money, and also that if they did not receive the Christian message attentively and comply respectfully, they would have to face the fierce vengeance of their Polish conqueror.

In some cases the Pomeranians responded very positively and very quickly. In others they resisted or defected after initially complying. Even then, Otto worked with them patiently and in one case assuaged the wrath of Boleslav, who was ready to punish them with great severity. There is no doubt that Otto made some use of his military and political support. However, it is also clear that evangelism was his priority. He much preferred a voluntary response to the use of force. His winsome, conciliatory personality was a fitting medium through which to transmit the Christian way. Largely because of his evangelistic style, the Pomeranians were not embittered and resentful toward Christianity as were, for example, the Wends. Subsequently, the process of Christianization was furthered by the ministry of German and Danish missionary monks and the settlement of many German immigrants among the Pomeranian people.[19]

Gaining the Conquerors

Not all Christianization during the middle ages was done from a position of political and military advantage. Throughout much of southern Europe during the fifth century, Christian territories were overwhelmed by Germanic tribes, many of whom were either pagans or Arians. The latter were a heretical form of Christianity that denied the true divinity of Jesus Christ. Some also were Catholics. (At this point in time "Catholic" refers to those who uphold the deity of Christ as defined by the Council of Nicea and subsequent councils—in other words, mainstream Christianity as compared with deviant groups.) These invaders and conquerors, though a relatively small minority, managed to dominate Christian Europe permanently. Christian influence filtered into these people, sometimes gradually and unintentionally, in other cases rapidly and dramatically. In the end, virtually all adopted the Catholic Christianity of their subjects. Many of their descendants became vigorous agents of Christian expansion.

To a large extent the conversion of the barbarians (Germanic peoples) in the west was the result of royal initiative and will be considered later in this section. However, it was also in part a process of acculturation. The religion and culture of the Germanic conquerors were much less developed than those of their Roman subjects. German rulers were eager to integrate their people into the Roman population, but the latter resisted, especially because of the religious differences. Gradually the conquerors began to conform religiously as well as culturally to the majority. Initially, this was not the result of evangelism because the Roman Christians were not yet ready to welcome them. Rather, it was the magnetism of a more impressive religion and a desire to be like those around them.

The conversion of Clovis, king of Franks (A.D. 502), and that of a number of other Germanic rulers, sped the process. They recognized that having the support of the Catholic church would greatly enhance their ability to rule successfully. Finally, a pope, Gregory the Great (A.D. 590—604), recognized the barbarians as a mission field ripe for the harvest and worked actively and creatively to win them for Catholic Christianity. His leadership helped to develop a more open and evangelistic attitude in the Catholics toward pagan and Arian Germans. He also launched a mission to the Anglo-Saxons, which will be discussed in the concluding section of this chapter. Although combined with royal and papal influence, acculturation was a major factor in the conversion of the Germans on the continent.[20]

Similarly, many Vikings were gained for Christianity through peoples whom they had conquered. In some areas, both on the continent and in Britain, the Vikings established colonies. Like the Germanic invaders before them, they gradually conformed to the religion and culture of those whom they had vanquished. Traders and other travelers brought Christian captives back to the Viking homelands. Soldiers and rulers became interested and involved in Christianity. During the 11th and 12th centuries, in ways to be described later, Christianity was imposed upon the general population of the Scandinavian nations. Christianity posed no political threat to the Vikings precisely because it was the religion of their captives, rather than that of military enemies. For them, to accept Christianity was not a mark of submission but the conscious or unconscious adoption of a religion and culture regarded as superior to their own.[21] Invaders and conquerors in eastern Europe—Slavs, Avars, and Bulgars—were also gradually absorbed into the form of Christianity that they encountered. This process was aided by the translation of the Bible and the liturgies into their Slavonic tongue.[22]

Rulers Christianize Their Subjects

At least a dozen nations or major ethnic groups were brought into Christianity during the middle ages primarily through the initiative or the support of their rulers. These were in every case people who lived outside the borders of the old Roman Empire or who had invaded and conquered its remote provinces. Some of these rulers actively engaged in evangelism themselves. The rest made it clear in other ways that they expected their subjects to become Christians. All imported or at least welcomed Christian missionaries, and many supplied them with material and political support. A few employed the threat of severe punishment to subjects who refused to accept Baptism and Christian instruction. Resistance of Christianization cost some people their lives. Appalling to the 20th-century person as these coercive methods of evangelism might seem, they were consistent with the social and religious traditions of the people involved.

Limitations of space permit only a brief review of these extremely interesting and significant developments. The first such case occurred already in the third century, when King Tiridates of Armenia was converted by Gregory the Illuminator and, with the support of his nobles, permitted Gregory to evangelize his subjects. They readily complied and very rapidly Christianity permeated Armenian culture.[23]

On Christmas Day, 496, Clovis, king of the pagan Franks, was baptized along with 3,000 of his troops. The encouragement of his Christian wife and a military victory in answer to prayer to the Christian God were contributing factors. He did not actively work for the conversion of his subjects. However, gradually many followed him into Christianity at least externally. This was the first Germanic ethnic group to become Catholic Christians after the conquest. Even though the faith was only superficially implanted among them, and the institutional church became weak and corrupt, the conversion of the Franks was of great significance. They were to become the leading power in western Europe, and their example encouraged other Germanic people to make a similar religious change.[24]

During the course of the seventh century, several pagan Anglo-Saxon rulers in Britain were converted. The first was Ethelbert of Kent, who also had a Christian wife. In 597 he permitted a group of Roman missionaries to evangelize his people. Soon he himself believed. Aided by his example and support, missionaries were able to make nominal Christians of the entire population. Edwin King, of Northumbria, was also introduced to Christianity by his wife. Her confessor, Paulinus, a Roman missionary, patiently evangelized the monarch and was permitted to establish the church in that land. After Edwin's death there was a pagan reaction. However, a later king, Oswald (634—42), who had been converted by Irish missionaries, enlisted their aid in evangelizing his people. Not only did he welcome and support their ministry, but he himself served as their interpreter on occasion. By his devout life and earnest witness Oswald greatly advanced the Christian cause and was, in the truest sense of the term, an evangelizing ruler.[25]

Several centuries later Scandinavian rulers who had been converted primarily through English influence worked vigorously to establish and consolidate Christianity among their own people. Anskar, the ninth-century missionary to the Scandinavians, had made a very small and short-lived beginning. It was not until late in the tenth century under royal auspices that the Christian movement flourished and prevailed. In Denmark, King Harold Bluetooth was converted about 945. He called missionaries and built churches. There was a revival of paganism and Christian persecution after his death. However, Svein and especially Knute the Great, several later rulers, put their power and influence behind the cause, and, by the time the latter had died in 1035, Denmark was largely Christian.[26]

The evangelization of Sweden was begun by German missionaries and furthered somewhat by commercial and political contacts with English Christians. However, a deep and widespread impact awaited the conversion of King Skötkonung in 1008. Subsequent pagan reactions were infrequent and brief. A century later under the rule of pious King Sverker (1130—1205) a cathedral was built, monasteries were founded, and the Church of Sweden entered into a relationship with the pope.[27]

In Norway several Christian rulers were especially energetic and aggressive in imposing Christianity upon their subjects. Norse Vikings and traders had encountered Christians in the course of their travels. Some Christian captives had spread their faith among the Norwegians, especially the aristocracy. Prior to seizing the throne, King Olaf Tryg-gvason (994—1000) was baptized and confirmed by English clergy whom he encountered in the course of his voyages. Once the throne was his, he went from region to region throughout his realm along with troops, leading nobility, and a number of English clergy. He met with the people and their regional leaders in public assemblies and encour-aged them to become Christians. Those who refused or who defected after Baptism were put to death. In most places people complied readily. In a few places resistance was stubborn, and was savagely put down. Idols and temples were destroyed, and mass baptisms were performed. A later king, Olaf Haraldson (1016—30), completed the Christianization of Norway. Assisted by English clergy, he went on tours throughout the land, investigating religious and moral conditions, appointing priests, and consecrating churches. After his death in battle (1030) against King Knute and the Danes, he continued to rise in popular esteem and was canonized as Saint Olaf.[28]

Rulers of many eastern European nations also took the initiative in Christianizing their subjects. Ratislav, prince of the Moravians, in about 862 asked the Byzantine (Greek) emperor for missionaries to work among his people. In the previous decade some western missionaries had brought many to a nominal profession, but the prince wanted something deeper. The emperor sent Cyril and Methodius, who prepared for their mission by reducing the Slavonic language to writing and by translating Scripture, liturgies, and other religious literature. This was resisted by German missionaries and the pope. Ultimately, Cyril and Methodius were forced out of Moravia, but their work of translation was a tremen-dous aid in evangelizing other Slavic people. Boris, king of the Bulgari-ans, accepted Baptism in 865 as part of a peace settlement with Byzantine Emperor Michael III. In keeping with this agreement he also furthered the mass conversion of his subjects despite opposition from his nobility. Slavonic was used as the language of the Bulgarian church, which ultimately became autonomous. This set the pattern that con-tinues in eastern Christendom to this day. Each nation or people orga-nized its own church with its own language and leadership, although the churches were in communion with one another. This is in contrast with the western (Roman) church, which pulled people of many nations into a single organization with a single leader, the pope, and utilizing a single language—Latin.

Late in the 10th century, Vladimir, ruler of what is now part of Russia, was converted and baptized. Missionaries both from the western and eastern churches had done some preliminary work, but Vladimir effectively extended and established Christianity among his people by encouraging conversion, building churches, and founding monasteries. Here too the church retained its autonomy, although it was in fellowship with and somewhat dependent upon the mother church of eastern Christendom in Constantinople. In the same century and in the next the Bohemians and the Poles, other Slavic groups, as well as the Magyars were brought into the western church through the initiative of their rulers.[29]

The factors that motivated these rulers to Christianize their subjects are reasonably evident. One was a sincere concern for their subjects' spiritual and eternal well-being. Most of these rulers themselves became Christians voluntarily as a result of compelling example and witness. They recognized Christianity as superior to their traditional religions, in fact, as the only true religion. To bring their subjects into this saving faith and fold was the only responsible thing to do, from their point of view, even if it required a considerable amount of pressure. Closely related to this was the realization that their traditional religion and cultures were already disintegrating. Confidence in and loyalty to the old gods was failing, and zeal for their old customs and ways was flagging as their people were exposed to Christianity and its cultural expressions. Then, of course, there were political advantages. For them and their people to be identified as Christians paved the way for improved relations with the strong and advanced Christian nations around them. Finally, sweeping away the old religious establishment and installing a new one of his choosing could help a ruler consolidate his power. It could symbolize his regime and provide a new center and dynamic for national life. In more than a few cases rulers declared themselves for Christianity after a crucial battle, which convinced them that Christianity was a more powerful and reliable military resource than their traditional religions. The balance between spiritual and political motivation varied from ruler to ruler and from situation to situation.

Attempts to Convert Jews

No aspect of the history of evangelism is more disappointing and shameful than some of the attempts to convert the Jews to Christianity. Jewish-Christian tensions in the early period have already been reported. During the middle ages, as Christianity became increasingly dominant and aggressive, the plight of the Jews became most unenviable. In both eastern and western Europe Christian rulers, usually with the approval and assistance of church leaders, tried to compel Jews to become Christian. Coercive measures ranged from social and economic sanctions to exile, torture, and death for those who refused. Toleration prevailed at many times and in many places. For example, leading churchmen such as Gregory the Great, Bernard, and Thomas Aquinas spoke out against the persecution and forced conversion of the Jews. For the most part, however, they were ignored. In addition to the official actions mentioned above, Jews were frequently subjected to violence by fanatical Christian mobs.

What fueled these cruel and un-Christian actions? A residue of resentment lingered from the conflicts of the early period. Christians were frustrated over the refusal of most Jews to respond to more friendly evangelistic methods. They were regarded as "Christ-killers" and, consequently, subject to God's curse. Vicious and unfounded rumors circulated, attributing atrocities and blasphemies to the Jews. Since Jews were forced out of most other economic pursuits, they became moneylenders and bankers, thus gaining the hatred that frequently attaches to those to whom others owe money. In addition, virtually every society likes to have a scapegoat. To medieval Christians, Jews seemed to be the logical candidates.

Although most Jews remained steadfast in their ancestral faith, some conformed to Christianity. The power of the Gospel, acculturation, and persecution were among the chief agents of change. However, even when conversion was sincere, it was often suspect. Jewish converts to Christianity sometimes rose to prominence in both church and state, evoking the envy of those less successful. Many were suspected of secretly practicing Judaism. Late in the 15th century the Inquisition was launched in Spain in order to ferret out secret Jews as well as secret Muslims. This brief and general summary can only begin to suggest the tragedy and disgrace of most medieval attempts to convert Jews.[30]

Monastic Evangelists

Evangelism in the middle ages was carried out primarily by members of monastic orders. We have already noted how they led the way in calling their fellow Christians to renewal, to a more complete commitment of heart and life. In this section we trace the outreach of monastic evangelists to non-Christians. Although originally this was not an objective of monasticism, by the sixth century we see monks engaged in the conversion of pagans as a by-product of other pursuits. From the eighth century we encounter monastic groups primarily devoted to this kind of evangelism. After medieval Christian rulers imposed Christianity on their subjects or conquered peoples, they would almost inevitably establish monasteries among them with the expectation that from these centers Christian influence would spread and penetrate.

Irish Missionary-Evangelists

In several respects Irish monasticism was unique. It was the dominant element of the Irish church rather than an auxiliary agency. It was tribal rather than diocesan. It was devoted to learning more than any other contemporary form of monasticism. Most important for the purpose of this study, it was characterized by an inclination toward ascetic pilgrimages. Small groups of Irish monks, usually a leader and 12 followers (after the example of Jesus), would leave their home monastery and familiar surroundings for some distant and strange place in order there to lead a life of austere seclusion. To the usual monastic sacrifices they added this peculiar form of deprivation. Their primary purpose on these pilgrimages was to further their own spiritual and eternal well-being. In the process, however, they became a significant force for the conversion of pagans as well as for strengthening the commitment of only partially Christianized people.

Their procedure was to secure permission from a local ruler to occupy some remote and valueless area. There they would build crude shelters and establish their regimen of worship, work, and study. Their piety, purity, self-denial, and charity were in striking contrast with the idolatry, savagery, and immorality around them. People noticed them and were impressed. Many were drawn to Christianity and monasticism by their example and requested instruction. After they became known and respected in an area, the monks would then go out among the people proclaiming the Christian message and modeling the Christian life. The evangelization of Ireland, Scotland, and northern England, as well as parts of France, Switzerland, and Italy, was accomplished by Irish missionaries in this way. Among their outstanding leaders were Columba (521—97), who went to Scotland, Columbanus (ca. 543—615), who went to the continent, and Aidan (d. 651), who went to Northumbria (England).[31]

Roman Missionary-Evangelists

The earliest Roman missionary monks were different from the Irish in several respects. They had no inclination toward ascetic pilgrimages. In fact, when they left Rome for the purpose of converting the Anglo-Saxons of Kent in southeastern England, it was with considerable reluctance and apprehension. They were afraid of those strange and warlike pagans. Only the insistence of Pope Gregory the Great kept them on their mission. Much to their surprise and relief, King Ethelbert received them cordially when they arrived in 597, due undoubtedly to the influence of his Christian queen, Bertha.

In this new and pagan environment the Roman missionaries resumed their monastic way of life. Using the monastery as a base, they traveled about the countryside preaching, usually out-of-doors, and, when appropriate, gathering people for Baptism. Their outstanding characteristic was order, discipline, and a close working relationship with the pope. In less than a decade all of Kent was nominally Christian. Through the combined efforts of Roman and Irish monks most of England was externally Christianized by the end of the seventh century, complete with a hierarchy and numerous monasteries.

An important evangelistic principle urged upon the Roman monks by Gregory, and probably observed by them, was that of accommodation. Heathen temples, festivals, and other practices need not be utterly eliminated from the lives of new Christians. Rather, they should be adapted to the worship of God. The monks were to remove only that which was clearly idolatrous and demonic and substitute Christian elements. Such an approach, Gregory contended, would aid their transition into the Christian faith and way.[32]

English Missionary-Evangelists

Inevitably, during the course of their missionary labors among the Anglo-Saxons, Roman and Irish monks met. There were some minor differences between them over church practices as well as some rivalry. However, by the end of the seventh century these two streams of missionary effort had merged under Roman leadership. At this point English Christianity became a distinct entity combining some of the best qualities of the parent movements. English monasticism reflected this. From the Romans it inherited a strong sense of organization, discipline, and loyalty to the pope. From the Irish it inherited a fervent zeal, learning, and the impulse to travel. Out of this heritage English monasticism soon developed an evangelistic commitment and effort that has rarely been surpassed.

The field to which the English monks were drawn was the continent of Europe—initially Frisia (Netherlands)—and from there to those parts of the Frankish kingdom east of the Rhine and north of the Danube. The inhabitants of this area were, for the most part, nominally Christian, although there were also sizable and hostile pagan elements. The work to which the English monks gave themselves unsparingly was the conversion of pagans and the spiritual deepening and strengthening of those already partially Christianized.

Hundreds, perhaps even thousands of English missionary monks, both males and females, ventured into strange, primitive, and dangerous territories intent upon evangelism. They traveled the major rivers, roads, and forest trails, living off the land. Upon entering a new area they would seek to make contact with the local leaders and upper classes, assuming that if they responded, the masses would follow. Because they were related ethnically and linguistically to these Germanic people (the English were descendants of the Anglo-Saxon conquerors of Britain), the missionaries were able to communicate effectively with them. Wherever possible, they established monasteries that drew local people into this earnest and rigorous Christian life-style and prepared them for missionary service. In addition, the monasteries became centers of learning and spiritual leadership radiating a reform influence throughout the society.

Political and material support for this work came from the Frankish rulers. At the beginning that support was limited, but as the eighth century progressed interest and involvement grew significantly. In fact, the work of the English missionaries flourished only where they enjoyed that support. The Frankish dynasty that increasingly sponsored this work was ultimately known as the Carolingians, named after the greatest of the line, Charlemagne, whose forced conversion of the Saxons we have already considered.

Certainly, the most outstanding medieval English missionary was Boniface (ca. 675—754), whose given name was Wynfrith. Born of Christian Saxon parents in Wessex and educated in several excellent English monastic schools, Boniface became an accomplished scholar, priest and ecclesiastical leader. At age 41 he left behind excellent opportunities for advancement in both church and monasticism in order to attempt mission work among the pagan Frisians of the Netherlands. Political disturbances interrupted that. After a brief interlude back in England at his home monastery of Nhutscelle, he returned to Frisia and worked for several years assisting the missionary archbishop Willibrord, a fellow Saxon with an established work among the Frisians. Before beginning an independent evangelistic effort, Boniface traveled to Rome and received a commission from the pope to work among "the savage Germans." With that credential, and with political support from Frankish rulers as well as prayer and workers supplied by English monasteries, he undertook his great work.

He began among the largely pagan Hessians and then moved to the semi-Christianized Thuringians and Bavarians. He preached, destroyed idols, planted monasteries, recruited workers, and established churches. Ultimately he was made archbishop of Mainz, from which position with royal support he improved order and discipline among the clergy and was an effective force for the reform of the decadent Frankish church. Furthermore, it was due primarily to his encouragement that the Frankish church was consolidated under the authority of the pope.

At age 78 he resigned his archepiscopal office and resumed missionary work among the pagan Frisians, with whom he had begun his evangelistic career. While preparing for the confirmation of a group of recently baptized people, he and his companions were attacked by an armed band of pagans. His companions prepared to take up arms in their own defense, but Boniface forbade it, urging them joyfully to accept the crown of martyrdom. It was a fitting conclusion to a life of courageous and effective evangelistic ministry. Fourteen years before his death he reported that as many as 100,000 Germans had been gained through his ministry.[33]

Friars as Evangelists

English missionary monks continued their evangelistic work among the Germans for five or six decades after the martyrdom of Boniface (754). This was followed by two centuries of monastic decline and decay. When monastic reform occurred in the form of the Cluny movement in the 10th century, evangelism was not part of it. Some concern to reach non-Christians was evidenced by the Cistercian order, which was founded at the end of the 11th century. However, it was not until the appearance of a new type of religious order early in the 13th century— the friars—that evangelism once again became a high monastic priority.

Of the numerous orders designated as friars, the Franciscans and Dominicans were most prominent. Although each had its distinctive emphases, they were similar in that both were activistic, devoted to a life of service in society rather than to one of contemplative withdrawal. Furthermore, that service in the case of both orders included evangelistic preaching. They traveled throughout Europe and far beyond in pairs or small groups with the express purpose of Christianizing their hearers. Earlier in this chapter we referred to their evangelism for the renewal of Christians. At this point we focus on their attempts to gain non-Christians. Virtually all recorded evangelistic outreach to non-Christians done by or among western Europeans late in the middle ages was the work of Franciscans or Dominicans.

The scope of their evangelistic work was vast, including ventures among the Muslims of North Africa and the Mideast, pagans on the Baltic shore, Turks, Mongols, and even the people of India. Some of that work, especially among the Muslims, resulted in few converts. Even rather substantial and flourishing beginnings elsewhere, such as among the Mongols, were subsequently wiped out by a resurgence of native religions or the rise of Islam. Little remains of their efforts during this period. However, their dedicated, energetic, and creative evangelization was commendable and cannot be overlooked even in this brief study.

Only two examples will be cited. Raymond Lull (1232—1316), member of a Franciscan auxiliary group, was moved by a vision of the crucified Savior to dedicate himself to world evangelism. He tried to persuade church leaders to found monastic orders specifically for the evangelization of non-Christians. By studying the languages and cultures of the people whom they proposed to reach, Lull believed that future missionaries could dramatically increase their effectiveness. His ideas were not well received, but he was determined to put them into practice personally. He traveled through North Africa engaging Muslims in dialog. He made few converts and was ultimately stoned by an angry mob. Despite his meager results, Lull's courage and vision continue to be a source of evangelistic inspiration.

The other example is that of the missionaries to the Mongols. During the course of the 13th century those people under the leadership of Genghis Khan and his successors accomplished one of the most spectacular conquests of all times. In a series of sweeping victories, they created an empire that included almost everything from the Pacific on the east to the Euphrates and Dnieper rivers on the west. During the first three-quarters of the century their attitude toward Christianity was hostile. However, after the way was prepared by western merchants and other Christians who had filtered in from adjacent countries, and after a more tolerant ruler, Kublai Khan, came into power, the missionaries were permitted to enter. Most were Franciscans. There was tension between the Franciscans and the Nestorian Christians, who during the middle ages had established small Christian outposts throughout much of the Middle and Far East. The Nestorians were spiritual descendants of Nestorius, a fifth-century patriarch of Constantinople denounced as a heretic by the Council of Ephesus (431) for his Christological views. Despite their long and extensive work in the Orient, it appears that the Nestorian churches did not convert many natives but primarily served Christian immigrants and their descendants.

The first Roman Catholic to reach the Mongolian capital, Cambaluc (now Peking or Beijing), was John of Montecorvino, a Franciscan. He arrived in 1294 and was received by the emperor. Within a decade he had established a church and translated the New Testament and the Psalms into the language of the Mongols and had made about 6,000 converts. Christian centers were also founded in three or four other major cities and many more were received by Baptism. By the mid-14th century, there was a cathedral and several additional churches in the capital. The evangelistic work of John and his Franciscan successors from the west was supported, in part, by the state. The missionaries, at least in Cambaluc, actually ate at the emperor's table. The depth and extent of their evangelistic impact cannot be measured accurately from the surviving records. However, with the benefit of royal endorsement and subsidy and the ability of the missionaries to work in one of the native languages, it may have been significant.

Regrettably, it was soon to be undone. During the last half of the 14th century the Chinese revolted against their Mongol overlords and purged their land of all foreign influences, including Christianity. Elsewhere, surviving heirs of the Mongol empire turned primarily to Islam and adopted severe repressive measures against whatever Christian presence remained.[34]

Russian Missionary-Evangelists

During the Mongol occupation of Russia beginning in the 13th century, many people moved north to escape their oppressive rule. Among them were numerous monks, both hermits and communities, who pushed far into the northern forests, beyond the reach of the Mongols, for safety and solitude. Pagans of that area and refugees from the south were attracted to the monastics. As in the west, people were drawn magnetically to monks, awed by their sanctity and eager for the protection of their God. Most eastern monasticism was contemplative, but these Russian monks in the far north evangelized the pagan population, provided pastoral care, introduced them to improved agricultural methods, taught them the Russian language, and integrated them into Russian culture. By the end of the 15th century the north was the political as well as the ecclesiastical center of Russia.[35]

The Evangelistic Message

What did these medieval evangelists say as they preached and witnessed to non-Christians? What was the content of their communication to those whom they wanted to bring to Christ and into the church? We have already briefly considered the messages of the ascetic, the monk, and the mystic as they called fellow Christians to renewal. Now we attempt to reconstruct the call to conversion as it was addressed to those still outside the Christian fold.

From the limited sources that survive we can discern some clear shifts in emphasis and even in content from the evangelistic message of the early period. First of all, by actions (often violent) and argumentation the missionaries tried to demonstrate the superiority of Christianity to paganism. Pagan deities were exposed either as human fabrications or demons or both. Missionaries frequently destroyed pagan idols and places of worship, challenging these deities to retaliate, if they existed. Furthermore, the Christians pointed to their own political, material, and technological success as evidence of their religion's validity.

Above all, they held out the prospect of eternal rewards and punishments as compelling incentives for becoming Christians. In terms of uniquely Christian theological content, they affirmed the triune nature of God, although in practice they often dwelt almost exclusively on the Second Person. They proclaimed both His justice and His mercy. They urged people to avail themselves of the cleansing power of Baptism, which removed the guilt of all previous sins, and to accept divine regulations for their conduct and worship along with divine power to abide by them. The end result of such faith and works would be the unsurpassed joys of the life to come.

Where did Jesus Christ fit into all this? He is God incarnate come to reveal Himself and to rescue us from evil. He is the divine Warrior-King with power to help us in every need, as well as to obtain forgiveness. His death and resurrection for human sin was mentioned occasionally and obviously believed. However, there is no evidence to suggest that this was the central element of their message. A fifth-century inscription refers to Baptism as the cleansing fount of life flowing from Christ's wounds. An inscription on a tomb of about the same period describes the deceased as redeemed by the death of Christ. Martin of Braga (ca. 574), in a letter to another bishop on how to convert the heathen, includes a solid paragraph on the atoning work of Christ. Bede (734), in a letter to a bishop, urges him to instruct clergy in the Apostles' Creed in their own language, presumably so that they could instruct their people. This would necessarily focus on the person and work of Christ.[36] Pope Boniface V, in a letter to King Edwin of Northumbria, speaks of the Cross by which the human race has been redeemed and of God's only Son whom He sent for redemption.[37] Otto of Bamberg preached to the Pomeranians about the coming of the Holy Spirit, the gifts of grace and the divine compassion and mercy revealed in Jesus.[38]

Such references are notable for their infrequency. The basic thrust

of the message to the non-Christians during the middle ages was that
they should submit to Christianity and its political and ecclesiastical
authorities for protection from evil and the prospect of benefits now and
hereafter. However, enough of the Gospel was conveyed along with all of
this to ignite faith in at least some. In various individuals and movements, from time to time, that flame flared up with great warmth and
brilliance. Even when only a dim spark, it was transmitted widely and
from generation to generation.

*   *   *

Evangelism in the middle ages was first of all a challenge addressed
to those who were already Christian in some sense. By dramatic examples of sacrificial dedication, as well as by the spoken and written word,
ascetics and monks stimulated others to respond to Jesus Christ with radical commitment. Some of this encouragement centered in the suffering
and saving love of Jesus as the motivating factor. More of it was strongly
works-righteous in orientation. By what they did and endured people
were led to believe that they would compensate for sin and merit God's
favor in this life and the next. Mystics fostered a form of Christianity
that emphasized the inner personal relationship with God and often
dwelt upon the atoning love of God in Christ as the source of that relationship. On the other hand, they also blurred the distinction between
Creator and creature and assumed that only by one's spiritual exertion
could God be found and experienced. However, in the calls to renewal
extended by these movements large numbers of Christians were transformed. The process of Christianization was advanced.

The evangelization of non-Christians frequently accompanied political change. Nations conquered by Christian powers often had to accept
Baptism and participation in church life as terms of surrender. Sometimes this was combined with persuasion and even bribery. In other
cases Christians used force to obtain agreement and compliance. Understandably, the more force was used, the greater the resistance and
resentment on the part of the non-Christians. An opposite phenomenon
was also common. Pagan conquerors were converted by the Christian
people whom they had subjugated. Both acculturation and evangelization were at work in these cases. In addition, some rulers newly converted from paganism imposed Christianity upon their still pagan
subjects. To accomplish this they used pious encouragement and example, imported missionaries, and also threats and violence. The most
offensive episodes of evangelism by force are those involving Jews.

The people who did most of the evangelistic proclamation during the middle ages were members of monastic orders. The earliest of these, the Irish (sixth and seventh centuries) were primarily ascetic pilgrims. However, pagans and semi-Christianized people whom they encountered were so interested in these monks and impressed by their example that the monks could hardly avoid testifying. The English missionaries (eighth century) were deliberately and vigorously evangelistic. A decline of monastic vigor and rigor from the ninth to the 12th century accounts largely for their lack of evangelistic involvement during this period. During the 13th century and beyond, a new type of monastic—friars— became heavily involved in evangelistic ministry especially among the Muslims and the Mongols, without lasting results. The spread of Christianity to northern Russia was primarily the work of monks who had fled from religious oppression imposed by their Mongol conquerors. Their monasteries became centers of Christian influence through which other Christian refugees were nurtured and pagans were converted.

In the message of medieval evangelists, the Gospel of reconciliation with God and newness of life solely through the work of Jesus Christ was significantly obscured and dangerously mingled with concepts of works-righteousness. However, enough was preserved and transmitted that Christianity not only survived but, at times, spread widely and even flourished.

III/Evangel Recovered and Disseminated: The Reformation Era
(1500—1650)

Reform is a prominent theme in church history. Periodically Christians have perceived a need for radical improvement in the church. A variety of reform movements have appeared in response to that need. Prior to the 16th century virtually all focused on moral, financial, and administrative abuses. However, early in the 16th century a new kind of reform impetus was felt. In northern Germany and then in Switzerland reformers arose whose criticism was aimed primarily at the church's message. Luther, Zwingli, Calvin, and their associates were convinced that the most threatening and debilitating problem facing the church was the distortion and obfuscation of its Gospel. Since the very early centuries, they believed, this process of doctrinal deterioration had been underway. In their own time it had become so serious as to jeopardize the salvation of those who relied on what the church proclaimed.

The church's error, as they saw it, consisted in requiring of the sinner what only God Himself can do, namely, to compensate for sin and make the guilty person righteous before Him. The theology and piety of the middle ages were thoroughly permeated by works-righteousness. Although salvation was regarded as primarily the work of God through the obedience and sacrifice of Christ, the contribution of the sinner was thought to be essential. There was a considerable amount of diversity in the teaching of medieval theologians about the relation of God's work to that of the sinner. However, on certain basics there was a consensus. God helps us to help ourselves, for instance. He has done the most difficult and painful part of the salvation process in the redemptive work of Christ. However, in order to get the benefit of Christ's work the sinner must move toward God. He must love God and obey God to the best of his ability.

This movement itself is, to a certain extent, the work of God. With a touch of His grace (understood primarily as transforming power) God enables the sinner to respond. If the sinner does the best he can with the resources available to him, God rewards him with another application of grace which will enable him to do still better. The process continues— more enabling grace following each satisfactory effort—until the sinner has improved sufficiently to be worthy of the blessed vision of God here- after in eternity. The sinner who does not respond to God's grace with adequate love and obedience secures no additional grace and does not merit the beatific vision.

The emphasis on works of merit in popular piety and practice was even greater than in medieval theology. Confessional manuals and cate- chisms of this era fostered a morbid preoccupation with sin and made relentless demands on the sinner for reparation. Continuous, extensive self-examination and frequent interrogation by the confessor were designed to produce awareness of sin and uncertainty of salvation. Relief and release were to be sought in acts of devotion, personal deprivation, and even cash payments. There is good reason to believe that resentment against this oppressive, works-righteous system was widespread.[1]

Salvation by God's grace plus human merit is a false gospel, accord- ing to the Protestant reformers, even if grace is the larger element and human merit is comparatively small. For, regardless of quantity, as long as the human component is considered essential, the self as well as the Savior is the object of faith. To the extent that faith rests on self it can never be secure. Even if one's contribution is minimal, how can he ever be sure that he has actually paid or done enough? If the only effective shield against the wrath of God is the merit of His crucified and risen Son, how will one survive if he replaces even a small part of that shield with his own flimsy merits?

Drawing especially on St. Paul and Augustine, the Protestant reformers affirmed that salvation is entirely God's work of grace (here understood as God's undeserved generosity) and in no sense that of the sinner. In an act of incredible humility and sacrifice, God's eternal Son joined the human race and endured the accumulated punishment of all human sin. By what He did and endured, Jesus justified us and declared us right with the Father, who is justly wrathful on account of our sins. This salvation, because it is complete and because it is a gift of grace, can be received only by faith. That is, having been made aware of God's gift of salvation and our desperate need for it, we can accept it as our own in personal trust. However, not even this acceptance is our work or accomplishment. The Holy Spirit, through the Gospel, both awakens and sustains this faith. Because they found this Good News of salvation by grace alone through faith in Christ clearly articulated in Scripture, the reformers were confident that it was correct. Authorities of the Roman church tried to suppress this recovered Gospel. Traditional teaching and practice of the church largely contradicted it. Faced with the necessity of choosing, the reformers took their stand on Scripture alone as the source and norm of the Christian message.

Although the Protestant reformers intended to correct and improve the ecclesiastical organization of which they were dutiful sons, the actual effect of their challenge was fragmentation. By the end of the 16th century, instead of being embodied in one major institution with the bishop of Rome at the head, western Christianity was divided between Catholicism and Protestantism, with the latter subdivided many times. Furthermore, rivalry and animosity were intense, not only between Protestants and Catholics, but among the various kinds of Protestants.

Extremely important to the purpose of this study is the realization that each of these Christian groups, Catholics as well as various kinds of Protestants, was convinced of its own correctness and was concerned about the harm that the doctrinal errors of the other groups inflicted on those who believed them. The result was the attempt on an unprecedented scale to convert people from one kind of Christianity to another. Most evangelistic effort in Europe during this period was of this kind. Opportunities to evangelize non-Christians in Europe were limited simply because not many admitted to being such. Furthermore, liberated and exhilarated by their newly recovered Gospel, many Protestants were eager to share it with others still in bondage to works-righteousness. The term "evangelical" soon came to designate the Protestant position with its Gospel orientation as compared with the works-righteous emphasis of Roman Catholicism.

For their part, once they recovered from the initial trauma of the Protestant challenge, renewed and invigorated Roman Catholics launched aggressive efforts to regain people and territories that had defected to Protestantism. In connection with vast colonial expansion, several Catholic nations launched the most massive world-mission programs that Christians had ever attempted. They were not content simply to compete with European Protestants, but were determined to Christianize multitudes inhabiting huge, newly-acquired American territories as well as those in their more limited African and Asian holdings.

Protestant Origins and Outreach

The brief survey of Protestantism undertaken here will not attempt to explore even the most important aspects of each of the major movements. Rather, in view of the specific focus of this study, we will concentrate on the processes by which people were drawn into the various branches of Protestantism and, in turn, induced others to follow them. What was it about the message, the messengers, the media, the political and cultural environment, that made it possible for these new Christian movements to survive and then to spread rapidly and extensively? Within less than 50 years Protestantism expanded from one dissenting individual to a position of numerical dominance in most of northern Europe and, in addition, was widely represented in central Europe. How did the reformers secure such a following? How did Protestantism grow?

Lutheran Expansion

The Reformation began as one man's search for spiritual peace and security. Anxious about death and divine judgment, Martin Luther was determined to get right with God. True to his Roman Catholic heritage, he turned to monasticism as the surest way to gain divine approval and prepare for the life to come. However, even the most severe deprivations and disciplines of monastic life brought Luther no assurance. He could never feel confident that his efforts were sufficient to compensate for his sins. Similarly, the sacrament of penance left him uncertain and frustrated. How could he know that he had remembered and reported everything he had done wrong? Neither did he find consolation in mysticism. This approach requires that one surrender, in love, to the infinite love of God. Luther's problem was that he could not love the God who demands the impossible (perfection) and then punishes the person who can not attain it.

A sensitive and sympathetic superior, John Staupitz, arranged for him to become a student and ultimately a teacher of Scripture in the hope that this would be an answer. It was in connection with his study of the Psalms and especially the Pauline literature that Luther came to realize that we do not have to make ourselves right with God by monastic, penitential, or mystical exertions. God makes us righteous by forgiving our sins for the sake of Christ. A deep and lasting sense of relief grew in Luther as the implications of this Good News became evident. Freed from fear of God's wrath and from the necessity of self-justification, Luther was eager to emancipate others.[2]

Popular Support

He began where he was—at the University of Wittenberg. He was popular among students and respected by his colleagues. During the course of his academic activities in the classroom, in faculty discussions, and personal conversations, Luther shared his discoveries and newfound convictions. Within three or four years after his recovery of the Gospel, both student body and faculty came to support his position. As he developed his grace-centered theology and, on the basis of Scripture, attacked everything in Catholic teaching and practice compromising it, he gained the assistance and support of that academic community. The significance of this for the spread of Lutheranism should not be underestimated. From 1520 to 1560 about 16,000 students were enrolled in the little institution. Two-thirds of these were from outside northern Germany. The evangelical theology and spirit absorbed at Wittenberg were carried far and wide throughout Europe and beyond as these students transferred to other universities, entered professional life, traveled for pleasure, or even undertook missionary journeys. Furthermore, as church reform was carried out in Lutheran territories, much direction came from this citadel of evangelical learning.[3]

Among the townspeople of Wittenberg Luther made his impact primarily through preaching. In 1515 the town council invited him to preach at the city church as a substitute for the regular pastor, who was ill. For the rest of his life Luther held this position in addition to a chair of biblical studies at the university. He was an earnest, colorful, interesting preacher with a gift for communicating effectively with the common people. In this dual role he was compelled on a regular basis to translate profound and complex theological issues into down-to-earth language and apply them to the needs of people. The recovered Gospel and its implications for life were the central and integrating theme of his preaching. Through his work as a parish preacher Luther helped spread the evangelical faith and life beyond the ivory tower of the university into the grass roots.

His influence as a preacher extended far beyond his congregation. To the future pastors who heard him he became a model as well as an inspiration. In addition, Luther wrote numerous sermons that were published for the benefit of those pastors who were ill-equipped to prepare their own. These were quality messages based on careful exposition of the Biblical text, clear Gospel orientation, and timely application to the individual and society. They were consulted, not only by parish preachers, but by scholars and other Reformation leaders. In these ways the influence of Luther's pulpit was magnified enormously.[4]

Key figures in the Reformation movements were Roman Catholic priests, who joined Protestant ranks in large numbers. Some had experienced a change of heart through exposure to the doctrine of Luther and the other reformers. For others it was a matter of expediency. As was already indicated, some of these had a very minimal grasp of evangelical truth and needed a great deal of help in getting it across to their people. However, others were able, knowledgeable, and committed. In the towns and villages of Europe they were the ones who imparted the recovered Gospel to the congregations and thus helped Lutheranism become a vital, growing movement.[5]

The printing press brought Luther and his doctrine to the attention of a large public and gained for him a host of followers. Although printing with movable type had been invented in 1484, this was the first instance of a major movement utilizing its potential. The importance of printing as a medium for disseminating the Reformation can scarcely be exaggerated. The translation and distribution of the 95 Theses throughout Europe in the course of a single month turned the obscure monk of Wittenberg into a celebrity. Luther's literary productivity was staggering—amounting to 100 volumes in the monumental Weimar Edition—and most of it was quickly published and widely read. In his writings he addressed the whole reading public. To scholars and church leaders he wrote in Latin, to the masses he wrote in German. Cleverly illustrated tracts, a magnificent translation of the entire Bible, catechism, and theological treatises all came from his ready pen and onto the press. Interesting and controversial works like those of Luther were in great demand. Through print Luther was able to make a deep and lasting impression on Christian minds and hearts. Few have used print more effectively. Nor were his the only writings that advanced the cause of Lutheranism. Philip Melanchthon, as well as numerous other authors (including some who remained anonymous), contributed to a literary flood that threatened to inundate the opponents.[6]

Still another reason for Luther's rapid rise in prominence and influence was his style. Not only did he have a powerful, substantial message, and marvelous gifts for communicating it, he also lived out his convictions with great courage and drama. He dared to defy the highest authorities in western Europe: the pope and the emperor. Both threatened him with their ultimate sanctions in order to compel him to back down. Condemned as a heretic, excommunicated by the church, and placed under the imperial ban, Luther nevertheless stood by his evangelical convictions and his criticisms of churchly corruption.

The personal and professional risks were as high as could be, and yet his conscience would not allow him to surrender or to compromise. He burned the feared papal bull of condemnation in a public demonstration when it finally arrived in Wittenberg on December 10, 1520. Four months later he stood alone at Worms before the emperor and the highest political figures of Germany and firmly refused to recant. He captured the imagination and evoked the respect of people of all stations in life. To the masses he became something of a folk hero. Even after the tragedy of the Peasants' Revolt in 1525, many common people felt that he was expressing their concerns and fighting their battle. His style added tremendously to his credibility.

The time was right for the Reformation-revolt that Lutheranism became. For more than a century sensitive and sensible people realized that there was something radically wrong with the church. The precise nature of the malady was a matter of dispute, but most agreed that the condition was grave. As will be seen, political developments provided a relatively secure environment in which Lutheranism could survive and grow. Revived linguistic skills and tools enabled Luther and others to study Scripture and the early Christian writers in the original languages. On the basis of such study they were confident that the Gospel they recovered and were sharing was authentic.

Social conditions were also favorable. The rise of an increasingly educated and competent middle class had created a receptive audience. The peasantry, especially in Germany, were chafing under oppressive economic disabilities and were ready to rally around almost any leader who would challenge the status quo. Intellectual ferment was generated in and through the universities. Popular religious movements, some stressing a mystical approach to God and others the awareness of sin and the need for salvation, revealed both dissatisfaction with existing conditions in the church and a readiness to move in a new direction. The stage was set for bold action.[7]

Political Support

If both pope and emperor were against Luther and determined to stamp out his movement, how was Lutheranism able to survive and grow? Luther's writings were to be burned. Anyone who supported him, regardless of rank or class, would also come under papal condemnation and excommunication. Declared an outlaw by the emperor, Luther was to be seized by any subject and turned over to the authorities, or done to death at will. His followers and supporters were liable to the same penalties. Printing, selling, buying, reading, or even owning any of Luther's writings was sufficient cause for severe punishment. In view of these threatening consequences, who would dare to stand by Luther and his cause? How could popular support continue to grow virtually unhindered?

Among those who could afford to support Luther and Lutheranism were strong German princes. Germany at this time was part of the Holy Roman Empire, of which it has been said that it was not, in any meaningful sense, holy, nor was it really Roman, nor even much of an empire. It was a loose confederation of hundreds of states, largely autonomous, as well as dozens of free cities. The emperor was elected. The position carried with it considerable prestige but little real power. The incumbent had to rely on the financial and military resources of his hereditary domain. Many territories were small and weak. However, some were large, relatively strong, and ruled by princes who were as capable as they were jealous of each other's authority. Even an emperor as determined and powerful as Charles V (1500—58), who outlawed Luther and Lutheranism, would think twice before attempting to enforce his edict against the will of such a prince.

But regardless of the cost, Charles was committed to the destruction of Lutheranism and would have moved against it except for several major distractions. Wars with France, the pope, and the Turks took him away from Germany for a decade and allowed the German princes to deal with the movement largely as they saw fit. Luther's own prince, Duke Frederick of Saxony, although ostensibly a Catholic, felt it his duty to protect Luther against both pope and emperor. He was succeeded in 1525 by his brother, John, a Lutheran by conviction. By the end of the decade six other princes had come into the Lutheran camp. Political considerations were unquestionably a factor. To assert and maintain independence of pope and emperor in some cases could enhance the stature of an ambitious prince. Furthermore, in all of these territories, Lutheranism was gaining at the grass roots, and even strong rulers can benefit by shifting with winds of change. There were economic advantages in becoming Lutheran, not the least of which was relief from heavy financial obligations to Rome and the opportunity to seize church properties, especially those belonging to monastic orders.

However, in the case of most princes who turned Lutheran, spiritual and theological factors appear to have been dominant. At the Diet of Augsburg in 1530 the Lutheran princes presented a confession to the emperor declaring what they believed and what was being taught in their churches. Although this confession was written by a theologian, Philip Melanchthon, on the basis of several earlier doctrinal statements, the princes had made it their own. The Augsburg Confession, as this document is called, became the foundational expression of Lutheran witness. With justification by faith as its central and integrating theme, it remains a lively and formative influence in all of Lutheranism and beyond.

The princes provided two services vital to the survival and spread of Lutheranism. One was protection. Individually and later also collectively in the Smalcaldic League, they prevented the forced repression of the movement by the military might of the emperor and Catholic princes. The other was administration. Initially Luther leaned toward a free church concept. All believers in a community should gather in a congregation for the Lord's worship and work. All authority would rest in the members of the congregation. Pastors would function by virtue of their call and in the congregation's name as well as in the name of Jesus. Policies and practices would be decided by a democratic process. Before long, however, Luther became convinced that this arrangement was impractical and unsafe. As a temporary expedient he called upon the princes to assume administrative leadership of the churches in their territories. They complied and this arrangement became permanent.

Under princely leadership all religious life in these territories was adjusted to Lutheranism. Teams of visitors authorized by the prince toured the parishes. Unworthy clergy and those who would not conform to Lutheranism were dismissed. Steps were taken to purify worship of Roman errors, to introduce education, and to provide for the physical maintenance of the church and pastor. The principle of religious uniformity was adopted. Although no one was forced to become Lutheran, no other type of Christianity could be practiced publicly. Dissenters were expected to leave. The line between vigorous leadership and coercion and manipulation is fine, and certainly elements of coercion were present in these Lutheran territorial churches. However, it was far from the forced imposition of religion by rulers that was prevalent in the middle ages.[8]

Lutheranism gained acceptance in free cities of the empire as well as in the northern principalities. There were 65 such municipalities during the Reformation era. In more than half of them Lutheranism became legal and in most cases the religion of the majority. Since these cities enjoyed a considerable amount of self-determination, Lutheranism could attain this status only by generating a groundswell of popular support. The experience of most cities was similar. The initial impetus came from preachers or educated laity, who, having been caught up themselves in the new religious movement, were eager to share it with others. From them Lutheranism spread, especially through the lower and middle segments of the population. In general, the aristocracy, magistrates, and councilmen resisted. Only when popular support became sizable did the agencies of government legitimatize it, and then only gradually. The earliest and some of the most significant Lutheran growth took place in the cities, where it took the form of a contagious popular movement.[9]

Lutheranism was carried to the Scandinavian countries both through students who had been at Wittenberg and by German Lutherans who had settled in large Scandinavian commercial centers. However, only by royal mandates motivated primarily by political and economic factors did the churches of these northern nations become officially Lutheran. In eastern Europe where there was no royal support the gains were limited and, in many cases, temporary. Lutheran students and merchants launched the work there too, but competition from other Protestants and especially the Counter Reformation by a revitalized Roman Catholicism reduced the Lutheran movement to relative insignificance.[10]

Reformed Protestantism Spreads

Shortly after the Lutheran Reformation erupted in Germany, similar and related movements began elsewhere. The most important of these originated in Switzerland. One, led by Ulrich Zwingli in the German-speaking canton of Zürich in the northeast, developed just a year or two behind that of Luther. Another, led by John Calvin in the French-speaking city of Geneva in the southwest, took hold in the mid-1530s, a generation after Zwingli's reform began. The two Swiss movements eventually drew together, although without obliterating some of their distinctive characteristics. Ultimately, the term "Reformed" was attached to this group of Swiss Protestants and their spiritual descendants in order to distinguish them from the Lutherans.

Theologically, the Reformed had much in common with the Lutherans. They looked to the Bible as their supreme theological and ethical authority. They affirmed justification by God's grace alone through faith in Jesus Christ without equivocation and rejected everything that seemed to compromise it. They were committed to cleansing the church's teaching and worship according to evangelical norms.

There were, however, significant differences between the Reformed group and the Lutherans, differences which proved to be irreconcilable. The central and integrating themes of their theologies were different. For Zwingli Biblical authority was preeminent. For Calvin it was the sovereignty of God. Luther, on the other hand, constructed his theology around justification by faith. While each accepted the central doctrines of the others as essentially true, they disagreed about which doctrine was the central and controlling theme of theology. Furthermore, they disagreed strenuously about the doctrine of the Lord's Supper. Lutherans held to the real presence of Christ's body and blood. The Reformed taught either a symbolic or spiritual presence.

Their approaches to traditional practices were also at odds. Lutherans believed that Catholic practices not forbidden by Scripture and useful as effective media of the Gospel could be retained. This included statuary, stained glass, musical instruments and compositions, vestments, liturgy, the confessional and the like. The Reformed, on the other hand, were convinced that only that which was specifically commanded or permitted in Scripture could be utilized, thus abolishing all of the above.

The rise and spread of Reformed Protestantism in Switzerland went hand in hand with movements of political liberation. The cities and cantons of Switzerland had attained extensive autonomy from their princes, bishops, and the emperor well before the Reformation era. When the Reformation was launched it became an occasion both for asserting their independence and for increasing it. In each community there were councils of several sizes elected by the citizens. Although nominally under the authority of higher political and ecclesiastical powers, these councils assumed the prerogative of evaluating and implementing changes in doctrine and church practice advocated by reformers. Ultimately, as the Reformation progressed, the councils carried out functions of both princes and bishops, having declared their independence of both and, where necessary, having successfully maintained that independence with military force.

Influences conducive to reform flowed into Switzerland from all directions. Luther's writings and followers arrived from Germany at a very early date. Intellectual movements designated as "humanism" were also well represented. Originating in Italy and developing in a somewhat different form in the north, humanism stressed a return to the original sources of culture. In order to discover and experience human cultural achievement at its best, one must return to the literature and art of classical antiquity, preferably through the original languages of Greek and Latin. In order to discover and experience Christianity in its pristine purity (and thus to realize how far its present forms had deviated), one must return to the literature of early Christianity, both the New Testament and the writings of the early fathers, again preferably in the original languages—Greek and Latin. The southern humanists were largely secular in interest, focusing their attention on pagan classics. Many in the north were Christian humanists. They hoped to stimulate church reform by uncovering and sharing the treasures of Christian antiquity. In the Netherlands, Germany, England, and France, Christian humanists paved the way for the Reformation and were initially supportive of it.

The Swiss Reformation was triggered everywhere by preaching. On the basis of insights gained from Scripture with the assistance of skills and tools provided by Christian humanists, preachers challenged people to reject the corrupt doctrine and practices of the established church and to find pardon, peace, and freedom in the Gospel. Some, like Zwingli and Calvin, were officially appointed preachers. Others were independent, itinerant agitators for reform. In addition, there were parish priests who, upon being converted to Protestantism, shared their changed beliefs with parishioners. Lay people also proclaimed the recovered Gospel in public and in private.

The Reformation message changed beliefs, church institutions, and practices, as well as personal piety. Regulations about fasting were ignored. Monasteries were emptied. Religious statues were toppled and stained glass windows smashed. Clerical marriages were celebrated. The confessional was abandoned. When ecclesiastical authorities tried to check the tide of change, the city councils set themselves up as arbitrators. Public disputations were held in order to resolve the issues. Those arguing for reform prevailed. The councils made Protestantism official and in so doing rejected the authority of their bishops. The reform process occurred in stages. The vestiges of Catholicism, especially the mass, were not eliminated entirely for several years in some places. In the case of Geneva the change to Protestantism went hand in hand with a political revolution against the Duke of Savoy.

It was at Geneva under Calvin that the most significant development in Reformed Protestantism took place. Calvin took the lead in reorganizing both church and community according to Protestant ideals. His monumental *Institutes of the Christian Religion*, revised and expanded over a period of more than 20 years, presented Reformed theology in a clear, coherent, and convincing form. On the basis of this remarkable work, hundreds of Reformed pastors were indoctrinated so thoroughly that they were able to plant and extend Calvinism even in areas very hostile to it.

Another factor adding to the strength and appeal of Calvinism was the model community that Geneva became. Under Calvin's leadership all of life was made to conform to Protestant spiritual and moral standards, as he articulated them. Here was a place where rigorous Reformed

Christianity was not only preached but lived, at least externally. Protestants from all over Europe came to Geneva, often as refugees, to experience this ideal, and many carried it from Geneva with the hope of relocating it elsewhere.

Reformed Protestantism spread widely. It became the religion of the majority in Holland, Scotland, and parts of southern Germany, and a significant minority in parts of northern and east central Europe. In both Holland and Scotland it rose to dominance in connection with political revolutions against foreign Catholic regimes. In France it began as an underground religious movement, but soon was combined with political and military movements challenging the centralization and extension of royal power. Before the period under consideration in this chapter ended, Reformed Protestantism was firmly planted not only in Europe, but also in the New England colonies of North America, and even in the Far East. With confidence, zeal, and even force, vigorous representatives of Reformed Protestantism evangelized for their faith.[11]

England is Protestantized[12]

In some respects the English Reformation began in the 1530s when the clergy and Parliament, compelled by King Henry VIII (1509—47), rejected papal jurisdiction and declared the king to be head of the church in that nation. The reason for this was the refusal of Pope Clement VII to annul Henry's marriage to Catherine of Aragon, who had failed to provide him with a male heir. Henry was determined for political as well as emotional reasons to marry his paramour, Anne Boleyn, who hopefully would bear a son to succeed him on the throne of England. After the break, Henry secretly married Anne, and an ecclesiastical court sometime later declared his marriage to Catherine null and void.

Apart from the matter of papal jurisdiction, the Church of England still did not become Protestant until after Henry's death, for he was thoroughly committed to traditional Roman theology and practice and would tolerate no deviation. On one occasion, for political reasons, he made some doctrinal concessions to the Lutherans, but a few years later reasserted his Catholic orthodoxy in unequivocal terms. Apart from rejection of the papacy, the most significant change in the direction of Protestantism allowed by Henry was the sale of the Bible in English translation and even the placement of that Bible in all the churches in order to make it available to the public. In the long run this did much to facilitate the spread of Protestant ideas and attitudes.

Even before the king and government severed administrative ties with Rome, a small group of scholars at Cambridge University began to test and even to undo theological ties. Under the leadership of Robert Barnes, who had studied for a time with Martin Luther, this group met regularly at the White Horse Inn as early as 1520 to discuss Lutheran doctrine. Among the participants were some who later played leading roles in the Protestantization of England. At Oxford University Lutheran books were being sold early in 1520, but there is no evidence of a Lutheran circle comparable to the White Horse gatherings at Cambridge.

Another center of Lutheran influence was the business community in London. There, also about 1520, followers of the 14th-century pre-reformer John Wyclif (known as Lollards), moved into Lutheranism and actively promoted it through the distribution of literature and personal witnessing. They reached out from London to numerous surrounding communities. They had become acquainted with Lutheranism through the travel of some of them in Germany and the Netherlands. In addition, they had been in touch with German merchants located in London who sold Lutheran books and disseminated Lutheran doctrine.

Tremendous impetus for the growing Protestant movement in England came from wide distribution of a new translation of the New Testament into English by William Tyndale beginning in 1525. Tyndale had met Luther and largely followed his theology until 1530, when, in connection with his work on the Pentateuch, he began to place greater emphasis on works of the Law. In any case, his fresh and meaningful translation of Scripture enabled large numbers of laity to discover for themselves the validity and power of the Protestant message and, in general, reinforced high views of Biblical authority.

During the reign of Edward VI (1547—53) the Parliament began to adjust the worship and teaching of the Church of England toward Protestantism. Political leadership for this came from the duke of Somerset and later from the earl of Warwick, who exercised much of the authority of the sickly boy king. Theological and ecclesiastical leadership came primarily from Thomas Cranmer, archbishop of Canterbury. Many of the new views and practices were embodied in and implemented by the *Book of Common Prayer*, which by law was to be followed in all the churches. The earliest edition of this book, known as the "First Prayer Book" of Edward VI, issued in 1549, reflected Lutheran influence as well as some of the traditional Roman practices. By 1552 Calvinist influences dominated, and a revised prayer book incorporating these influences was published and its use enforced. While a significant element of the population was becoming Protestant by conviction, the majority were still largely indifferent and accepted these external changes without much difficulty.

Extremely important in the transition to Protestantism were hundreds of theologians and clergy from the continent, whom Cranmer invited and encouraged to come to facilitate the Reformation in England. Most were Reformed and came from Strassburg, Zürich, and Geneva. The most distinguished of these was Martin Bucer of Strassburg. Not only Cranmer's invitation but also anti-Protestant pressures from Emperor Charles V accelerated this migration. In England they were granted not only refuge but also positions of academic and ecclesiastical leadership from which they exerted strong Protestant influence.

Ironically, one of the most powerful surges of radical Protestant influence came to England as a result of a later monarch's attempt to restore Roman Catholicism. Mary Tudor (1553—58), Edward's half-sister and the daughter of Henry VIII by Catherine of Aragon, remained steadfastly Catholic despite the changes made during her predecessor's reign, and she was firmly convinced that she had been put by God on the English throne in order to bring England back to her traditional faith. This she accomplished by force, including the burning at the stake of nearly 300 Protestants who refused to comply with Roman Catholicism, among them some revered leaders. Many earnest Protestants fled for sanctuary to Reformed communities on the continent. There, during Mary's brief reign, they experienced and absorbed a form of Protestantism that to them seemed much more thorough than anything they had known in England. Meanwhile, Mary's persecutions backfired. They generated a much deeper and stronger anti-Catholic sentiment in England than any Protestant leaders had managed to cultivate. Upon her death, Catholicism was rejected immediately, and Protestantism was once more established by her successor and half-sister (daughter of Anne Boleyn), Queen Elizabeth I (1558—1603).

The form of Protestantism imposed by the Elizabethan Settlement, as religious adjustments under this monarch are designated, was a compromise. Certain Catholic usages—kneeling to receive the Eucharist, vestments, and church ornamentation—were retained, while moderate Protestant views and practices were also incorporated. The issue of Christ's presence in the Sacrament was left open by a formula that was deliberately ambiguous. The "Second Prayer Book" by Edward VI was revised accordingly, and its use in all the churches was required by law in 1559. This religious compromise, designed to secure acceptance from those of both Catholic and Protestant persuasions, actually pleased few who were earnestly devoted to either position.

Among the most dissatisfied were those who had returned from their self-imposed exile during the reign of Mary Tudor. To them the Elizabethan Settlement was a halfway reformation. Inspired by their experience with the Genevan model, they were determined to purify the Church of England from the vestiges of Catholicism and to make whatever other changes were necessary to vitalize English Christianity. Here we have the beginnings of Puritanism, a movement within the Church of England further to reform and energize it. In addition to anti-Romanism, they were characterized by commitment to Scripture as the only source of doctrine and ethics, by active and responsible lay involvement (including a voice in the selection of preachers), by insistence on more earnest and spiritual pastors, and, in the case of many, by rejection of episcopal polity and commitment to either presbyterian or congregational forms of church government. There were several different types of Puritans, and they were never more than about 10 percent of the population. As both the crown and Church of England tried to repress them, they became increasingly militant. Some left the Church of England and formed illegal free congregations. For a brief period in the mid-17th century, they spearheaded a political revolution that abolished both the crown and Church of England for a decade and introduced limited religious liberty. Ultimately they were overthrown politically and forced either to conform to the reestablished Church of England or to continue as separate non-conformist churches.

The importance of Puritanism from the perspective of this study is that it was one of the most vigorous, aggressive, and contagious forms of Protestantism to emerge from the English Reformation. The first stages of Protestantization were imposed from the top, for reasons that were largely political, without much regard for developing support at the grassroots. The English people and most of the lower clergy went along with the rejection of the papacy, then accepted a rapid shift to increasingly radical Protestantism followed by a return to Roman Catholicism, and then adjusted to moderate Protestantism. This incredible flexibility seems to indicate massive indifference. With the rise of Puritanism, however, we see earnestness, commitment, the urge to share, and even the readiness to suffer and sacrifice for one's convictions.

In addition to the Puritans, numerous other even more radical Protestant groups appeared in 17th-century England, the most significant of which were the Quakers. Rooted solidly in Calvinist theology and morality, committed to church reform and spiritual renewal, and motivated and guided by a sense of mission as God's covenant people, these radical English Protestants were to become the source of great new waves of evangelistic effort. This occurred not so much in England as in North America, to which many migrated.

Anabaptists—The Most Evangelistic Reformation Movement

No Christians of the Reformation era were more committed to and active in evangelism than the Anabaptists. The Great Commission (see Matt. 28 and its parallels, Mark 16 and Luke 24) became central to their theology, especially their understanding of the church, as well as the agenda for their lives. Furthermore, unlike most of their contemporaries, they were convinced that the command of the Lord to evangelize the world applied to *all* Christians. With great conviction and courage Anabaptist laity as well as leaders proclaimed the Gospel to those around them, and they traveled far and wide with that message. They were feared and hated by virtually all governments and established churches for reasons which will be discussed below. As a result, they often faced persecution entailing imprisonment, torture, and death. Nevertheless, for a decade they maintained their aggressive pattern of outreach despite the martyrdom of hundreds. After most of their responsible leaders had been killed, fanatics drew some of them into a political revolution at the city of Muenster in 1535. This was crushed with great severity by the legitimate authorities and, subsequently, survival rather than evangelism became the Anabaptist priority. However, while it lasted their evangelistic fervor was impressive.[13]

Who were the Anabaptists? The name (which means "rebaptizers") refers to the issue over which they began to emerge as a distinct entity in Protestantism. They contended that infant baptism is not Scriptural, and, furthermore, that Baptism is not a channel of God's saving grace. Rather, they believed Baptism to be an act whereby a Christian confesses his faith and enters the community of God's people. Therefore, infant baptism is invalid and converts were to be rebaptized.

Anabaptists did not constitute a large or homogeneous movement, but rather a variety of small, loosely connected movements with some important commonalities. They surfaced in Zürich in the mid 1520s and soon were found in central and southern Germany, Moravia, and the Netherlands. Although widespread, they were never numerous. Despite their tireless and courageous witness they apparently gained no more than about 300 converts per year, or about 30,000 during the first century of their existence. Unrelenting repression by both Catholic and Protestant governments inhibited growth and even exterminated the movement in many places. Only where there was a degree of religious toleration or conditions of religious unsettlement did they make more substantial and permanent gains.[14]

Certain key doctrines set the Anabaptists apart and also set them against much in their society. They were extremely critical of both church and state, which made them appear to be a serious threat to the common good. Along with positive motivation grounded in the Great Commission, their profound pessimism toward established religion and government helps to account for their incredible evangelistic zeal. Several of their basic convictions, which seemed so radical and threatening in the 16th century, have become generally acceptable and even normative in the 20th.

Separation of church and state was one of those key controversial doctrines. Since Constantine, governments in much of the Christian world had taken a prominent role in the affairs of the church. Their involvement ranged from protection and support to domination. This was consistent with traditional views and practices of most European peoples, who looked to their temporal rulers for direction in religious matters. In theory, the leading reformers favored the autonomy of the church, but in practice for reasons of expediency they went along with the state church system. As communities and territories turned Protestant it was with government approval, by government decision. In some cases, such as Scotland and the Netherlands, this approval came from a new government which followed a revolution. In any case, in virtually all of western Europe, whether Protestant or Catholic, churches were controlled to a significant degree by government and were, in effect, branches of government.

This, the Anabaptists contended, was a gross perversion. It represented the prostitution of the church, a fatal compromise of the sole lordship of Christ over the church. In accepting government control, the established churches, whether Protestant or Catholic, had apostatized and were in fact no longer the church. The conclusion following inexorably from this was that only those who separated from these false, state-controlled churches and followed Christ as their only Lord and Head were the true church, that is, the Anabaptists themselves. By such a claim the Anabaptists offended and outraged their fellow Christians. On the basis of such a conviction they felt compelled to evangelize and proselytize everyone around them. They alone were true Christians. Everyone else was deluded and damned. In so doing, however, they violated imperial laws against the propagation of unapproved religions and conducting illegal religious activities. Ancient laws making heresy a capital offense and condemning rebaptism were also reactivated against them in some places.

Underlying their objection to government control of churches was their concept of the church. To Anabaptists the church was a voluntary assembly of experiential Christians kept pure by discipline. One could become a member of the church only by conscious and free personal choice, specifically, by accepting God's grace in Christ, following contrite awareness of sin and God's wrath, and by firmly vowing to lead a holy life. One did not become a Christian and a member of the church by the accident of birth into a "Christian" society or by the rite of infant baptism decided by parents and the state. One became a Christian only by responsible decision. Furthermore, one remained a Christian and a member of the church only if that commitment was maintained and lived. Persons whose conduct contradicted their profession, who by sin or spiritual neglect revealed indifference toward or contempt of Christ, must be rebuked, and, if they remained impenitent, they were to be expelled from the Christian community. The established churches, hampered by government restrictions or their own neglect, had failed to maintain their purity by the exercise of discipline. Anabaptists practiced it with great seriousness and even severity.

A corollary to the above doctrines is the principle of religious liberty, which the Anabaptists affirmed with greater emphasis than any of their contemporaries. Here too the major reformers agreed in principle but were appalled at the extremes to which the Anabaptists wanted to carry this. If a valid relation to Christ and the church can be entered only by an act of free choice, it follows that individuals should be at liberty either to make that choice or to decline it. Governments should not prescribe what their citizens are to believe and practice in religious matters, nor should they prohibit the free expression of religious views. Every aspect of religion should be left to individual choice.

The inevitable result of this principle would be religious pluralism. Instead of one set of religious institutions and teachings in each community or territory, there would be many making conflicting claims and competing with one another. To most 16th-century people, especially leaders of church and state, this seemed dangerously confusing and divisive of society. It was seen as nothing less than religious anarchy, which, if tolerated, would likely breed political anarchy. For a thousand years Europe had been religiously monistic. The prospect of religious liberty and pluralism was threatening to most people. This also helps to explain the violent reactions against Anabaptism. They were regarded as anarchists. Ultimately their conviction about religious freedom gained wide acceptance. In the 16th century, however, it appeared to be dangerously radical.

Catholic Renewal and Missions[15]

Even before Luther triggered the Protestant movement, forces within the Roman church had begun to work seriously and effectively for renewal within that body. Unlike their Protestant counterparts, these reformers did not challenge traditional Roman teaching and practice. Rather they concentrated on correcting moral and administrative abuses as well as on spiritually revitalizing both clergy and laity. The Catholic reform began in Spain and spread throughout much of southern Europe. It was living and convincing proof that the Roman church could be reformed from within. By the third quarter of the 16th century, as a result of this movement, the Roman church had regained much of its integrity and confidence, and was able to stem and even significantly to reverse the Protestant advance. With determination and evangelistic zeal Roman educators, missionaries, and rulers combined forces to reconvert many individuals, communities, and territories to Catholicism.

Simultaneous with the rise and spread of this renewal movement was a vast program of world missions. As Catholic nations conducted campaigns of colonial expansion in the Orient and especially the Americas, they were sometimes accompanied and in other cases preceded by government-sponsored monastic missionaries. By the end of the 16th century the east was dotted with Catholic missionary churches, and in the new world large areas had been nominally Christianized.

The Spanish Model

While Spain was not the exclusive source of Catholic renewal and missions, it was certainly the major source. Initiative came from the monarchy—pious Queen Isabella (1474—1505) and her less pious but supportive husband, King Ferdinand (1479—1516). Direction came from Gonzalez (or Francisco) Ximenes de Cisneros (1436—1517), a monk of unwavering ascetic earnestness and a leader of unyielding determination. He was made confessor and advisor to the queen and archbishop of Toledo, the highest church post in Spain. Together they designed and implemented profound and extensive improvements in the Spanish church.

The major thrust of their reform efforts was directed at monasticism and the clergy. Both were riddled with corruption. The immorality, greed, and negligence of their spiritual leaders were a source of disillusionment and deprivation to Spanish Catholics. To correct these deplorable conditions, Ximenes, backed by Isabella, relied on a combination of discipline and education. Religious communities either shaped up or were shut down. Priests and bishops either stayed at their posts (many had been absentee incumbents) and performed the essentials of their ministries or were dismissed. Violations of Christian and clerical moral standards were dealt with promptly and severely. This sharp crackdown thinned clerical and monastic ranks for a time. However, it also dramatically elevated both the morale and external behavior of many who remained. In addition, Ximenes dramatically improved clerical education. At the newly established University of Alcala he introduced a curriculum for future clergy centered in the study of Scripture in its original languages and in the theology of Thomas Aquinas. The results were impressive. Disciplined and well-prepared at the top, the Spanish church entered a new era of strength and service.

Two paradoxical features of the reformed Catholic church of Spain are especially important to note. One is the limitation of papal authority in Spain. Convinced that the interference and ineptitude of popes was the cause of much corruption in the church, the Spanish monarchs insisted that they retain control of appointment to high church office. Too often papal appointees were selected for reasons other than qualities of spiritual and moral leadership. At the same time, reformed Spanish Catholicism was totally committed to traditional doctrine and piety. The spiritual and theological supremacy of the pope was retained; only his administrative interference was curtailed.

Renewal was also occurring at the popular level. An improved caliber of parish priest was preaching and teaching with greater sincerity and effectiveness. In addition, a wave of mystical piety was set in motion by people such as Theresa of Avila (1515—80) and her younger protege John of the Cross (1542—91). This was characterized by a self-renouncing quietism—lifting the soul in voiceless contemplation until union with divine love was attained in the form of ecstatic experience. Theresa and John traveled through Spain founding new houses of their Carmelite order or introducing spiritual renewal into existing houses. While their efforts were centered largely in monasticism, their influence extended to the laity. An extensive literature grew out of this mystical movement. Furthermore, many monks and priests who were drawn to it preached mystical piety into the hearts and lives of their hearers. Although it includes some emphasis on the redemptive love of God in Christ, Spanish mysticism suffered from an emphasis on the human initiative in furthering the God-relationship. It also emphasized subjective experience at the expense of the objective revelatory and redemptive work of God. Yet for many it became a source of warm, even passionate, devotion to God, leading to spiritual and moral renewal.

Agents of Catholic Reform and Anti-Protestantism

The impulse to reform the Roman church from within also appeared and spread outside Spain. Some of this was inspired by the Spanish model. Others arose independently. Especially important were developments in Italy, where the chief authorities of the Roman church—popes and councils—eventually took up the cause of reform. Supported by a vigorous, aggressive new order and armed with a terrifying instrument of repression, the church was able to put its house in order, take a clear and firm stand on matters challenged by Protestants and, with a combination of persecution and persuasion, win back many who had left the Catholic fold.

About 1517, while Lutheranism was still in its embryonic stage, a group of Italian evangelicals was formed in Rome. It was an informal fellowship called the "Oratory of Divine Love," in which several dozen concerned intellectuals, both clerical and lay, gathered to pray and work for reform. Similar groups arose elsewhere in Italy. The study of the New Testament in translation and even the doctrine of justification by faith were important items of consideration. Some participants were open to doctrinal adjustment in the direction of Protestantism as well as moral and administrative reform. Others were committed only to the latter and were opposed to any compromise of traditional Catholic doctrine. The second element prevailed and ultimately shaped the character of the Catholic reform through the election of one of their number to the papacy.

Jesuits

Among the forces contributing to Catholic renewal and advance, the Society of Jesus (Jesuits) was preeminent. Founded by Spaniard Ignatius Loyola (1491—1556) in 1540, this religious order became an awesome agency of reform as well as a powerful counterforce against Protestantism. The foundation of the Jesuit order was the personal spiritual renewal of the individual members by the use of Loyola's *Spiritual Exercises*, a month-long process of deep reflection on sin, redemption, and obedience. Originally the purpose of the order was the propagation of the faith, but in 1550 the defense of the faith—combatting Protestantism—was added and became the primary objective. The order grew rapidly as did its influence.

Education was the chief method by which Jesuits accomplished their objectives. They established quality schools for children and youth. Initially they served primarily the poor. However, as the aristocracy and royalty of southern Europe discovered the excellence of the Jesuit schools, they sent their children to them in increasing numbers. The emphasis shifted to higher education. Soon their many colleges and universities enjoyed a near monopoly among the upper classes. Attractive and effective pedagogy combined with fervent devotion to traditional Catholic theology produced a new generation of fiercely loyal Catholic rulers in southern and central Europe. Many chose Jesuits for their personal confessors and advisors. Inevitably, these rulers were offended by the mass defections to Protestantism that had occurred in some of their territories. Encouraged by their Jesuit mentors, they used the power and resources of their positions to try to bring their Protestant subjects back into the Roman fold. Eventually this led to the devastating Thirty Years' War (1618—48), in which Protestant and Catholic states fought bitterly over the forced restoration of Roman Catholicism. The intellectual impact of Jesuit education was at least as powerful as its political impact. Quality education conducted by brilliant and learned teachers in a way that reflected and supported traditional Catholic theology added substantially to the Roman church's credibility among thinking people of all kinds.

Reform-Minded Popes and Council

Even this growing royal and intellectual support could not have achieved a massive shift back to the Roman church in central Europe had the church itself not been noticeably and significantly improved. Such improvements did, in fact, take place in the 16th century, initially under the auspices of pious Catholic rulers and ultimately with the backing and direction of the popes and a council. For example, Pope Paul III (1534—49) appointed a council of distinguished churchmen to investigate conditions in the church and make recommendations. Their findings officially confirmed what was already obvious—there was much monastic decay, abuse of episcopal power, failure properly to educate both clergy and laity, sexual laxity, and buying and selling of church offices. The report condemned these evils and called for swift and decisive remedy. However, since the report fell into the hands of Protestants, to the embarrassment of Roman authorities, it was never acted upon.

Permanent and thorough measures for Catholic reform came out of the Council of Trent, which met sporadically from 1545 to 1563. The dual purpose of this council was to respond both to the theological critique put forward by Protestantism, and to the corruption lingering within the Roman church. For decades Protestants and Catholics alike had been pressing for a general council in the hope of resolving Catholic and Protestant differences as well as correcting evils within the Roman church. The hard line taken at Trent against key Protestant doctrines and practices shattered prospects of reunion. In an uncompromising manner, Trent reaffirmed the traditional Roman positions and condemned those things regarded as essential by Protestants, such as justification by faith alone and the sole authority of Scripture. On the other hand, by taking a traditional stand the council provided the kind of decisive and authoritarian leadership required for aggressive conservation and expansion.

Trent also made provision for sweeping improvements in the church. Indulgence abuses were curtailed. Bishops were given expanded powers of supervision and discipline and were expected to use them. Above all, bishops were required to provide adequate seminary education for prospective priests, emphasizing not only theological development consistent with the church's position, but also spiritual and moral development. It was recognized at Trent that to a large extent the Reformation was a reaction to a crisis in pastoral care. As a result of the council there were growing numbers of well-prepared and pious priests ministering in Catholic parishes. However, Catholic success in this regard, like that of the Protestants, was limited. Many bishops dragged their feet in implementing these regulations, either for lack of interest or money. In areas such as France and Spain, temporal rulers controlled the appointment of bishops, and their commitment to reform wavered at times. The areas most effectively reformed as a result of Trent were Italy, and southern Germany.

Inquisition

The Inquisition was an institution that utilized terror and torture as a means of discovering and exterminating heresy. It was established during the 13th century and directed especially against the Cathars, a Gnostic-like movement that had succeeded in drawing large numbers of people away from the Catholic faith and fold. The Inquisition was revived in Spain during the late 15th century in order to deal with large numbers of Jewish and Muslim converts to Christianity suspected of continuing secretly in the practice of their former religions. In the 16th century in Spain and especially in Italy Protestants became targets of the Inquisition and were effectively eliminated.

Church and state cooperated in the inquisitorial process. The inquisitor was a churchman learned in theology—usually a Dominican. He was accompanied and assisted by enforcement personnel provided by the government. By careful interrogation the inquisitor attempted to discover heresy in those accused of secretly adhering to it. At his discretion he could employ torture in order to extract confessions and recantations from the unwilling. However, anything admitted or renounced under torture had, in theory, to be confirmed apart from torture in order to be valid. Those who later retracted what they had confessed and recanted under torture could be tortured again. If the inquisitor was convinced that the suspect was guilty, his prospects were bleak either way. If he confessed under torture and repudiated heresy, he faced imprisonment and loss of property and civil privileges because he had not confessed and renounced the heresy readily and voluntarily during the early stages of the process when this could be done with little or no penalty. On the other hand, if he did not confess, the inquisitor could confine him indefinitely and interrogate under torture repeatedly in order to secure the desired admission of heresy. The Inquisition was not supposed to kill suspects, although this did, in fact, happen. The purpose was to terrify people into exposing and rejecting their error. Those who confessed and would not renounce their heresy died by fire.

What possible rationale could earnest Christians (which many inquisitors were) use for this abhorrent institution? Given their assumptions, the case for the Inquisition is easily constructed given the presuppositions of those who directed it. First of all, enforced religious uniformity in various forms had been accepted as valid by European Christians for a thousand years. There was no fundamental aversion based on ideals of personal and religious freedom such as became widespread in later centuries. In addition, heresy was regarded as a hideous crime against both God and man—against God because it perverted His sacred truth, against man because it infected his soul in such a way as to lead to eternal condemnation. A person guilty of distorting an earthly king's decrees would be interrogated and punished with great severity. A person who poisoned the water supply of a village causing illness and death to others would be sought out relentlessly and punished mercilessly. How much more necessary it seemed to discover and deal with those who perverted the truth of God and thereby caused the eternal suffering and death of innocent people. Even the heretics' own well-being seemed to require these harsh measures. Just as a doctor might have to employ painful measures to remove a tumor or set a broken bone, so the inquisitor used pain to try to save the suspect from the terrible consequences of his heresy.

Before the third quarter of the 16th century had passed, the Roman church had recovered from the trauma of the Protestant revolt, regained its integrity and confidence, and even recouped some of its losses to that movement. Various factors contributed to the revitalization of the Roman church. Some zealous Catholic rulers (most notably Spaniards) took the initiative in correcting moral and administrative abuses in the church. At the popular level movements of mystical piety revived the spirituality of many. The Society of Jesus was a highly dedicated, well-disciplined task force that educated a new generation of militantly loyal, reform-minded Catholics, especially among the ruling class. The Council of Trent clarified Catholic theology on controverted points and enacted measures to improve the church, especially the quality of pastoral care. In Italy and Spain the Inquisition effectively discouraged or eliminated anything that was suspected of deviating from approved Catholic teaching and practice. At every level the Roman church experienced significant purification and strengthening, without, however, undergoing the type of doctrinal reform that Protestants regarded as crucial. The Gospel of God's saving grace through faith in Christ was still obscured by prominent elements of works-righteousness.

From the perspective of this study the importance of the Catholic Reformation is that it resulted in aggressive outreach. As long as the church was degraded by corruption and worldliness, the incentive to promote or even to protect it remained low. However, once it was being rehabilitated, once sincere and responsible leadership was restored, people began to respect their church and its beliefs. Furthermore, highly committed individuals and groups within the Roman church began zealously to try to reconvert those who had defected from Catholicism, sometimes by witnessing and thoughtful argumentation, in other cases by political and even physical force. The impulse of Catholics to share their faith, to defend and extend their church, was a direct consequence of the 16th-century renewal.

Methods of Global Expansion[16]

More spectacular even than Roman Catholic recovery and expansion in Europe was the worldwide missionary work undertaken with considerable success by representatives of this reinvigorated church. We will examine several of the more important methodologies by which Roman Catholics of this era tried to make Roman Catholic Christians of others in parts of the world that up to this time had had little or no contact with Christianity.

Patronage

Direction and support of Catholic world missions during this era was exercised by the Catholic monarchies of Spain and Portugal in an arrangement called the patronage system. Late in the 15th century these two nations were in conflict over which parts of the world each would colonize and conquer. They submitted their case to Pope Alexander VI (1492—1503) for arbitration. His decision was that Portugal would have exclusive access to the eastern hemisphere and Spain to the western. Because of miscalculations and previous agreements the eastern hemisphere included Brazil and the western the Philippine Islands. These grants were made with the provision that the Christian faith would be propagated wherever these powers extended their influence. The agreements were honored.

Monastic missionaries—Dominicans, Franciscans, and later Augustinians and Jesuits were the most numerous—accompanied these forces of European expansion and attempted to gather native peoples into the church. Usually the missionaries confined their activity to areas already controlled by their patron nations, but there were some who ranged into other areas for evangelistic purposes. The distinctive feature of the patronage system is that not the church but the state was responsible for converting the heathen. With authorization from the pope, the representatives of the kings recruited and financed workers for this task and to a great extent determined how, when, and where the task would be carried out.

There is reason to believe that these Europeans were sincerely interested in Christianizing the natives peoples who came under their control. Prince Henry the Navigator of Portugal, who launched the colonial expansion of that nation, was an earnestly religious person. Virtually all who went out from both Spain and Portugal to conquer or to trade claimed a missionary motive. However, the desire for gain clearly surpassed that motive in most instances. Christianization was part of the process of subjugation and civilization and usually was not allowed to interfere with the cruel exploitation of converted people, especially in the Americas. Conquered peoples were organized into work forces under Spanish landed proprietors in order to mine precious metals and to cultivate plantation crops for export to Europe. Injustice, disregard for health and safety, and cruelty characterized the administration of many *ecomenderos*, as the Spanish overlords were called. In other ways, as well, the personal example of many Europeans contradicted the faith they were trying to impart. Sexual immorality, greed, and spiritual indifference were the rule with most, which could only create confusion and cynicism in the minds of the natives when they compared these behaviors with the Christian ideals.

On the encouraging side was the work of Bartolome de Las Casas (1474—1566), the most conspicuous of numerous Dominicans who denounced the ill-treatment of conquered peoples. He not only admonished the offenders and exercised church discipline upon them but actually secured decrees from the Spanish monarchy forbidding such abuse. Unfortunately, these decrees were frequently ignored.

In general, the patronage system worked best in the Spanish possessions and proved to be fraught with problems in the Portuguese possessions. The Spanish were more deeply affected by the Catholic renewal and had the resources with which to hold and control the areas they entered. Although Spanish Christianity in the Americas and the Philippines was superficial, syncretistic, and passive, there were continuing serious efforts to improve the situation during the period under consideration here. The Spanish monarchy sent hundreds of capable and devoted missionaries to these possessions. Unfortunately, other missionaries were of low character and commitment. Although their impact was limited, their efforts were largely commendable.

On the other hand, Portugal was a declining power during most of this era and never did experience the spiritual renewal that touched Spanish Christianity so deeply. Under Portuguese patronage there were mass movements into Catholicism in Ceylon, and Francis Xavier (1506—52) carried out his vast and visionary work in India and Southeast Asia. In addition, for a time the Jesuits worked earnestly and effectively in Brazil. However, for the most part Portuguese missions were weak and even counterproductive. Especially in the Orient, the Portuguese colonial authorities were very jealous of their authority over the mission enterprise. They tried to control even those missionaries who worked outside their territories, and after the 16th century they were in constant conflict with Rome over this. In addition, as their power waned they were displaced throughout much of the Orient by the Dutch, who turned Roman Catholic missions into Reformed Protestantism wherever possible.

Coercion

In an approach reminiscent of the middle ages, both the Portuguese and the Spanish, especially the latter, frequently relied upon force in order to convert the heathen. By royal decrees the practice of Hinduism was forbidden in Portuguese India. Idols and places of worship were destroyed. The natives, particularly their religious leaders, were compelled to receive Christian instruction. Although not demanded, Baptism and participation in Catholic worship were strongly encouraged. In the civilized portions of Spanish America the imposition of Christianity was also quite direct. In connection with their conquest of the Aztecs in Mexico and the Incas of Peru, the Spaniards destroyed idols and temples and encouraged Baptism. By overt threats Indians were induced to conform religiously to their conquerors. Most readily complied. They were traditionally submissive to the religious leadership of their rulers, and, apparently, their old religions were disintegrating. Mass conversions occurred in many places, often with little or no instruction. Missionaries fanned out from the urban centers to surrounding towns and villages. Initially most worked through interpreters, but soon the need for learning the languages and customs of the people became apparent. There was little resistance to the new religion.

However, neither was it accepted with great conviction and ardor. Since instruction was minimal and pastoral leadership sparse, Christianity was often combined with remnants of traditional religions. As the work unfolded, ecclesiastical structures were developed to support it. New dioceses were created and bishops appointed to oversee ministry in hundreds of new parishes. Despite the steady influx of European missionaries, there never were enough priests to cover these parishes adequately, and the quality of some left much to be desired. Few native clergy were trained, and no native bishops were consecrated during this period. Furthermore, little or no evangelism was done by the converted natives; only the European missionaries engaged in outreach.

Reductions

An entirely different missionary approach was employed with the more primitive natives in remote areas. In their case, conversion was deliberately separated from conquest. After the bitter experiences in the West Indies, where whole tribes were destroyed by the aggression and oppression of the *conquistadors*, missionaries, backed by legislation, determined to protect primitive peoples elsewhere from this fate. When Spanish forces reached the mainland, missionaries were prepared with methods that could protect primitive peoples, bring them into the Catholic fold, and incorporate them safely into the structure of Spanish colonial life. The institution growing out of this concern was the *reduction*, a mission community, designed not for the profit of the Spaniards, but for the well-being of the Indians.

A team of two or three missionary monks accompanied by a small armed guard and often by a few already Christianized Indians would enter a new area and establish a station. With gifts and food they would attract local Indians and induce them to settle there. They would teach them to raise crops, do handicrafts, and involve them in Christian instruction and worship. The purpose was to gather the Indians into a largely self-sufficient community under the leadership of the missionaries, wherein they would be introduced into a totally new way of life as well as a new religion. As much as possible they were divested of their old culture and religion. Every effort was made to keep out other Spaniards, for fear of their corrupting influences and exploitative practices. In general, the Indians complied rather willingly with the *reduction* system. However, there was resistance to some of the required religious practices, such as memorization of prayers and catechism as well as private confession.

The basic appeal of the *reduction* was that it provided the Indians with food, clothing, shelter, and protection (from hostile Indians as well as rapacious Spaniards) in exchange for labor and submission to missionary leadership. The institution was unquestionably paternalistic and chauvinistic. It reflected little sensitivity toward or appreciation of the Indians' cultural heritage. Once the people in a given mission community were regarded as sufficiently civilized and Christianized, they were incorporated into the main structures of the Spanish colonial church and society. The *reduction* was reasonably effective in Mexico, Central and South America, and in parts of what is now the southwestern United States. Elsewhere in North America and in the Philippines it met with little success.

Spanish expansion into the Philippines during the last quarter of the 16th century was strikingly different from its earlier counterparts in the Americas. Here missionary concern superceded the desire for conquest and commercial gain. The expedition, headed by Legaspi, originated in Mexico and was directed by men with colonial experience from that field. However, measures were taken to prevent the evils and abuses that marred the American experience. Very little force was used in the Philippines, and the natives' rights were protected by law. All Spaniards were to conduct themselves in such a way as to honor Christ and commend His church to the inhabitants. Destructive rivalry between missionary orders was prevented. Missionaries were required to work in the vernacular languages. Despite a shortage of missionaries, hundreds of thousands were baptized before the end of the century. Ecclesiastical structures and educational programs were established in order to conserve and nurture the new converts and their descendants. Christianity spread more rapidly and extensively in the Philippines than anywhere else in the Orient. Part of this was due to circumstances—the primitive level of the native religion and culture as well as the weak and divided political situation—which offered little resistance to the higher religion and culture of the invaders. On the other hand, credit must also be given to the more humane, just, and spiritual approach of this new generation of Spanish adventurers.

Access via Rulers

Portuguese missionaries in a number of instances gained entree to people by converting or at least securing the support of their rulers. Late in the 15th century a native chief in the Congo, West Africa received Baptism. Although he later defected, his son and successor, Alfonso, was a zealous, witnessing Christian. At his encouragement many of his subjects were baptized, and his son, Henry, was consecrated a bishop in 1518, the first black African known to be elevated to that position. Other blacks were ordained into the priesthood. However, this experimental indigenous church did not prove successful. Many Congolese were only superficially Christianized, and others appeared to defect through lack of pastoral care. In addition, the Christian monarch engaged in slave trade with the Portuguese. Despite the efforts of new waves of missionaries to revive it, the church in this place had disappeared by the end of the 17th century.

Similarly in Ceylon during the 16th century there were mass conversions after several kings and their nobility were baptized. Although the motivation of many was clearly political (they were seeking support or other advantages from the Portuguese), intensive work by Franciscans and Jesuits led to sound and steady growth. By the mid-17th century, when the Portuguese were displaced by the Dutch, some parts of Ceylon were predominantly Catholic.

The beginnings and rapid spread of Christianity in Japan were also related to the favor of rulers. When the great Jesuit missionary Francis Xavier (1506—52) entered Japan in 1549 with his interpreter, he first approached a local feudal lord and made converts among members of his family. Elsewhere, too, Catholic missionaries enjoyed this advantage. Two factors account for the openness of the Japanese to the missionaries. Their traditional religion, Buddhism, had been weakened by moral decay and controversy as well as by involvement in political conflicts. In addition, Japan was in the process of looking to the west, especially to Portugal, for commercial opportunities. The identification of the missionaries with that nation gave them a distinct advantage.

From the 1560s Christianity was supported by the leading military and political figure in Japan, Oda Nobunaga (d. 1582). Nagasaki became the chief center of Christianity, and by early in the 17th century it was said to be predominantly Christian. Although hostility surfaced in 1587 with the rise of Hideyoshi, Christianity continued to grow, even though the number of missionaries was usually less than a hundred. The total Christian population by the early 17th century was about 200,000. There were many churches, schools, and seminaries. Persecution began in earnest in 1612, and by 1650 Christianity appeared to be completely eliminated by the expulsion or execution of its leaders and the prohibition of its practice. However, when Japan was reopened to westerners in the mid 19th century, communities of secret Christians were discovered in remote hills and islands, one of the most remarkable examples of Christian survival in all history.

Accommodation

Most missionaries of this era reacted negatively to the cultures and religions of the non-Christian peoples whom they sought to convert. What was mentioned in the discussion of *reductions* above took place also where other missionary methods were employed. New Christians were compelled or induced into a new culture and life-style as well as into a new religion. Their traditional values, views, and practices were replaced with those of the missionaries. The assumption was that their cultures were either so inferior or permeated by pagan religion as to be beyond rehabilitation. There was little interest in maintaining continuity by retaining whatever did not violate Christian theology and moral standards. Instead of attempting to permeate and transform their cultures from within, the missionaries usually did everything possible to displace or even to destroy those cultures. Consequently, non-Christians had to surmount cultural barriers as well as religious barriers on their path to Christ. In addition, those who did become Christians were culturally separated from their non-Christian fellow-countrymen and thus were in a difficult position from which to evangelize them. Also tragic was simply the loss of much that was rich and meaningful in the cultural heritage of these newly Christianized peoples.

Some interesting exceptions to this culturally insensitive approach were attempts at accommodation undertaken by Jesuit missionaries to the Orient. The first notable example was Matteo Ricci (1552—1610), who began his work in China in 1582. Although other missionaries had preceded him in China during this era, Ricci soon emerged as the leader. He approached the task with imagination and sensitivity. By means of his scientific and mechanical knowledge he gained the respect and friendship of the ruling classes. In addition, he adopted the garb and life-style of Confucian scholars, the most esteemed social class in China. What is more, he decided that the custom of venerating ancestors and Confucius was not idolatrous, and, consequently, he permitted his converts to continue this practice. In addition, he employed as names for God terms from ancient Confucian classics. His basic policy was to retain everything from Chinese culture that did not clearly conflict with Christianity. In questionable areas he gave the culture the benefit of the doubt. The work in China flourished as long as this policy of accommodation was pursued. A number of important scholars and officials were converted, including a prince. Missions were started in most provinces. Institutions of Christian higher education were founded. By 1664 there were 250,000 Chinese Christians.

The other pioneer of accommodation was Robert de Nobili (1577—1656), who began work in India in 1605. His predecessors in this field had worked exclusively among the lower classes. Nobili's assumption was that influence trickles downward. Consequently, he determined to concentrate his efforts upon the uppermost class—the Brahmins. He identified himself with them as much as possible (without violating Christian essentials) in diet, dress, and social custom. He learned their languages and expressed Christian concepts in terms borrowed from their religious vocabulary. He observed caste restrictions by establishing separate churches for his Brahmin converts so that they would not have to worship and fellowship with those of lower classes. He did not neglect the lower classes but felt that all the people of India would be reached most effectively through their natural leaders. By the time of his death more than 1000 adult converts were being baptized each year. By the end of the century the Christian population of India numbered about one million. Also significant is the fact that some of this success occurred outside areas of Portuguese control.

From the beginning the principle and practice of accommodation was controversial and, in 1704, was repudiated by the Roman church, only to be reinstated in the 20th century. Interestingly enough, neither in China nor in India were many converted from the higher classes, although identification with the higher classes seemed to make Christianity more appealing to others.

Catholic missions during the Reformation era reflect tremendous dedication and energy. During the space of a century and a half, Catholic Christianity was permanently planted worldwide in areas where

Jesus Christ had been unknown. The problems and limitations of this vast outreach do not outweigh its positive contributions. The great religious orders, primarily with the support and direction of Catholic rulers, did what no one else had ever attempted successfully and what no one else was able to do at the time—they made Christianity a truly global religion.

*   *   *

By the dawn of the 16th century pressure to reform the Roman church had been building up for more than a century. It rose sharply when a new type of reformer appeared on the scene, one who went beyond the usual complaints against moral and administrative abuses and attacked the very heart of the church's message. In place of the traditional Roman salvation system, which required that God's grace be supplemented by works of human merit, the Protestant Reformers proclaimed salvation by God's grace alone through faith in Jesus Christ. When the leadership of the Roman church backed by Catholic political powers tried to repress the reform movement, a series of ecclesiastical explosions followed, resulting in the fragmentation of western Christianity. The Protestant-Catholic split was followed by many additional divisions on the Protestant side. The Christian church appeared to be disintegrating.

In reality, however, it was expanding. Protestants were renewed and energized by the Gospel which they had recovered. Convinced from Scripture that this was God's own truth, many were eager to share it with others still caught in medieval error. New media were utilized for the dissemination of this Gospel. The concept of the priesthood of all believers was reborn and put into practice by some in the form of zealous evangelism. Despite the sin and the pain that inevitably accompany Christian controversy and separation, the Reformation undoubtedly increased the number of earnest, witnessing Christians in western Europe.

Nor was this only among the Protestants. Within the Roman church, too, reform and renewal were underway among those who had no quarrel with official theology and no desire to break with the papacy. Clerical and monastic life were significantly improved and financial abuses mitigated first in Spain and, ultimately, throughout Catholic Europe. Able defenders rose up to answer the Protestant challenge. By mid-16th century the highest authorities in the Roman church were committed to reform, and the church had recovered its self-respect. With that came the determination not only to regain as many as possible who had been lost to Protestantism, but also to establish the Roman Catholic Church and faith worldwide. As two Catholic nations launched programs of vast colonial expansion they were accompanied by missionaries who succeeded remarkably in fulfilling that dream.

IV/Revivals and New Expansion

(1650—1789)

In time, reform movements themselves almost inevitably need to be reformed or, at least, renewed and revitalized. So it was with Protestantism. During the last half of the 17th century all major branches were displaying signs of stagnation. In the opinion of some, the 16th-century Reformation had never been completed. Although it dealt effectively with the reformation of doctrine, it did not, in their judgment, effectively implement the reformation of hearts and lives. Most of Protestantism was hindered by government control or restriction. There was a general decline of spiritual earnestness among both clergy and laity as well as widespread neglect of Christian morality. Specific causes and symptoms varied from denomination to denomination and from area to area. Prophetic voices rose up to decry these conditions and to call for renewal. Some currents of piety continued to flow even in times and places of great stagnation. However, it was not until the final decades of the 17th century that impulses of renewal strong enough to effect dramatic change began to stir and surge throughout parts of Protestantism.

Revival movements spread far and wide. As one subsided another would begin, or the momentum of still another would accelerate. Although there was a considerable amount of diversity among them, all movements stressed religion of the heart and life—the personal experience of being in a saving relationship with God and the necessity of Christian obedience. Many thousands in Europe and North America were deeply touched by these revivals. Their faith was warmed and strengthened and their conduct was transformed. Beyond this, whole denominations were profoundly affected and some new denominations were born. The face of Protestantism was decidedly changed.

Among the most noticeable and significant changes was a tremendous increase in evangelism. A large and growing army of zealous preachers devoted themselves primarily to gaining the lost or revitalizing the lax. Even more revolutionary was the readiness of increasing numbers of lay people to witness to Jesus Christ both for conversion and for renewal. Not since the early church had so many Christians been so eagerly and actively involved in carrying out the Great Commission. In addition, these revivals eventually sparked an interest among Protestants in missions to those who had never been exposed to the Christian Gospel. By the end of the 18th century Protestants were organizing foreign missionary societies, although several more limited ventures had been undertaken earlier. It is in these Protestant revivals of the 17th and 18th centuries that we find the origins of the modern evangelistic and missionary movements.

During this same period Roman Catholic world missions were still very much alive. There were new problems as well as new opportunities. Although the rate of expansion slowed considerably and some painful losses were sustained as a result of the decline of the Catholic European colonial powers, the Roman missionary effort was still awesome compared with the fledgling Protestant ventures. Although inertia gripped many fields, in others there were new evidences of earnest and imaginative outreach.

The Protestant Revivals

Three major currents may be identified in the revival movements under consideration here. Although they were centered in three different parts of the western world and possessed distinctive characteristics, there was a considerable amount of interaction and each was influenced by the others. They were: (1) Pietism in Lutheran Germany; (2) the Great Awakening among various kinds of Calvinists in the North American colonies; and (3) the Evangelical Revival in the Church of England of which the Methodist movement was most prominent. The first part of this chapter examines each of these to determine the nature and extent of the evangelistic impulses they generated. This will be done against their social and religious backgrounds and will indicate the manner in which each was affected by the others.

Pietism (1675—1727)[1]

On the surface, church life in Lutheran Germany was flourishing during the last half of the 17th century. In a society that was recuperating from the ravages of the Thirty Years' War (1618—48) worship services—weekdays as well as Sundays—were well attended. The pastoral office enjoyed prestige. Theology was an important branch of learning and much significant literature was being produced in this field. Some notable hymns were composed. Commendable examples of Christian charity were performed by many individuals. However, in the opinion of some sensitive observers, other very obvious factors pointed to serious underlying maladies.

During the last decades of the 16th century and for a hundred years thereafter, much of Lutheranism had been dominated by the theological movement called Orthodoxy. At its best, this movement contributed significantly to the clarity of Christian thought by articulating Scriptural truth with great precision and thoroughness over against false alternatives. The analytical tools of Aristotelian philosophy were employed in the process, which helps to account for the precision. It also accounts for the static and abstract character of much of that theology. Orthodoxy was, in fact, a new scholasticism, a Protestant version of what Luther had rejected so vehemently in medieval Roman Catholicism. Essentially an intellectual approach, Orthodoxy often degenerated into sophistry and hairsplitting. The effect of these excesses on preaching was deadening. Preachers delivered long, learned theological lectures far removed from the lives or even the understanding of their hearers. Preoccupation with heresy often left the impression that it was the only evil worth getting excited about. Pastors regarded themselves primarily as theologians and guardians of truth, rather than shepherds of souls, and as the only ones authorized to communicate the Gospel. The laity were regarded as consumers of doctrinally pure theology and correctly administered sacraments, rather than participants in the church's ministry.

In the judgment of Orthodoxy's critics, to an alarming degree spiritual death had settled in. The symptoms seemed obvious. Much theology and preaching was dominated by crude and loveless polemics. Concern for pure doctrine, however, as valid and necessary as it is in itself, was crowding out concern for personal spiritual growth and holiness of life. Dry formalism and intellectualism deprived worship of meaning. The laity were relegated to a passive role. In the preparation of candidates for the pastoral office little was being done to cultivate a warm faith and a loving, moral life. On the basis of all this, the conviction began to grow that many in the churches—clergy as well as laity—were not true Christians.

Although others before him had expressed such views, Philip Jacob Spener (1635—1705) stated them with unprecedented clarity and power and launched Pietism as a movement. He came out of a home that was permeated with the popular German devotional literature of John Arndt

(1555—1621) as well as that of the English Puritans. He studied in Strassburg under orthodox Lutheran teachers but also absorbed some of the Reformed spirit so evident in that community. He traveled in both Switzerland and the Netherlands, where he became further acquainted with the persons and practices that shaped Reformed piety. His first pastoral appointment was to Frankfurt as senior minister of the local clergy. Subsequently he served in Dresden and Berlin.

Immediately upon beginning his pastorate in Frankfurt, Spener initiated measures designed to quicken and deepen his people spiritually. He introduced a period of catechetical instruction for children on Sunday afternoons and tried to revive the rite of confirmation, which had fallen into disuse. What turned out to be even more influential and consequential was his use of the conventicle. This was a small group designed to awaken and strengthen people spiritually and morally by means of religious discussion, Bible study, mutual confession, exhortation, and prayer. Spener's conviction was that the best hope for renewing the church was to begin with the remnant of true Christians in every congregation. As they were gathered and edified they would become a leaven through which others would be reached and changed. Initially these meetings were held in the company of the pastor and even at times on church premises. The very first were held in Spener's home. They were intended to renew the church from within. However, in more than a few instances they became elitist and divisive. Participants tended to become so enthusiastic about what was happening to and among them in their little groups that these gatherings became substitutes for regular worship in church. In addition, they frequently disparaged the spirituality of outsiders, even the clergy, regarding them as unconverted. Spener tried to check these trends, but with limited effect. Conventicles of both kinds, churchly and separatistic, spread widely. The term Spener applied to them was *collegia pietatis* ("study classes in piety"). Some trace Spener's use of conventicles to comparable groups employed by various Reformed movements such as Puritanism. Though plausible, this has not been established conclusively.

Important as they were, the above events were only preliminaries, preparation for the emergence of Pietism as a full-blown movement. That was heralded by Spener's publication in 1675 of *Pia Desideria* (Pious Wishes). In this work Spener called attention to the corrupt conditions in the church which he diagnosed as moral laxity, mechanical and formalistic use of the sacraments, excessive polemicism, barren intellectualism, and the neglect of love and good works. His proposals for correcting these conditions included: more extensive devotional use of

Scripture; recovery of the priesthood of believers; emphasis on the *practice* of Christianity as the necessary result of theological knowledge; a more loving and restrained approach to controversy; revised pastoral education emphasizing piety as well as academic achievement; practical assistance in sermonizing enabling pastors to stimulate faith and its fruits. Although all had been said before, Spener communicated it with freshness, earnestness, and persuasiveness. It was received enthusiastically by many and fuelled a new drive for renewal. The term "Pietist" was first used in 1677 as a term of derision, but ultimately it was claimed proudly by those who identified with the movement.

Out of Pietism came evangelistic motivation, skills, and agencies. Like the Anabaptists before them, Pietists assumed that most people around them, both laity and clergy, although externally connected with the church, were not authentically Christian. Therefore they were lost and in need of conversion—a vast mission field. The Pietists, on the other hand, having deeply experienced their own lostness and God's saving grace, realized that they had something vital to share. Tremendously encouraging in this connection was Pietism's emphasis on the priesthood of believers, which assured lay people that they too had a ministry to exercise. The privilege and responsibility of sharing the Gospel was theirs, both for the comfort and strength of believers and for the conversion of the lost. Preparation for such sharing was received in conventicles, in which ordinary Christians helped each other to find meaning and direction from the Bible. It was natural and inevitable that earnest Pietists would also share the Word apart from the conventicles, and that they would invite others to participate in these edifying gatherings. Unquestionably, the transformed attitudes and conduct of many Pietists gave credibility to their witness. With contagious enthusiasm and confidence Pietism spread from person to person, from community to community and from nation to nation. An outpouring of pietistic literature and hymns soon complemented this personal outreach.[2]

If Spener was the patriarch and visionary founder of Pietism, August Hermann Francke (1663—1727) was its theoretician, chief organizer, and practical implementer. His higher education included Reformed, orthodox Lutheran, and pietistic influences. At the University of Leipzig in 1687 he assumed a leading role in the *collegium philobiblicum*, a group of students and professors who studied the Bible in the original languages. At Spener's suggestion the group turned from the scholarly to the devotional approach.

In the same year, while preparing a sermon on John 20:31 at Lueneberg, Francke experienced what he regarded as a true conversion.

Stricken with the realization that he lacked the living faith referred to in the text, he fell to his knees and pleaded that God would save him from this wretched condition. Suddenly all his doubts were dispelled. Sorrow and restlessness of heart vanished, and he was filled with joy. From that moment he found it easy to resist sinful inclinations and to live a godly and joyful life. As a result, he realized that authentic faith such as he had received was of infinitely more value than the erudition he had previously cherished.

Following his conversion Francke became associated with groups of Spener's followers, and late in 1688 he traveled to Dresden where he visited Spener in his home for several months. The two men became very close, and Francke's understanding of Pietism developed significantly. He then returned to the University of Leipzig where his teaching and preaching became tremendously popular. Powerful orthodox opponents drove him from Leipzig and subsequently from a pastoral position in Erfurt. However, Spener succeeded in getting him a pastorate in the village of Glaucha and a professorship in the newly established University of Halle nearby. From these positions, which he held simultaneously, he soon became the intellectual and institutional leader of the rapidly developing pietistic movement.

Francke's strategy for renewing and reforming the church differed from that of Spener. The latter hoped to accomplish this through conventicles. Small groups of earnest, witnessing Christians planted in many congregations, Spener believed, would penetrate the church with pious influence until the whole body was revitalized. Francke, on the other hand, set out to revise the entire educational system in such a way as to inculcate pietistic views and values in upcoming generations of clergy and laity. His educational efforts were carried out at various age levels and in various kinds of programs—from technical-vocational to professional. He made Halle a model educational community and hoped that it would become an inspiration to other communities. Furthermore, he educated thousands of pastors and teachers there who eventually carried out spiritual and moral renewal throughout much of Germany and beyond. As his vision and plans unfolded it became clear that his goal extended beyond church reform. He was determined to work for the religious and ethical betterment of all society.

In order for this to happen, Francke realized, institutions of learning must offer educational excellence in an atmosphere of true godliness. To a remarkable degree he succeeded at both. He was a sensitive, imaginative, and practical educator—able to make learning appealing and to adjust it to individual interests and aptitudes. Convinced that teachers were the key to effective education, Francke selected his with great care. Since the type of teacher he desired was scarce, Francke trained some while they taught. He used students from the university, especially theological students. The latter committed themselves to a five year program. The first two years were devoted to study of the humanities and the last three combined the study of theology with teaching. Along with academic and pedagogical progress, these student-teachers also were engaged in exercises designed to foster their spiritual and moral development.

This educational experiment was remarkably successful. Students at the lower levels had the benefit of earnest, able, and energetic teachers. Future pastors gained marvelous practical experience in the education and spiritual formation of the young. Despite the strong spiritual and practical thrust that Francke gave to theological education, there was no relaxation of intellectual requirements. Traditional theological disciplines were pursued with rigor. Only subjects in the classical, humanist tradition were neglected—no mean loss, to be sure.

Rulers and powerful government officials did much to advance the course of Pietism in Germany and beyond. The most important of these was Frederick of Prussia (elector, 1688—1701; king 1701—13). Spener had established relationships with those in high places quite unintentionally. Francke deliberately cultivated them. Prussian rulers especially were supportive of Pietism, not only because of their friendship with leaders of the movement or because of their personal preference for the pietistic approach to religion, but also out of political considerations. They wanted to utilize religion as a unifying force within their emerging empire. Reformed and Lutheran elements within the state were often in conflict. To minimize this, rulers promoted the rise of Pietism, which was anti-polemical and more open to cordial interfaith relations. During the first half of the 18th century, pastoral appointments in Prussia and other parts of northern Germany were largely reserved for men of pietistic orientation, providing them with the opportunity to dominate the Lutheran church. The Scandinavian countries, especially Norway, were also penetrated by pietistic influence.

In the south, especially in Wuerttemburg, Pietism was more a grassroots movement. Early in the 18th century restrictive legislation against conventicles was somewhat inhibiting to its spread. However, this was lifted in stages, with the result that in almost every village and town there sprang up one or more cell groups, most under lay leadership, with their memberships primarily from the working classes. This was in contrast to other sections of Germany where the nobility especially were attracted to the movement. Theological leadership came from the University of Tuebingen, where several very influential scholars interpreted and promoted Pietism.

Both Spener and Francke made the Bible the book of the people. Ordinary lay people were encouraged to study it devotionally and to share its contents. To facilitate this a disciple of Francke in 1710 raised money for the publication and distribution of inexpensive Bibles. This developed into a large program that by 1800 had made 2.5 million Bibles and Bible portions available at low cost. Financial support and patronage came chiefly from Pietists. Some were drawn into the pietistic movement through use of these Bibles. Inspiration for the great national and international Bible societies founded in the next century came primarily from this venture. Virtually every major evangelistic and missionary effort in the modern era has been supported by Bible study made possible by the massive translation and distribution programs these societies sponsor.

The reform of the church, initially the Lutheran church of Germany, was the specific concern of Pietists especially in the early stages of the movement. Although some split with the external institution of the church, this was not the purpose of the founders of Pietism. They wanted to awaken and transform the church from within. By promoting the devotional use of the Bible in private and in conventicles, they tried to bring "dead" and inactive members to more vibrant and zealous personal faith, obedient lives, and responsible participation in the ministry of the church.

Although Pietist theologians repeatedly affirmed their unswerving commitment to orthodox and confessional Lutheran theology, their concerns inevitably resulted in a shift of emphasis from the objective to the subjective. They did this consciously with the conviction that it was necessary to counteract an imbalance introduced by Orthodoxy. Instead of emphasizing the external Word and its traditional interpretation, they stressed the internal testimony of the Spirit and the personal interpretation of the illuminated heart. Instead of emphasizing the broader community of the church, they stressed conventicles and personal experience. Instead of emphasizing justification, they stressed sanctification—the new birth and the new life.

Orthodox opponents were quick to sound the alarm on the dangers of this subjectivism and even overreacted to it. However, the dangers were real, and some radical pietistic individuals and groups did deviate seriously from the historic and Biblical Christian faith. On the other hand, from a historical perspective it seems undeniable that Pietism in many ways provided some desperately needed correctives in stagnating segments of Protestantism. Not only did it recapture a warmer, more relevant vision of the individual Christian life and revive some neglected aspects of the church's mission, but it also released energies that prompted many to put both into practice.

Quite inadvertently, Pietism also became involved in foreign mission work. King Frederick IV of Denmark wanted to establish missions in India at his colony of Tranquebar. He had difficulty in locating prospective missionaries among his own people. Concern for missions developed much later in Protestantism than in Roman Catholicism. Both opportunities and resources were lacking. Protestant contacts with non-Christian peoples through colonial enterprises lagged behind those of Catholicism by a century. Furthermore, they had no ready-made mission force comparable to monastic orders. Although the major reformers developed the proper theological foundation for foreign missions in their doctrines of the church and of the universal priesthood of believers, they did not develop an appropriate application of this to the non-Christian multitudes throughout the world.

During the 17th century several prominent lay people attempted to awaken a sense of missionary obligation, but they were put down hard by the theologians of Orthodoxy. The theological faculty of Wittenberg University, for example, argued: (1) that the Great Commission applied only to the apostles and has already been fulfilled; (2) the heathen have a natural knowledge of God and are, therefore, without excuse; (3) not the church but the state is responsible for carrying the Gospel to people of faraway lands.

In view of attitudes like these that were characteristic of theological faculties, it is not surprising that King Christian had difficulty finding pastors to staff his proposed mission in India.

However, two men who had studied with Francke and had been sensitized at Halle to their high privilege and responsibility of reaching out to the lost with the Gospel were presented with this missionary call and accepted it. In 1706 Bartholomaus Zeigenbalg and Heinrich Pluetschau arrived in India and began their work. Their correspondence with Halle was widely publicized, and financial support for their work flowed into Halle from all over Europe. Shortly thereafter, Halle missionaries were also at work in the East Indies. During the 18th century 60 foreign missionaries went forth from Halle institutions, making it one of the major sources of the rise of Protestant missions. Those who were so committed to converting the lax and the lost in "Christian" Europe could hardly remain indifferent to the plight of unnumbered millions throughout the world who were living and dying without Christ.[3]

Even a brief discussion of Pietism such as has been given above is not complete without reference to the renewed Moravian Brethren who became associated with it early in the 18th century and constituted a vital link to Protestant revivals elsewhere in the world. Paradoxically, the founder of the renewed Brethren was not a Moravian, but a German Lutheran Pietest, Nicholas Ludwig, Count of Zinzendorf (1700—60). A group of Moravian refugees whose religious roots reached back to the pre-reformer, John Huss, were permitted to settle on Zinzendorf's estate of Berthelsdorf in Saxony in 1722. The count soon began to get involved in their community and religious life. In their new environment these refugees organized as a Christian community apart from the world, dedicated to the service of Christ and people wherever they might be needed. This process culminated in a communion service of great spiritual power on August 17, 1727, which is regarded as the birthday of the Moravian church.

During the course of all this, Zinzendorf emerged as their leader. He came into this role out of a rich pietistic background. A native of Dresden and a godchild of Spener, he was reared by a loving and devout grandmother. From early childhood he displayed unusual spiritual interests and sensitivities. For six years he was a student at Halle, where teachers tried to curb his assertive and arrogant style of piety. Even in the citadel of Pietism Zinzendorf came on too strongly in his spiritual and moral encouragement of others. During these trying years and whenever he was under stress, Zinzendorf found solace in an extremely close and experiential relationship with his Lord. He also studied at Wittenberg, where he gained both a respect for theological substance in this bastion of Orthodoxy and a distaste for what he regarded as excessive intellectualism and dogmatism. He desired to study theology in preparation for the pastoral ministry. However, he deferred to the wishes of his family and studied law. During his student years he worked zealously to convert his peers to more experiential and zealous faith, and he gathered those who responded into small groups under his leadership. For several years he traveled through various pietistic centers in Germany and then on to the centers of Reformed piety in the Netherlands and Switzerland. He also visited Paris where he consulted with Roman Catholic leaders. An important result of these interfaith contacts was that they made him aware of the possibility of loving, meaningful interaction with people of other confessions. An ecumenical vision was born. After a short period of government service he devoted his full attention to the Moravians, whom he had permitted to settle on his land and who were soon joined by

Bohemian refugees and even German Lutheran Pietists, Reformed, Anabaptists, and Schwenkfelders.

Under Zinzendorf's leadership, this diverse group was welded into a community centered in religious ideals in which civil and spiritual authority were combined in a single structure. The community was divided into major groups called "choirs" according to people's station in life—married people, single women, widows, widowers, children. Each choir in turn was divided into smaller groups called "bands" consisting of five to seven members. Choirs met for instruction; bands for the exchange of religious experiences and for mutual spiritual encouragement. Theoretically the confessional posture of the Brethren was Lutheran. Zinzendorf was a Lutheran and had even managed to secure recognition of the Brethren as part of the state church of Saxony. However, in both teaching and practice the Moravian Brethren drifted significantly from these moorings and in 1756 assumed the status of a separate church.

The central and overriding purpose of the Moravians was evangelism. Not only the leaders or certain designated specialists, but all members saw themselves as people devoted primarily to God's worship and work, specifically outreach to the lost. Already in 1727 members were traveling throughout Europe on evangelistic missions. Five years later Zinzendorf met some natives of the Spanish West Indies and Greenland, which precipitated Moravian missions in foreign lands. In 1733 a sizable group of Moravians settled in Georgia. Zinzendorf himself traveled to some of these places and also to Pennsylvania, where he initiated work among the Indians and founded a number of Moravian congregations. Other mission fields were entered in quick succession. At the peak of its missionary effort the proportion of Moravians actively engaged in the work was one in 60, as compared with one in 5,000 for the rest of Protestantism. Furthermore, they characteristically chose difficult fields requiring much patience, devotion, and courage.

The evangelistic approaches of the Moravians grew out of their central theological emphases. The task of theology, according to Zinzendorf, was to understand and express the Biblical revelation in a way that will evoke a genuine and lasting experience of God's love. Feeling is the organ by which God's love is received, but not the criterion of God's truth. Meaningful faith is trust in God as revealed in Christ, based on the Biblical witness, verified in personal experience, and resulting in a felt identification with Christ. Moravian piety centered on the suffering and death of Jesus, sometimes carried to morbid extremes. Conversion was viewed as a conscious experience. However, in contrast with elements of Lutheran Pietism, which emphasized the struggle leading up to it, Moravians viewed conversion as a gift of God given instantaneously and completely. The result of conversion, they taught, is a condition of great blessedness—serenity, joy, confidence—filling the heart and flooding into the life of the believer. Hymns reflecting the message and piety of Moravians, some composed by Zinzendorf, have been included in the hymnals of many denominations.

The Moravian way to do evangelism was to demonstrate to all who would receive it the happiness that had come to them as a result of their attachment to Jesus. They made it clear that this happiness was available to all through faith in Him. Their chief goal was to preach the crucified Savior into men's hearts. Early lay evangelists received no special training. If they had authentic "heart religion," it was assumed that they could share it effectively. Areas into which they entered were determined by lot. Their goal in preaching and witnessing to people was not to gather them into the Moravian church, but rather to warm their hearts, create a small circle or spiritual support group, and then encourage them to be a spiritual influence within their ancestral churches.

These societies scattered throughout Europe and beyond devoted to the renewal of individuals and churches were called the *Diaspora*, after the name given to Jews scattered throughout the Roman Empire in the early centuries. *Diaspora* societies maintained close contact with the home congregations, sustaining their interest and sense of involvement, and stimulating their prayer support. Activities in the societies were similar to those of pietist conventicles—devotional Bible study, prayer, sharing experience, and mutual encouragement.

From this it is obvious that the Moravians were not interested in the success and growth of their ecclesiastical institution, but rather in spiritually revitalizing individuals and churches. They had a strong sense of the unity of all experiential Christians. If hearts are truly warmed by a personal relationship with Jesus, confessional and denominational differences are of minor significance, the Moravians believed. In Pennsylvania Zinzendorf tried to gather scattered Protestants into a nondenominational fellowship, but without success. Others were not so ready to ignore historic differences.

In the foreign mission fields preaching and witnessing were combined with medical, agricultural, and even commercial assistance. Many missionaries demonstrated their commitment to the cause by supporting themselves through the practice of a trade.

The importance of the Moravians to the development of Protestant evangelism is way out of proportion to the size of the group or the number of their converts. Although their theology and practice were not above reproach, the Moravians provided a marvelous example of joyful dedication to the evangelistic task and a high sense of privilege about sharing their Savior with others. At a time when most Protestants were just beginning to awaken to this important mission, Moravians were already alert, committed, and vigorously at work.[4]

The Great Awakening (1726—76)[5]

Just about the time that German Lutheran Pietism began to lose momentum, a somewhat similar and related movement got underway among Calvinists in the English colonies of North America. As the name "Great Awakening" indicates, it was viewed as a rousing from spiritual torpor or even death to vital Christian faith. During the half century before the War of Independence in a series of dramatic evangelistic events eventually reaching into most sections of the colonies, tens of thousands were converted and hundreds of new churches were established.

Even after these revivals ran their course, they remained an extremely important factor in American religious life. As a result of the Great Awakening, the goal of gaining all for Christ was accepted at least in theory by virtually all American churches. Some made the attainment of that goal their chief endeavor. Others at least periodically pursued that goal with renewed commitment and zeal. In addition, the conversion experience became normative for most Protestants, and inherited Christianity became suspect. The church was viewed increasingly as a voluntary association of like-minded believers, as opposed to the concept of an inclusive or established religious community. Partly as a result of this, the laity became more active and reflected a greater sense of ownership in their churches. The moral standards advocated by leaders of the Awakening were adopted by many individuals and even noticeably affected social regulations and mores. With the conversion and moral transformation of so many Americans, the notion grew that the glorious millennial reign of Christ was being ushered in on these shores, and that this would be accomplished before His visible return.

The Great Awakening took place during a period of sweeping social change. Population increased sixfold, from about 400,000 to 2.5 million during these 50 years, largely as a result of Scotch-Irish and German immigrations. The resulting pressures led to the expansion of the frontier westward and southward. Community consciousness and close family structures crumbled as individuals broke away to claim free lands on the frontiers. Wars with Spain, France, and the Indians were costly and disruptive. The economy was hampered by lack of a standard and stable currency. Insurrections among growing numbers of black slaves were put down savagely. Religious conditions were appalling. Fifteen percent is probably a generous estimate of the church-affiliated portion of the colonial population. Many immigrants lost their religious interest and involvement in the process of relocation. Others who came over had either never possessed an ardent and active faith, or they were influenced by the rationalism that was settling over much of Europe. Among the descendants of the Puritans indifference and moral laxity were widespread. Individual spiritual leaders and church assemblies deplored these conditions and tried with limited success to correct them. A factor working against improvement in some denominations was the chronic shortage of committed and qualified pastors. Although groups such as the Congregationalists and Presbyterians had a reasonably adequate number of clergy, the earnestness and spiritual strength of many was increasingly questioned. Preoccupation with the challenge of eking out an existence in the wilderness distracted many colonists from spiritual concerns. The management and enjoyment of their abundance competed with Christianity all too successfully with those who were already well established. It was in this environment of spiritual languor amid swirling currents of social change and ominous social tensions that new signs of life began to appear in some of the churches. Soon there was a general and vigorous awakening.

Some interpreters see the Great Awakening as a process of adaptation to cultural and social change. It is viewed as spiritual and emotional upheaval in people who, drawing on a core of widely held beliefs, forged a new religious and ethical rationale that enabled them to cope with the collapse of old ideas and institutions and to build new ones. The position taken in this study is that while social and cultural confusion added to the intensity of the Awakening, they were not its chief stimuli. These are to be found rather in an earlier religious movement that we have already briefly considered—Puritanism. Elements in the Puritan ideal were being neglected in colonial churches. The Awakening was, in part, a return to some of those ideals.[6]

Puritanism in colonial America was a complex phenomenon with social, political, and even economic aspects of considerable importance. Although in its narrowest definition the term applies only to the Congregationalists of New England, its influence permeated many other churches also in the middle and southern colonies. Interpretations of the nature as well as the causes and consequences of Puritanism differ drastically. The discussion that follows will leave most of that aside and focus on several major spiritual concerns in the Puritan heritage that clearly provided both direction and motivation to the Great Awakening.

One such concern was that every member personally experience his conversion and then reflect this event in an earnestly spiritual and moral life. From its inception in 16th-century England, Puritanism was as opposed to formalistically imparted church membership as it was to vestigial Romanistic ceremonial practices. The genuine Christian will *know* existentially that he had been delivered from God's judgment by His grace in Christ. To a degree not common in England, colonial Puritans emphasized that this occurred in a specific conversion experience. Marks of conversion and, more importantly, of God's election as its ultimate cause were sustained attention to spiritual things—Scripture, prayer, public worship—and a life conscientiously conformed to the divine will.

Children of such experientially converted persons were regarded as partially included in God's covenant of grace through their parents. This was signified rather than effected by Baptism. However, at some point during their youth or adulthood, the children were expected to enter that covenant fully by means of a conscious, felt experience to which they would testify publicly. On the other hand, persons could maintain partial membership in the church indefinitely even as adults, if they professed agreement with the church's doctrine, submitted to its discipline, and led upright lives. However, their membership privileges were limited. They did not have the right to vote in the church, receive the Lord's Supper, or have their own children baptized. These rights were originally reserved for full members.

The problem was that growing numbers already late in the 17th century never got beyond partial membership because they never underwent a conversion experience. The pressure to receive their children by Baptism mounted. Before the century was over, such Baptisms were officially sanctioned and widely practiced in both Connecticut and Massachusetts. Soon thereafter they were also admitted to the Lord's Supper. The designation for this arrangement of accepting people with no conversion experience at the Lord's table and of baptizing their children was the "Half-Way Covenant." Through parents or even more remote ancestors they had in some limited sense entered God's covenant of grace. Their doctrinal agreement with the church, submission to its discipline and conformity to its moral standard seemed to authenticate that covenant. The hope was that participation in the Lord's Supper would in some way promote a conversion experience. However, this was not generally the case. The proportion of "unconverted" members in Puritan churches increased with each succeeding generation. This rested uneasily on the consciences of earnest church leaders. In its early stages the Great Awakening was the mass conversion of many in the Half-Way Covenant as well as of those who had fallen completely away from the faith of their forebearers.

Another major concern of historic Puritanism was that their ministers be truly "spiritual" men. Part of their original dissatisfaction with the Church of England was that the clergy were unspiritual or even worldly, and that they were not preaching earnestly to the hearts of the people. As a result, Puritans raised up their own preachers, with or without formal theological education, who, in regular worship assemblies of the Church of England when possible or in separate meetings when necessary, would feed their souls with strong spiritual food. Contemporaneous with the perceived spiritual decline of Puritan membership was what seemed to be a despiritualizing of their ministry. Although they were well-prepared, respectable, and dutiful, many ministers seemed to lack contagious fervor and piety. Their preaching tended to be too cerebral. Sermons were increasingly read rather than delivered freely and directly. Whatever the specifics of their deficiencies might have been, it seemed clear that many were incapable of inducing spiritual revitalization and moral transformation. Some saw a causal relationship between the spiritual decline of the members and the unspiritual ministers. One leader of the Awakening put it very bluntly: the reason why so many congregations are spiritually dead, he said, is that they have dead men preaching to them.

This sense of need for a more spiritual ministry that was integral to the Puritan heritage was met in two ways by the Great Awakening. One was by itinerant preachers of considerable spiritual potency who traveled widely preaching both in churches and in the open air, providing what ordinary ministers presumably lacked. A few of the famous itinerants will be mentioned below. There were also sizable numbers of unknowns who crisscrossed the colonies stirring the multitudes with their fervent preaching. Some of them were extremists and fanatics, severely judgmental of the regular ministers and disruptive of parish life by infringing on the pastoral authority of others. For this, the itinerants themselves came in for much criticism. However, among those spiritually and even professionally transformed by the more responsible itinerants were many of the regular ministers who heard them. The Great Awakening stimulated personal spiritual renewal among Puritan preachers. It also inspired them to incorporate into their ministries something of the form as well as the content of the itinerants' approach.

The chief method employed in the conduct of the Great Awakening was the revival service. This consisted primarily of pointed and powerful preaching that portrayed in vivid terms the terrifying consequences of sin and the comforting marvel of God's redemptive love in Christ, along with an urgent plea to accept that love while the opportunity was there. These services were conducted in church buildings when this was permitted. Sometimes the preacher was the local minister. Having been revived recently himself, he was eager to duplicate the experience in his members. In other cases the preacher was an itinerant. Crowds frequently swelled to the point that no available building would hold them, and the open air became the sanctuary. The preaching was not necessarily emotional or even eloquent, but it was unmistakably earnest and frequently set off strong emotional reactions. Struck by the message, hearers would cry out with fear or joy and some would faint. These responses were viewed as evidence of the Spirit's presence and power. For many the revival meeting became a spiritual turning point, resulting not only in a powerful inner experience, but also in active church membership, reformed conduct, and eagerness to involve others in a similar transformation. Aside from its spiritual appeal the revival was a dramatic, exciting social phenomenon. The entire community as well as many from the outside were often completely absorbed in the event.

The Great Awakening broke out in the Raritan Valley of New Jersey in 1726 under the preaching of a Dutch Reformed pastor, Theodore Frelinghuysen (1691—1748). Having come under the influence of both German Pietism and Puritanism in Europe, Frelinghuysen was dissatisfied with the formalism and indifference of his flock. After years of preaching for deep spiritual and moral change, he finally saw many of his members revived and renewed. Through his preaching and that of others who adopted his style, this revival continued among the Dutch Reformed, despite opposition, for several decades.

It also spread to some English Presbyterian Puritans nearby. Gilbert Tennent (1703—64) of New Brunswick, New Jersey, utilized the revival approach in his church, and other Presbyterians of that tradition followed suit. They were resisted by Scotch-Irish Presbyterians who traditionally stressed correct doctrine over experience. Ultimately this resulted in a split between the "Old Side" and the "New Side" (revivalist) Presbyterians.

New England was the scene of the most remarkable and extensive awakening. Jonathan Edwards (1703—58), a Congregationalist preacher in Northampton, Massachusetts, precipitated it in 1734 with a stirring sermon on justification by faith. This was preceded by a period of anxiety in the community about the worldliness of the youth and was followed by numerous conversions, increased attendance and attentiveness at worship, and a pervasive atmosphere of holy joy. Reports of the revival spread, and the experience was replicated in communities all along the Connecticut River. About 40 parishes were affected. As in Northampton, the revival preaching was done by the local ministers. The revival crested in 1735 and had subsided everywhere by 1737. In that year Edwards published *A Faithful Narrative of the Surprising Work of God in the Conversion of Many Hundred Souls,* in which he described the phenomenon. This was read widely in all the colonies as well as in England and Scotland, creating considerable interest and expectancy.

A new burst of revivalism was ignited in 1739 with the arrival in the colonies of George Whitefield (1714—70), a young clergyman of the Church of England who had begun his astonishing career as a preacher only three years earlier following a deep personal religious experience. After a triumphant tour through the middle colonies he came to New England in the fall of 1740, where the way had been prepared by numerous newspaper articles about his work as well as the publication of his writings. He was met everywhere by large and sometimes unruly crowds, whom he often addressed in the open air. The first wave of the Awakening in New England had been confined largely to the Connecticut Valley. This second wave washed over the entire area. It was a great and general awakening—150 congregations were touched by it and as many as 50,000 new members added.

The following summer a fanatical itinerant, James Davenport (1716—57), brought disrepute upon the movement by his wild and denunciatory preaching. Anti-revivalist forces were already building up and a division developed among New England Congregationalists. Anti-revivalists ("Old Lights") criticized leaders of the Awakening for enthusiasm (claims to direct contact with and revelation by the Spirit), emotionalism, censoriousness, and excessive, irresponsible itinerary. Charles Chauncy (1705—87) of Boston was head of the "Old Lights." The pro-revival party ("New Lights") survived the attacks, however, and the clergy in this party outnumbered their opponents three to one.

An unexpected and highly significant result of the Great Awakening in New England was the emergence of the Baptist churches as a vital and growing element of colonial Christianity. At the outbreak of the revival in 1740 they were a small, demoralized group and even opposed to the revivalist approach. Nevertheless, increasing numbers of those converted to Congregationalism in the Awakening began to make their way into Baptist congregations. The emphasis on experience, so characteristic of the Awakening, seemed inconsistent with even the moderate sacramental views and practices of the Congregationalists. In addition, the anomaly of an established, inclusive Congregationalist church led many to feel that this church was only partly reformed. Furthermore, after their initial resistance to revivalism, the Baptists adopted it whole-heartedly and were able to keep the Awakening going in their midst long after it was quenched elsewhere in New England. Not only thousands of individuals but entire congregations came into the Baptist fellowship from the Congregationalists. Along with numerous converts from the outside, they tripled the number of Baptist congregations in New England during the last half of the 18th century. From this body many preachers moved out into the frontiers where, especially in the south, they reaped a great harvest.[7]

A variety of denominations preceded these New England Baptists into the southern colonies—Anglicans, Presbyterians, Lutherans, and even several other kinds of Baptists. There had also been some minor revivals. However, the enormous challenge of reaching the settlers coming in a large and steady stream to the southern frontiers was met most effectively by these Separate Baptists ("Separate" because many had originally separated from the Congregational church). In 1755 Shubal Stearns, a Bostonian converted by Whitefield, led a small group of fellow believers, mostly family, to Sandy Creek in Guilford (now Randolph) County, North Carolina. They founded a church that soon "mothered" nine others. Stearns and his associates were fervent revivalists. They traveled far and wide on evangelistic missions, converting many and inspiring some of them in turn to take up itineracy. They were as eccentric as they were effective. Their revival meetings were characterized by emotional and behavioral extravagance, but at the same time they insisted on strict spiritual and moral discipline. They united with some Regular Baptists whose tradition included concern for correct doctrine and some limitations of congregational autonomy. Their preachers generally lacked formal education.

A unique development among these Baptists was the farmer-preacher. This was a farmer who, after having been "born again," believed that he possessed both the gifts and the call to preach. Without leaving his farm he would begin to preach, gather a flock at any simple meeting place—in a home or barn or under a tree—be ordained, and begin a part-time ministry. Because of his earnestness and his closeness to the other settlers the farmer-preacher was able in a unique way to meet the evangelistic opportunities of the southern frontiers. As various sections of the south filled up and groups of farmers would decide to move on to new frontiers, there would often be farmer-preachers among them ready to plant the church in the new locations.

Parallel with the Great Awakening, and somewhat related, was a significant work of outreach to immigrants. The two most numerous groups were the Scotch-Irish and the Germans. About 400,000 of the former and 300,000 of the latter settled in the English colonies of North America during the first three-quarters of the 18th century—most of them in Pennsylvania. This represents 28 percent of the entire colonial population at the outbreak of the Revolution.

The Scotch-Irish were traditionally Presbyterian, but most immigrants exhibited very little commitment to or interest in that faith. They became a fruitful mission field for the colonial Presbyterian churches, which, by the time the Scotch-Irish were arriving in mid-century, were resolving some of their differences over revivalism and were ready to meet a new challenge. The "New Side" element dominated the reunited Presbyterians. Their style of revivalism was more subdued than that of the New England Congregationalists. Although interested in a conversion experience, the real goal of the Presbyterian revivalists was changed lives. Much pastoral energy was invested in the attainment of that goal. A key role in the expansion of Presbyterianism was the College of New Jersey (today Princeton University), which educated many of the ministers that served their existing churches and who founded new ones. The growth of the denomination was substantial—to about 200 congregations and about 170 ministers. Much of the growth consisted of Scotch-Irish immigrants and their descendants.

The German immigrants were religiously more diverse, consisting of Reformed, Mormons, Dunkers, Mennonites, and Schwenkfelders as well as Lutherans, who were the largest group. The vast majority were from a pietistic tradition. Among the German immigrant churches only two engaged in vigorous outreach—the Moravians and the Lutherans, both of which were profoundly influenced by Pietism. The Moravian venture was surprisingly extensive: congregations in 31 localities, 50 missionaries to Indians, and three semi-communistic settlements that contributed substantially to the material support of their outreach. However, by 1775 they had only 3,000 members in colonial America.

Ministry to German Lutheran immigrants did not begin in earnest until the arrival of Henry Melchior Muhlenberg (1711—87) in 1742. Previously pastors were in very short supply, and the dedication and competency of many who were available left much to be desired. Lacking leadership, many German Lutheran immigrants drifted into other churches or, more frequently, into spiritual indifference. Muhlenberg was a Halle missionary—zealous, tireless, wise. His motto was: the church must be planted. He traveled through German settlements in Pennsylvania and beyond, ministering to whatever existing congregations were there. He gathered new congregations, recruited additional workers, erected buildings, made peace between warring factions, developed a liturgy, and founded the first Lutheran body in America— the Pennsylvania Ministerium—in 1748. By 1771 there were 101 Lutheran congregations throughout the middle and southern colonies. From the very beginning Muhlenberg's goal was to establish a united, independent, self-supporting Lutheran church in America. To an astonishing degree this was accomplished during his lifetime.

His style was not revivalistic, but rather one of churchly Pietism. He was an earnest shepherd of souls concerned about the spiritual well-being of individuals and groups. He reached out with Word and Sacrament to gain people, feed them spiritually, and to organize them for the Lord's work.[8] To a greater degree than some Pietists, he was committed to maintaining the theology and practices of historic Lutheranism.

To a large extent the story of evangelism in colonial America is the story of revivalism. In both New England and in the southern colonies itinerant revivalists as well as resident ministers preached stirring messages of sin and forgiveness into the hearts of marginal Christians and unbelievers, often with transforming results. Emotion-charged revival meetings induced conversion experiences in many and led some beyond this to active church membership and an eagerness to share the Gospel with others. Congregational and Baptist churches especially grew through revivalism. Among the Presbyterians in the middle colonies there was also a strong revivalist element. However, their approach was more reserved, combined with a concern for doctrinal substance and the desire for a learned ministry. In this respect they were more like the Congregationalists than the Baptists. With this modified revivalism the Presbyterians gathered in tens of thousands of Scotch-Irish immigrants.

The evangelization of the Indians in the 13 colonies was a concern of some Christians from the very beginning. The charter of the Massachusetts colony, for example, stated that this was its chief purpose. Virginia professed a similar objective. In 1646 John Eliot (1604—90), having learned an Indian language and translated some prayers and Scripture portions, began preaching to Indians near Boston. His hearers were quite responsive, and those who were converted or in process of conversion were gathered into European-type villages under the leadership and care of missionaries. This arrangement was strikingly similar to the *reductions* of the Catholic missionaries to South America but was probably not a conscious imitation. His efforts, along with those of other missionaries, brought the number of Christian Indians in this area to about 4,000 by 1675. However, disease and the French and Indian Wars were extremely destructive to the work, and numbers declined after this date. About the same time a Swedish Lutheran pastor, John Campanius, launched a less successful effort among the Indians of the lower Delaware valley. A variety of similar ventures were carried out elsewhere in the colonies.

The Great Awakening stimulated new outreach in the 18th century. Eleazor Wheelock (1711—79), an active revivalist, began a program to educate Indians as missionaries to their own people, which eventually developed into Dartmouth College. Jonathan Edwards himself was a missionary to the Indians at Stockbridge, Massachusetts (1751—57). David Brainerd (1718—47), having been touched by the Great Awakening, evangelized Indians in Massachusetts, New York, and New Jersey. His diary was published and widely read, stimulating others to undertake missionary work in North America and throughout the world. Anglicans and Dutch Reformed worked with some success among the Iroquois and Mohawks of New York. Moravian efforts have already been mentioned. Financial support for much of the work came from Europe, but the missionaries were colonists. Enduring results were minimal. The vast and increasing pressure of white settlers, combined with factors mentioned above, decimated, dispersed, and disillusioned the Indian population, making evangelism among them difficult and unproductive.[9]

The Evangelical Revival (1739—91)[10]

The British counterpart of Pietism and the Great Awakening was the Evangelical Revival. Basically it began with the outdoor preaching of Whitefield and Wesley at Bristol (early 1739) and concluded with Wesley's death (1791). However, the first stirrings of the revival were felt a generation earlier, and the movement was far from spent when Wesley died. What began as an effort to revitalize the Church of England ultimately resulted in two new dissenting churches, both bearing the name "Methodist. " However, the Church of England was also profoundly affected by the revival. An evangelical party was formed, which, during the next century, became the dominant force within that church. In addition, some of the other dissenting churches—especially the Baptists and Congregationalists—were revived and activated. The Evangelical Revival of the 18th century was probably the deepest and most powerful Christian movement ever to touch England.

Its significance extends far beyond that land. Out of the Evangelical Revival came strong and lasting impulses for Protestant world missions, which in various forms continues to grow and produce fruit two centuries later. The Methodist church, transplanted to North America, was uniquely suited to meet the needs of settlers on the ever expanding frontiers of the United States. More recently, Methodism spawned some new vigorous and rapidly growing movements, the most important of which is Pentecostalism.

Deplorable religious and social conditions in 18th-century England were important elements in the background of the revival. Religious rationalism had taken root in the previous century and continued to spread, especially among the educated and affluent. Many clergy of the Church of England were affected as well as those in several of the dissenting churches. Those who regarded human reason as the chief source and criterion of truth inevitably surrendered belief in Christ's deity, His redemptive death, His resurrection, and anything else in Scripture that was supernatural in character. Much preaching degenerated into intellectualistic moralizing. Spiritual lethargy set in. Virtually nothing was done to reach the unchurched. The lower classes especially were alienated. Their lives were hard. Poverty, illiteracy, and alcoholism were widespread. There was much immorality, crime, and violence. Remote and irrelevant, the Church of England was unable to meet their needs, and most clergy were not interested enough even to try.

Other concerned Christians, however, did rise to this awesome spiritual and moral challenge. In London about 1678 the phenomenon of religious societies appeared. These were support and service groups of earnest Christians devoted to Scripture study, prayer, mutual encouragement, and preaching, as well as ministry to those in spiritual and material need. By 1700 there were about 100 such societies in London alone. The number declined shortly thereafter, but many survived and became a vital element in the Evangelical Revival. William Law (1686—1761) issued an urgent, widely read appeal to Christian piety and morality entitled *Serious Call to a Devout and Holy Life*. Isaac Watts (1674—1748) wrote numerous hymns that reflected and fostered religion of the heart and life. In both Scotland and Wales revival preaching, limited but significant, began during the first decades of the 18th century.

These developments revealed serious concerns about the state of British Christianity and, in some sense, prepared the way. However, the Revival itself in its distinctive forms and with its astonishing power began in Bristol, mid-February, 1739, under the ministry of George Whitefield. We have already commented briefly on his part in the Great

Awakening the following year. The reputation he gained in connection with the English Revival (to be described in this section) preceded him to the colonies, arousing interest and magnifying his impact upon audiences. Although John Wesley (1703—91) soon eclipsed him as leader of the Evangelical Revival, Whitefield must be recognized as its founder. The events that signaled the dawn of a new era in British Protestant religious life was the beginning of Whitefield's open-air preaching at the coal mining community of Kingwood near Bristol.

Open-air preaching was not new. Throughout Christian history it had been used, often very effectively. Howell Harris (1714—73), an itinerant Welsh lay preacher, had adopted this approach several years earlier, and it was from him that Whitefield got the idea. What sets Whitefield's outdoor preaching apart is the rapid and phenomenal popularity it enjoyed. Initially this could be attributed to his personal charisma. However, he inevitably committed his work to successors who, in most cases, were able to sustain and even increase it. The Evangelical Revival was not a personality cult dependent upon one spectacular individual; rather, it was a new style of evangelistic ministry exercised by many.

Whitefield was already a celebrity when he began his open-air ministry. In 1737, a year after his ordination to the diaconate, he had preached to large and responsive congregations in London, Bristol, and Gloucester. He was also much in demand as a speaker at religious societies. During most of 1738 he was in Georgia, where he determined to found an orphanage. Upon his return to England at the end of that year, he began a preaching tour that had as one of its purposes to raise funds for the proposed orphanage. At Oxford, early in January 1739 he was ordained as a priest of the Church of England, but without a specific parish assignment. From there he traveled to London where he spoke to many societies and churches. Opposition was rising, however, because of his unconventional message and style, and growing numbers of churches were closed to him.

Changes in Whitefield, both theological and homiletical, occurred during this period. Up to this point he preached salvation by grace and works, but grace alone became and remained his theme ever after. In addition, he began to emphasize the gradual sanctifying work of the Holy Spirit in the believer. These doctrines reflect the Calvinistic orientation that became increasingly important to him. His preaching style also underwent a transformation during these months. Previously he had read his sermons from manuscripts. Now he began to preach more freely and spontaneously. Although only 25 years old, he was becoming one of the most articulate, artful, and magnetic preachers of all times.

To return to Bristol in February 1739, Whitefield seized on field preaching both out of necessity and for the advantages it offered. It was a necessity because more and more pastors refused to let him use their churches, and even when permission was granted many buildings were not large enough to hold the growing crowds that were attracted to his preaching. It was advantageous because with the whole outdoors as his sanctuary he could go wherever the people were, take advantage of established gathering places, and reach people who were little inclined to enter a church building. There were also disadvantages. In the minds of some, outdoor gatherings of this sort were associated with fanaticism and civil disorder (e.g., the Puritan uprising of the previous century). In addition, there was always the possibility of unfavorable weather.

Whitefield was nevertheless convinced that conditions warranted the risks. When he became aware of the crying needs of the coal miners of Kingswood—no church, no school, abject poverty, hostility toward outsiders and vicious in their dealing with one another—Whitefield decided that this was where he would begin his open-air ministry. On a cold Saturday afternoon in February, he went to this wretched mining community and called people out of their grimy hovels, caves, and mines to an open place called Rose Green to hear a Gospel message. About 200 came. Encouraged, he announced another open-air meeting several days later, which 2,000 eager listeners attended. Shortly thereafter the attendance surpassed 5,000, and within a month no less than 20,000 were gathering. The people were deeply moved. Tears of repentance streaked their unwashed faces and songs of praise came from hearts rejoicing in God's grace. During these six weeks of open-air preaching at Kingswood, Whitefield became a master of this new evangelistic style and an inspiring model followed by thousands of other evangelistic preachers down through the centuries.

With great success he also conducted similar meetings in more civilized and advantaged communities—Bristol, Gloucester, and even London. In the parks of London, which were centers of coarse entertainment, rowdiness, and crime, Whitefield preached regularly over a period of several months to enormous crowds (as large as 40,000) that were incredibly attentive and responsive. In addition, he preached frequently in religious societies as well as in those churches where he was still welcome. During these months of his London ministry (May and June 1739), the celebrated young preacher became a sensation, surrounded by adoring multitudes, sought out incessantly for his spiritual counsel by people of all classes and ages. Although he was not immune to egotism, Whitefield remained remarkably humble and unselfish despite all the acclaim.

George Whitefield launched the Evangelical Revival within five months. Not only the spectacular preacher and his gripping message, but the changed hearts and lives of many hearers were very much before the public eye. It soon became clear that this phenomenon was no flash in the pan. Whitefield's effectiveness and appeal lasted for decades. Although some claim that his work yielded only meager permanent results, there is much evidence to the contrary. The fact is that White-field was deeply concerned about sustaining the work he began. He carefully selected successors to assume control and direction of the fields he had opened. The most notable example of this is his enlistment of John Wesley (1703—91) to carry on the burgeoning revival in Bristol and Kingswood when Whitefield was preparing to leave for Georgia.

Wesley and Whitefield had become acquainted at Oxford University six years earlier (1733), when Whitefield was an undergraduate and Wesley, 11 years his senior, was a Master of Arts, lecturer in Greek, Fellow of Lincoln College, and an ordained priest. The two met when John's younger brother, Charles, invited Whitefield to breakfast. This was unusual in itself, since Whitefield was a servitor, a poor student who earned his tuition by functioning as a personal servant of several students of rank and means. Custom forbade social interaction between servitors and other students, and between servitors and tutors. Despite this, friendship immediately blossomed, and Whitefield soon became part of the Holy Club in which John and Charles played leading roles.

This small group of scholars and students was devoted to the rigorous practice of devotion, discipline, and service through which the participants sought to further their salvation. Since the general climate of the university was spiritually and morally lax, members of the Holy Club were subjected to a considerable amount of ridicule and even hostility. A secondary but significant aspect of the Holy Club was the promotion of academic excellence among the members.

In the Wesleys Whitefield found much needed friendship. In the Holy Club he found stimulus for the spiritual earnestness already growing within him. However, he did not find the Gospel or adequate relief for his longing for a secure and saving relationship with God. Neither did the other members. Their approach was thoroughly works-righteous. By extraordinary spiritual and moral exertion they were striving to convince themselves that they were acceptable to God and safe for eternity.

John and Charles Wesley were sons of a rector of the Church of

England, born and raised at Epworth. The home was characterized by religious earnestness, firm but loving discipline, and also some tension between the parents. Their mother, Susanna, was an able, strong-minded woman who personally provided individualized elementary education for each of her 11 surviving children. (Eight others died in infancy.) Whitefield was the son of a prosperous Gloucester innkeeper. The family suffered financially after the father's early death and the failure of the mother's second marriage. During his early youth Whitefield went through a period of worldliness, but at age 17 he began to get serious about his relationship with God. The Wesley brothers, during their early youth, also manifested some rebellion and spiritual neglect.

A good preparatory education at Charterhouse prepared John and Charles for scholarly excellence at Oxford. Spiritual concern lagged until 1725, when, at the encouragement of his mother, John decided to prepare for holy orders. He developed an interest in mysticism through reading Thomas a Kempis' *Imitation of Christ*. Bishop Taylor's *Rule and Exercise of Holy Living and Dying*, prompted him to try the ascetic way. After his ordination in 1728 John left the university briefly. During his absence Charles and several others organized a little club primarily to aid one another in their studies. A moderate spiritual dimension was added. When John returned a year later he assumed leadership and redirected the purpose to fostering William Law's ideal of a fully consecrated life. This was the character of the Holy Club when Whitefield joined in 1733.

Although he appreciated and respected the Wesleys and the objectives of the Holy Club, Whitefield found no spiritual peace in either. After a period of distressing inner struggle to attain it through extreme ascetic practices that finally broke his health, Whitefield experienced the relief and joy of salvation through awareness of God's gift of Christ in 1735. The source from which he gained this Gospel insight is not known, but its effect upon him was profound and lasting. The following year he was ordained as a deacon in the Church of England and immediately began his astonishing preaching career.

John Wesley's conversion occurred three years later (1738), after his return from a humiliating and frustrating missionary assignment in Georgia. A lasting benefit of the experience, however, was his contact with a small group of Moravians whose joy and confidence in the Gospel impressed him deeply. From them he was introduced to justification by faith. Not long afterward, at a meeting of the Aldersgate Society in London on May 24, 1738, while listening to a reading of Luther's preface to his *Commentary on Romans*, Wesley felt his heart strangely warmed and realized that he did have certainty of salvation through trust in Christ alone. Charles had had a similar experience several days earlier.

John became better acquainted with the Moravians through a visit to Germany. His respect for them never wavered, but he did find himself at odds with some points of their theology and practice, specifically their quietism. They held that while awaiting the dawn of true faith a person should remain passive, using neither the means of grace nor prayer, but leaving all the initiative to God. In time other differences also surfaced. However, for their remarkable example of joyful assurance in Christ as well as for the Gospel of God's justifying grace, John Wesley was permanently indebted to the Moravians. Shortly after his return from Germany, Wesley read Jonathan Edwards' account of the revival in and around Northampton, Massachusetts and began to wonder if God might not have something similar in store for England.

We now return to Bristol in mid-March of 1739. Whitefield was preparing to leave for Georgia. In four short weeks his open-air ministry had mushroomed to the point that tens of thousands regularly gathered to hear his preaching. Money had been collected for a school at Kingswood. Religious societies were vibrant and growing. His mind turned to John Wesley. They had met the previous December after a separation of three and a half eventful years. Whitefield learned of Wesley's conversion experience and of his work in the societies both at London and Oxford. Well aware of Wesley's intellectual and organizational abilities as well as his spiritual seriousness, Whitefield urged him to come to Bristol and assume leadership of the revival that had attained such astonishing size and strength.

Reluctantly, Wesley accepted. He could not hope to match Whitefield's eloquence and charisma. He was somewhat repelled by the informal, unconventional style of revival ministry. However, after observing Whitefield in action and having been commended by Whitefield to his followers, Wesley began his outdoor ministry. Although the crowds he drew were not as large as Whitefield's, they were sizable and very responsive to his preaching. Emotional reactions, far more intense and bizarre than Whitefield evoked, marked Wesley's preaching from a very early time. Not only in the Bristol area but also later in London Whitefield presented Wesley to the assembled multitudes as his successor. Immediately this thrust Wesley into prominence and at the same time provided the revival with a source of continuity and momentum. Although Whitefield's commendation gave him his start, Wesley's personal qualities and performance earned him lasting and growing stature in the revival.

In order to give stability to the Revival, Wesley added two features. One was a new kind of religious society. Those who were converted or deepened spiritually at the mass meetings were gathered into support groups (societies) that were subdivided several ways into smaller groups for instruction and mutual encouragement. A variety of lay leaders exercised supervision over the small groups and special ministries of each local society. Traveling preachers were in charge of clusters of societies. At the head of all units and personnel was Wesley himself. Members whose participation or moral behavior wavered were admonished and, if they did not improve, were dismissed.

These highly structured and tightly disciplined Methodist Societies (named after the highly methodical approach of their leader) were not regarded as churches. They were a renewal movement within the Church of England, a supplement to, rather than a substitute for, the worship and sacramental ministry of that body. Only in later years, after unremitting opposition from the ecclesiastical establishment, did separation occur. It did not become final until after Wesley's death simply because he would not stand for it.

The other stabilizing factor that Wesley introduced was preaching houses or chapels. These were meeting places large enough to hold the assembled Methodist society members at a given location. With the rapid growth of society membership, private homes and other available facilities soon became inadequate, so the chapels met an urgent need. These buildings were not regarded as churches, and the activities within them were not intentionally competitive with the worship services of the Church of England. They were intended as renewal centers designed to augment and support the work of that church.

Wesley's theology was distinct from that of Whitefield to the point that controversy broke out between them, and their followers divided. Wesley was Arminian, stressing the freedom of the sinner to move toward God, as opposed to the Calvinist concept of human helplessness in conversion. He believed that Christ's atoning work was for all sinners, as opposed to the Calvinist teaching that Christ had died only for the elect. He taught Christian perfection, meaning that when the Holy Spirit works the highest level of sanctification, original sin is overcome and the believer is capable of purely loving motives. Calvinists, on the other hand, taught the continuing power of sin in the believer. Above all, Wesley rejected the Calvinistic doctrine of election—that from eternity God predetermined the final destiny of both the saved and the lost. Wesley believed that on all of these points Calvinism cut the nerve of evangelistic impulse. Although Whitefield did not feel compelled to emphasize these doctrines, he did believe them and resented Wesley's outspoken opposition to them. Whitefield's followers eventually became the Calvinistic Methodists and Wesley's the Wesleyan Methodists. Despite the controversy and division the two leaders maintained reasonably good personal relations.

In order to understand Wesley and some of the movements that eventually descended from him, it is important to note some developments in his theology regarding the relation between faith, works, and assurance. During the first period of his religious pilgrimage (1725—38), he was seeking the assurance that he had saving faith by strenuous works of piety and service. As already noted, this quest failed. In the events culminating at the Aldersgate meeting, he found assurance in the Gospel of God's free grace in Christ and in the realization that faith itself is His free gift. At this point he identified the experienced assurance of pardon with justifying faith. Later he changed, recognizing that this felt assurance is only a companion of faith rather than its essence. Justification by faith came to mean simply trusting in the righteousness of Christ, which might or might not result in an assurance experience. Distinct but inseparable from justification is the new birth, an inward change from sin toward the image of God, the implantation of godly attitudes.

Although works did not produce assurance, assurance produced works. The stronger and fuller one's assurance, the stronger and more active one's love for God and for people. Wesley believed that assurance was a measure, not of justification, but of sanctification. Sanctification was a work of God's grace following justification and directed toward perfection. The concept of perfection as taught by Wesley focused primarily on motivation, specifically love. He believed that the Holy Spirit generated in some believers a love for God so complete and powerful that they no longer felt sin within or were aware of sin in their lives. This perfect love was inevitably joined to full assurance of salvation and, in fact, flowed out of it.

Motivational perfection did not result in behavioral perfection. Human ignorance remained even in the perfected Christian and at times caused him to sin inadvertently. All intentional and conscious disobedience, however, was eliminated in the person who had received the blessing of perfection. Although in these respects perfection was complete and instantaneous, there was also room for growth in the perfected person as he struggled against ignorance and external temptation. Wesley urged all Christians to be aware of this blessing of perfection—or "entire sanctification," as it was also called. They should be ready to accept and live in it, if it were granted to them. However, many, including Wesley himself, did not attain perfection in this life. Their experience of sanctification was a process of growth from partial to more complete love and obedience. Significantly, their sense of assurance was never complete either. Wesley's emphasis on sanctification and perfection as the most desirable form of it became increasingly prominent and eventually appears to have displaced justification as the central theme. This represents a significant departure from the theology of the 16th-century reformers.

Like the Pietists and leaders of the Great Awakening, Whitefield, Wesley, and their associates were subjected to constant and severe criticism. They were accused of fanaticism and excessive austerity, of violating the laws of the church about unauthorized worship activities, of manipulating weak souls, and of utilizing lay preachers. In addition, the doctrines of justification by faith, the new birth, and entire sanctification were condemned. The chief source of the opposition was the clergy of the Church of England, who recognized in the Revival an indictment of their own ineffectiveness and neglect. Adherents and advocates of rationalism also registered their disapproval, denouncing what they believed to be mere emotionalism and superstition. Much of the opposition was literary, but frequently it also took the form of mob attacks on both the preachers and their followers, instigated and encouraged by clergy of the establishment. In general, leaders and participants in the Revival accepted these attacks with patience and dignity and replied to their critics with commendable restraint.

Despite opposition, the Revival grew steadily. By Wesley's death there were more than 70,000 members of his Methodist societies in Britain alone, primarily from the lower and middle classes. Whitefield's group, although not as large, also made inroads into the aristocracy through the support and influence of Selina, Countess of Huntingdon (1707—91). Her example and financial backing were extremely important to the growth of these Calvinistic Methodists, who eventually were designated as the Welsh Methodist Church. In addition, many who remained within the Church of England, both clergy and laity, were affected by the Revival and incorporated some of its characteristics into their own lives and ministries—the emphasis on conversion, confident faith, and a life of Christian service. However, few adopted the more rigorous aspects of Methodist discipline.

Among the reasons for this growth are, first of all, the earnest, moving Gospel preaching of Whitefield, the Wesleys, and hundreds of zealous and effective but less prominent associates. The well-structured and disciplined societies founded by Wesley deserve much credit for conserving, sustaining, and also extending this growth. The extensive utilization of lay leaders and preachers gave a stronger sense of ownership and responsibility to the laity, which many found appealing and stimulating. The use of dedicated itinerant preachers provided flexibility and mobility of outreach, enabling the Revival to meet the needs of many who were not being served by the churches. Printed material helped a great deal. The journals and sermons of the great revivalists were published and widely read. The education of an evangelistic ministry helped assure the Revival's continuation and extension. Wesley prepared and compiled reading materials for the in-service training of his lay preachers. Lady Huntingdon founded a school for preachers at Trevecca in Wales.

From the very beginning, the Revival was characterized by what is now called social ministry. Material as well as spiritual needs of the poor and the distressed were met by concerned evangelicals. (At this point in history "evangelical," when used with reference to English Christianity, designates those identified with the Evangelical Revival.) This was both a living demonstration of the Gospel and preparation for verbal witness. Many who were aided in this way eventually believed. Finally, thousands of stirring hymns both expressed and fostered the spirit of the Evangelical Revival.

The basic approach of the Evangelical Revival, especially that of Wesley's wing, incorporated the main features of each of the other two Protestant revivals. Like Pietism it made excellent use of groups comparable to the conventicles, only more thoroughly organized and more carefully disciplined. In this way it had the benefit of small group support and a laity active in ministry to one another.

The Evangelical Revival also had a valuable outreach capability that the Pietists lacked—mass, open-air evangelism. Most conversions occurred in these outdoor meetings after which converts were drawn into the societies for nurture and activation. In its utilization of mass evangelism the Evangelical Revival was like the Great Awakening. The ministry of George Whitefield accounts for the outdoor ministry in both revivals. However, the Great Awakening did not include the extensive use of a follow-up agency to its mass evangelism comparable to the Methodist societies. There were some religious societies of the older Anglican type in the colonies, and they did perk up as a result of the Awakening. In addition, many congregations tried to follow up on those gained in revival services, but lacking the close connection with the revivalists that the Methodist societies enjoyed, as well as the discipline they maintained, the follow-up measures of the Great Awakening were less effective.

World Missions

Significant developments also took place in the mission fields during the era under consideration in this chapter. In some places missionaries of aggressive new Protestant colonial powers took over Catholic work and made it their own. In addition, destructive rivalry between the missionary orders and the temporary dissolution of the Jesuits took a heavy toll on the Catholic mission enterprises. Controversy over the principle of accommodation raged in the mission fields. Especially in the Orient, the patronage system became more of a problem than an aid. It became increasingly clear that direction of Catholic missions ought to be coming from the headquarters of the church, rather than from Catholic monarchs. Even at its best, the patronage system was often dominated by political and economic rather than evangelistic concerns. With the traditional sources of missionary ardor and energy failing, it was extremely helpful to the Roman cause that a new source opened up—France—and from that new source came the opening of new fields and the utilization of some fresh approaches.

The most important development in Roman Catholic world evangelization during this period was the creation of the Sacred Congregation for the Propagation of the Faith in 1622 (often referred to simply as "The Propaganda"). Not only did this agency centralize the control and coordination of the far-flung missions of the church and break the stranglehold of the Spanish and Portuguese monarchies on Catholic missions, but it also took a more enlightened approach to missions. From the first Secretary of the Propaganda, Francesco Ingoli (d. 1649), came the realization that evangelistic strategy must grow out of careful study of the mission fields. On the basis of such study he saw strengthening of missionary clergy as a primary need. More bishops must be consecrated for service in the mission fields. More secular clergy must be utilized to balance those from monastic orders. Above all, an indigenous clergy must be developed. In 1659 the Propaganda articulated very clear and strong support of the policy of accommodation: do not unnecessarily disturb the cultures and customs of non-European people. Do your utmost to adapt to them. Essentially, this was the approach of Matteo Ricci in China and Robert de Nobili in India, which was discussed in the previous chapter.

In order to bypass the control of Spanish and Portuguese patrons, the Propaganda established a new office, that of vicar apostolic. This was, in effect, a missionary bishop, an ecclesiastical official who exercised all the authority of a bishop, including ordination, without actually bearing the title. The difference was that the vicar apostolic had no fixed regional assignment but was charged to establish and oversee the work of the church in non-Christian areas and was responsible only to Rome. Even though these areas were outside the boundaries assigned to Spain and Portugal, the work of the vicars apostolic was resented and obstructed by them. In view of their extensive traditional missionary responsibilities, these nations felt slighted and even threatened by this change. With the increasing involvement of French missionaries (to be discussed below), they felt that this would be an opening wedge for French imperialism. However, the new arrangement was upheld and extended with the result that the leadership of the church was now directly in charge of growing segments of its evangelistic outreach.

During the 17th century France became the center of Catholic missionary interest and involvement. Alexander Rhodes, a French Jesuit who worked in Southeast Asia from 1623 to 1645, stimulated missionary awareness by reports of his activities and by recruiting workers—all with the hearty support of the Propaganda. Out of this came the Society of Foreign Missions and in 1663 the establishment of a seminary dedicated to the preparation of missionaries. Among the major contributions of Rhodes and his French associates was indigenization. He learned the Vietnamese language and reduced it to writing. Next he trained a group of native catechists. These were well-prepared, well-disciplined workers who lived in community and took vows of celibacy and obedience, although they were not ordained. Their work was extremely effective. By 1658 there were reportedly 300,000 Christians in Vietnam (probably an exaggerated count), although during some of this time European missionaries were expelled.

A major setback (at least numerically) to Catholic evangelization in the Orient was the complete reversal of the policy of accommodation. From the very beginning there were those who viewed this policy as an unconscionable compromise with paganism. Things came to a head in 1693, when the vicar apostolic of China ordered the Jesuits to discontinue use of the controversial Chinese terms for God (Tien and Shang-ti) and to forbid their followers to conduct their traditional ceremonial veneration of departed ancestors. The Jesuits appealed to Rome and offered testimony from the Chinese emperor himself that these challenged terms and practices in no way compromised Christian beliefs. Rome was unyielding, however, and in 1704 issued a decree supporting the restrictive position of the vicar apostolic. An inexperienced and insensitive papal representative carried this to China, leading the infuriated emperor to expel all missionaries who followed the decree. Subsequent appeals by missionaries to reverse or modify the decree failed, with the result that growth was impeded and decline set in where Catholicism had once flourished. The issues in the controversy are complex and technical. While Rome clearly overreacted to the accommodation policy, it also seems evident that the accommodationists had conceded too much to paganism and had become syncretistic.

Another area of French Catholic missionary effort was North America. From 1632 to 1763 earnest and heroic work among the Indians was carried on primarily by Jesuits. It extended from the northeastern Atlantic coast to the Mississippi and down that great river to the Gulf of Mexico. Some converts were made. The *reduction* system utilized widely in South America was not successful here. The Indians were far more mobile and independent than their southern counterparts. Missionaries learned the languages, lived among them, and provided medical and educational assistance. However, recurring warfare among the Indians as well as their involvement in wars among European colonists were most disruptive. In addition, the Indians tended to blame the missionaries for their misfortunes—wars, disease, famines—as they were accustomed to blame their previous religious leaders. Lasting results were limited and the missions ceased when French rule came to an end in 1762—63. Despite the disappointing harvest, these French missions represented the most ambitious and sustained attempt of any Christian group to evangelize the American Indians.

Far more significant in the long run was the planting of the Roman Catholic Church among French settlers of what is now eastern Canada. These immigrants began coming early in the 17th century, and by the end of French rule they were very numerous. Prominent in building the church among these settlers was Francois Xavier de Laval-Montmorency, who came to Canada in 1659 as vicar apostolic and became the first bishop of Quebec in 1674. Already in 1668 he founded a seminary to train secular clergy to augment the efforts of the monastic missionaries. By the time French rule ended there were said to be 70,000 Roman Catholics in Canada.[11]

During the period under consideration Protestant missions were just getting under way. As the Dutch colonial enterprise extended into the Orient, some provisions were made not only to supply spiritual care for Dutch people in the east but also to reach out to the natives. The Dutch East India Company founded a small seminary in Leyden that in a decade or so prepared a dozen ministers for this work. Motives and methods employed left much to be desired. Ministers were paid a cash bonus for each convert made, and converts received special advantages because of their Christian status. Numbers increased rapidly especially in Ceylon and Indonesia. Although most of the work was superficial and most Dutch missionaries were gone by the end of the 18th century, some substantial and enduring contributions are evident. The New Testament was translated into Malay in 1688 and became the chief textbook in many schools. Some Dutch clergy became proficient in that language. By the end of the 18th century, despite all the limitations of the effort, the Christian population of the East Indies was between 65,000 and 200,000—the largest group of Protestants east of India. During subsequent centuries vigorous new growth came forth from this beginning.

We have already mentioned the start of Lutheran missions in India in the Danish colony of Tranquebar by the German Pietist missionaries Ziegenbalg and Pluetchau in 1706. Under difficult circumstances they made a slow but solid beginning. They learned the language and the culture, translated parts of Scripture, established schools, worked for the personal conversion of individuals, and prepared a native ministry. In addition, they promoted awareness of and interest in the mission to India by the publication and translation of *Annual Letters,* which reported on their work. Translations of these letters were read with great interest in England. On one occasion, Ziegenbalg returned to Europe on leave, and among the dignitaries who received him were the king of England and the archbishop of Canterbury.

English involvement in missions to India were stimulated by these contacts with the German missionaries. The latter wished to extend their work beyond the confines of Tranquebar, but the Danish king refused to support this. The Anglican Society for the Propagation of Christian Knowledge (S.P.C.K.) agreed to finance these ventures, and English missions to India were underway. The missionaries, however, were pietistic German Lutherans who, in an unusual arrangement, conducted a full sacramental ministry for the Church of England without ever having received episcopal ordination. There had been an English commercial and military presence in India throughout the 17th century. However, whatever Christian ministry they provided was restricted largely to the English. The East India Company was initially opposed to missionary work among the Indians for fear of creating resentment that would adversely affect their business.

The outstanding English missionary to South India was Christian Friedrich Schwartz (1724—98), whose service in that area extended for nearly half a century. With extraordinary ability and dedication, he ministered to the Indian population as well as to the British community. In order to serve his constituents he became conversant in several Indian languages as well as English and Portuguese. He gained the acceptance and respect of all with whom he had contact. He stressed the education especially of the young and carefully prepared candidates for Baptism. The Tranjore church grew to a membership of about 2,000 under his missionary and pastoral leadership.[12]

Other Protestant missionary efforts have already been mentioned elsewhere in this chapter—that of the Moravians in various fields and that of the English colonists to the American Indians. There were also others that deserve mention. This brief report has been merely a sample suggesting some of the factors that prompted this important type of evangelistic outreach as well as some of the approaches employed. From these limited beginnings in subsequent centuries Protestant missions grew into a vast global enterprise that gained millions.

*   *   *

By the last quarter of the 18th century, many sections of Protestantism had undergone vast and dramatic transformation. The lethargic, passive, and even worldly mood that had settled over many by the end of the Reformation era was largely dispelled. Hundreds of thousands were taking their personal faith and morality with great seriousness. Above all, an evangelistic spirit was rekindled and spreading widely among Protestants to the extent that making Christians of others was recognized by many as their chief mission. These Protestant revivals mark the beginning of evangelistic and missionary movements that continue with great force to the present. Roman Catholicism did not experience anything comparable in size and scope to the Protestant revivals, and its foreign missions suffered some major setbacks. However, the central authority of that church began to assume responsibility for global outreach as never before. New concern and support for missions developed in France. Imaginative and heroic new efforts were launched, especially in Southeast Asia. As will be seen in the next chapter, these impulses for renewal and outreach were far from exhausted at the end of the 18th century. Rather, they were about to build up for yet another, even greater surge of evangelistic zeal and activity.

V/Worldwide Impact
(1789—1914)

Sharp contrasts characterize the state of Christianity during the century and a quarter covered in this chapter. On the one hand, in western Europe, which had been its stronghold for more than a millennium, Christianity faced massive decline, defection, and even hostility. On the other hand, in that same part of the world significant revitalization was under way. Among both Protestants and Catholics a variety of movements were stimulating many to new levels of devotion and service. Those affected were never more than a small minority, although they were probably a larger and more zealous minority than their counterpart in the previous era. Paradoxically, then, while the number of professed Christians in western Europe was shrinking, the number of concerned and witnessing Christians was apparently growing.

Outside Europe Christianity was experiencing vast numerical and geographical gains. Especially in North America and Australia many millions were gathered into the churches. In addition, during this era world missions became a major Protestant preoccupation. Major and promising new mission ventures throughout the world were added to the small and scattered beginnings of the 18th century. Despite a new surge of effort by Roman Catholics, Protestant missions surpassed them in terms of money and manpower expended by the end of this period. Much of the interest and motivation for this surge of Protestant outreach was a product of the 18th-century revivals. Opportunities for world evangelization accompanied the colonial expansion of Protestant nations such as England and Holland. Christian reverses in Europe were more than offset by these huge advances.[1]

The subject of Christian evangelization in the 19th century is as complex as it is large. The analytical review attempted here is neither comprehensive nor intensive. Rather, it explores four key developmen's of this era. While the contributions of some representative individuals and movements are mentioned, this is by no means a catalog of 19th-century evangelistic personnel or organizations. It is a broad, sweeping survey illustrated by some particulars. The four developments considered here are: (1) the revitalization of European Christianity; (2) ministry to transplanted Europeans; (3) expansion of American Protestantism; and (4) world missions. Each is discussed in relation to its own social and cultural background as well as in relation to the other developments.

Revitalization of European Christianity

Simultaneous with the religious revivals of the 18th century discussed in the previous chapter was the rise of forces that challenged and undercut European Christianity. Various kinds of rationalism that looked to human reason rather than to divine revelation as the source and criterion of all truth became fashionable, especially among those who were educated, wealthy, and powerful. Growing confidence in the scientific method and its findings led many in that field to question the accuracy of the Bible, particularly with regard to creation and miracles. A new and more critical approach to the study of history was applied by some to the Bible, further eroding confidence in its reliability and authority. Revolutionary political views and movements increasingly deprived the church of its traditional position of advantage and influence in western society.

During the 19th century, these forces continued to affect Christianity adversely and, augmented by others, resulted in the steady "de-Christianization" of western Europe. Technological advance accelerated the industrial revolution. This, in turn, speeded the process of urbanization. As multitudes flocked to the cities to take advantage of new employment opportunities offered there, they were separated from the social support for religion that still existed in many rural areas. Furthermore, in this industrial environment, many were subjected both to grinding poverty and galling regimentation. Demoralized and dehumanized, many turned to alcohol, vice, and crime. New philosophies and political theories antagonistic to Christianity became influential, among which those of Karl Marx (1818—83) and Friedrich Nietzsche (1844—1900) are some of the most prominent. Among the rising middle class as well as the upper class, who were profiting from the social and economic developments, a spirit of arrogance, optimism, and self-sufficiency often made Christianity seem superfluous.

Under these circumstances it was not unusual that many nominal Christians disregarded the faith and disobeyed its moral standards. This had happened in every previous era. More ominous and unique was the fact that growing numbers were disassociating themselves from the Christian faith and community, and some were even attacking it as worse than useless. Not forces from without but elements from within were rising against the church. "Christian" Europe was being secularized. Although this was especially obvious on the continent, it was also taking place to a lesser degree in the British Isles.

Paradoxically, while de-Christianization was underway among many western Europeans, spiritual revitalization was occurring among others. Christians in various nations and denominations began to take their faith and its implications more seriously. They cultivated a closer relationship with God and dedicated their lives more completely to His honor and service. They defended Christianity against its attackers. They reached out to those who were being swept away by currents of secularism. In the name of Christ they responded to the social and material needs of those who had been victimized by industrialization and urbanization. These revitalized Christians were not a large segment of the total population, but they were both earnest and active. Concerned and visionary individuals touched many with the love of God through their words and deeds. Vigorous movements, new and old, addressed the evangelistic mission of the church as well as its humanitarian and educational tasks. Among some there was a resurgence of conservative and confessional theology. Among others the recovery of historic worship forms and practices was central. Activation of the laity was a common emphasis. A number of new free churches were born. There was a new burst of pietistic fervor on the continent. In Britain the Evangelical Revival was pretty well sustained through the 19th century and was stirred up significantly during the last half of that century as a result of American influences.

Roman Catholicism[2]

In some respects the experience of the Roman Catholic Church in the 19th century was as traumatic as that in the 16th. Once again it was confronted by revolution and desertion on the part of many within its ranks. Some of this was a reaction against the worldy wealth and power of the church and its support of a corrupt monarchy. Such was the case in France during the revolution of the 1780s. In part it was an expression of anti-Christian rationalism, which viewed all Christianity (not only Catholicism) as superstitious, intolerant, and an enemy of progress. Although this too was most prominent in France, it was also well represented in the other Catholic nations of Europe. Furthermore, there was widespread resentment of the Roman church's control of education, marriage, and family life and of its opposition to the rising demand for democratic forms of government also in Catholic Europe. The details of this disaffection lie beyond the scope of this study. Suffice it to say that as a consequence the Roman Church lost not only its privileges and power, but much of its material wealth and in some places even its independence. All of this occurred in areas that historically had been staunchly faithful to and even aggressively supportive of the Roman Church. The losses were staggering, and the church's ability to recover appeared questionable.

However, new vitality and commitment did appear especially in France, where the opposition had been most severe. Grave defects and evils appeared in the rationalistic, revolutionary forces that had set themselves against the church. Despite their disillusionment and dissatisfaction with certain aspects of the Roman church, people also missed other aspects when they were gone or drastically curtailed. The turmoil and radical change ushered in by a revolutionary age made some long for the stability of an earlier age, and the Roman church was a symbol of that stability. Attacks against the church moved some to defend, uphold, and even extend her. Four areas, in particular, reflect this revitalization. Three of these will be discussed in the paragraphs immediately following and the fourth in the final section of this chapter.

Nowhere was new loyalty and life more evident in Roman Catholicism during the 19th century than in monasticism. More religious orders were founded during this century than in any previous century. In addition, many existing orders were revived from the lethargy that had overcome them in the 18th century and began to recruit new members and to resume their missions with restored zeal. The Society of Jesus, which had been disbanded under pressure from Catholic governments and other religious orders, was reorganized and began once again to function effectively. A notable feature of 19th-century monasticism was its emphasis on service to others, rather than merely on the salvation of the members' own souls. Even the contemplatives, whose chief activity was prayer, devoted themselves largely to intercession for others. Teaching, evangelization of the de-Christianized multitudes at home as well as converting pagans abroad, ministry to the poor, the oppressed, and the ill—these were all conspicuous concerns of revitalized Catholic monasticism.

Also among the secular clergy and the laity comparable developments took place. From a Protestant perspective not all of these can be evaluated positively. Devotion to the Virgin Mary rose through visions claimed by several women and the encouragement of several popes. This culminated in the decree of Pope Pius IX in 1854, which made the immaculate conception of Mary a dogma of the church. A popular focus of the cult of Mary was the healing Shrine of Our Lady of Lourdes established on the site where Bernadette Subirous allegedly received her visions. A parallel development, more consistent with the Gospel, was devotion to the Sacred Heart of Jesus. Although it originated in mystical movements of earlier centuries, this form of piety spread widely through all parts of the Roman church during the 19th. The physical heart of Jesus as seen in the visions became a symbol of His sacrificial love manifest in His incarnation and suffering. Many groups of laity, especially women, devoted themselves to the Sacred Heart of Jesus. They expressed this in prayer, sacrificial service, and frequent communion. A liturgical movement was born that had as one of its goals to nurture the spiritual life of the laity by promoting more meaningful and earnest participation in worship. Catholic Action, a lay movement designed to stimulate spiritual development and to influence public affairs, originated in Italy about 1868. As will be seen in a later portion of this chapter, much lay interest and involvement in foreign missions also appeared in this century.

Severe and damaging criticism of the Roman church during the 19th century came from academic circles, now thoroughly dominated by secular influences. To counter this and to demonstrate the intellectual respectability of the Roman faith, a number of institutions of higher learning were founded. These schools, staffed by Jesuits and other teaching orders, were characterized by a clear and unequivocal Roman Catholic commitment. Able Roman Catholic scholars acquired competence in the various disciplines, including those from which much of the anti-Catholicism was emanating. This enabled them to reply to the church's critics from a position of strength and knowledge. It also enabled them to interpret learning in their respective fields in a manner consistent with Roman theology and values. With loyal Roman Catholic scholars teaching and writing in virtually all subjects, with distinguished Roman Catholic educational institutions imparting knowledge from that distinctive perspective, confidence in the church's intellectual integrity was restored. Roman Catholic scholarship and education provided a viable alternative to secularism. It both expressed and fostered revitalization in that church.

Protestantism on the Continent

Rationalism dominated most Lutheran and Reformed churches on the continent of Europe during the last half of the 18th century and the first decades of the 19th. Germany was the center of Protestant theological thought. From its faculties, even from the University of Halle, the fountainhead of Pietism, a rationalistic reinterpretation of Christianity was promulgated. Rather than a religion of supernatural revelation and redemption, Christianity was presented as "natural" religion and morality implanted in every human being at birth, discoverable and even provable by human reason. An optimistic view of man and history combined with virtual rejection of revelation, miracles, and the saving work of Christ, resulted in a view of Christianity distorted almost beyond recognition. Christian Wolff (1679—1754) is generally considered the "father" of the German "Enlightenment," as this theological movement was called, although others even more radical than he also assumed prominence.

While many in the rank and file did not understand or identify with this rationalistic revision of Christianity, the officialdom of the Protestant churches generally did. Supported by sympathetic governments, they tended to place only those candidates for the pastoral office who were sympathetic to or identified with the Enlightenment. Church policies, literature, and worship orders reflected rationalistic influences. The prominence and prestige that Pietism enjoyed during the first part of the 18th century was drastically diminished. That movement survived, but only as a despised and even repressed minority.[3]

As the 19th century progressed, however, Rationalism itself came under attack. Various forms of Romanticism, which emphasized the importance of feeling over reason as a source of truth, challenged the basic assumptions of Rationalism. Friedrich Daniel Ernst Schleiermacher (1768—1834) developed a theology of religious experience which, though brilliant and appealing, departed as significantly from historic Christianity as it did from Rationalism.[4]

In addition, early in the 19th century, Pietism in its several forms rose up against Rationalism and the spiritual indifference it spawned. Although it never regained the size and strength attained in the previous century, Pietism displayed fresh vitality, creativity, and aggressiveness. Evangelists, preachers, and even theologians of pietistic orientation made numerous converts from Rationalism among the clergy as well as the laity. Leaders of considerable theological and organizational ability leveled criticisms against rationalistic doctrine and practice. They reaffirmed the divine character of the Bible, the reality of sin and the need for redemption through Christ, the importance of a felt conversion experience, and the inadequacy of reason to discover God or effect union with Him.

More importantly, Pietists established institutions and programs that expressed and fostered these traditional Christian beliefs and values, usually in pietistic dress. Bible, tract, and missionary societies multiplied. Local pastors as well as itinerant preachers stirred up renewed commitment in the large crowds that gathered to hear them. Some new pietistic hymns were composed, and existing ones were gathered into new compilations. Devotional literature was produced in abundance. Conventicles were reestablished and extended. From the stump of Pietism new shoots sprang up, both Reformed and Lutheran. Although combatting Rationalism and converting people from it was one concern of these Pietists, an even stronger drive was to rouse people from the spiritual apathy that had overcome so many. A particularly vigorous and aggressive form of Pietism, lay-directed and often anti-clerical, was that founded in Norway by Hans Nielsen Hauge (1771—1824).

Another countercurrent to Rationalism that flowed parallel to revived Pietism was a resurgent confessional Orthodoxy. Although its momentum had been checked and its influence diminished by the rise of Pietism in the 18th century, Orthodoxy had never disappeared. Early in the 19th century events provoked a new burst of loyalty to and appreciation for traditional Protestantism. Among Lutherans it was related not only to disillusionment with rationalism, but also to resentment against the forced union of Lutheran and Reformed churches by some of the German governments. A symbol and further stimulus of this neo-confessionalism was the publication by Claus Harms (1775—1855), on the tercentenary of the Reformation, October 31, 1817, of a new set of 95 theses attacking both Rationalism and unionism. Among the Reformed in both Switzerland and the Netherlands, conservative reactions protested the stranglehold of Rationalism on the state churches. In both places, some traditionalists separated into free churches that grew in number and influence throughout the 19th century.

This conservative renaissance cultivated strong commitment to specific and historic Christian beliefs and involved fervent and lucid testimony to these beliefs. It won converts, not only among the common people but also among parish clergy and leaders of theological thought. It recovered and articulated a clear, substantial, authoritative message, which could be communicated in a meaningful and compelling manner. It created a literature to transmit and perpetuate this message. It gave historic Protestantism theological and intellectual respectability. Adolf von Harless (1806—79) of Erlangen University is a worthy representative of the many distinguished leaders who prompted the conservative revival.

In some individuals and groups confessional Orthodoxy and Pietism came together. This required adjustment on both sides, since historically these movements had been at odds. At its best, this marriage of diverse partners (which may be called "Confessional Pietism") combined important strengths of both movements and compensated for their respective weaknesses. The warmth and zeal of Pietism balanced by the theological confidence and competence of Orthodoxy did at times result in vigorous and effective Christian movements.

An interesting and important example were the followers of Martin Stephan (1777-1846), pastor of St. John's Church, Dresden, Saxony from 1810 to 1838. Although educated in the rationalistic University of Halle and at Leipzig, Stephan persisted in the pietistic orientation acquired several years earlier. During his pastorate in Dresden he joined a pietistic society and rapidly assumed a prominent role in it. In time the group dissolved into Stephan's larger following. A personality of extraordinary power and magnetism, he drew large crowds of listeners to his services. His approach until the mid 1830s was typically pietistic—earnest but not unduly emotional, conversion-oriented, emphasizing the devotional use of the Bible and prayer, but not particularly concerned about a specifically Lutheran doctrinal position. However, in a search for theological substance he turned to the Lutheran Confessions, became convinced of their validity, and led his growing group of adherents into a form of confessional Lutheranism that retained significant elements of Pietism. The effect of his preaching and counseling was to convert many from Rationalism and indifference.

Unfortunately, appreciation for Stephan's ministry degenerated into excessive adulation. In 1838, as a result of conflict with the civil authorities over his questionable pastoral activities, Stephan convinced his followers that they should flee from this hostile rationalistic environment. A party of 665 persons emigrated from Saxony under his leadership to Perry County, Missouri, where they set out to establish a pure Lutheran community. Shortly after their arrival, Stephan was discredited and dismissed on charges of sexual immorality and maladministration.

After a tumultuous period of readjustment, the Saxons abjured "Stephanism" but retained their confessional Lutheranism. Reorganized under the leadership of C. F. W. Walther, this group ultimately founded the Missouri Synod, which championed the cause of conservative Lutheranism in North America. Their confessionalism and orthodoxy led the Missourians to contend against every form of Rationalism as well as every attempt to adjust Lutheranism in the direction of American Protestantism. From the pietistic elements in their background came the impulse to share the Gospel. As will be seen later in this chapter, they were extraordinarily successful in gathering into their churches great numbers of German immigrants who arrived during the last half of the 19th century.

The new vitality of continental Protestantism also appeared in the form of innovative approaches to urban ministry. Johann Hinrich Wichern (1808—81) founded and developed the Inner Mission, a multiform venture designed to meet the material as well as the spiritual needs of disadvantaged residents of the center city. The poor, the homeless, transient workers, prostitutes, orphans, alcoholics—all were served by a network of missions established throughout Germany and supported by volunteer societies. The Inner Mission's evangelistic purpose was complemented by its ministry to the material needs of people. It was a church, not just a social service agency. By preaching the Word to the downtrodden, Wichern hoped not only to save them eternally but also to rehabilitate them for this life and, in that way, to contribute to social renewal. Also, by the compassionate exercise of social ministries, he gave concreteness and credibility to the preached Word.

Still another aspect of the 19th century revitalization of continental Protestantism was a renewed appreciation for liturgy and the broader Catholic heritage. This included the enrichment of worship with historic forms and practices as well as increased emphasis on the sacraments, the authority of the pastoral office, and a high doctrine of the church. This movement took hold among both German and Scandinavian Lutherans. Its purpose was not merely aesthetic or nostalgic, but pastoral—to inspire and strengthen God's people through more meaningful and memorable worship experiences. The effect of the liturgical renaissance in many places was significantly to invigorate personal faith and parish life and was often accompanied by fresh commitment to the evangelistic mission of the church.

No individual personifies revitalized continental Protestantism in its major aspects more dramatically than Johann Konrad Wilhelm Loehe (1808—72). Into his life and ministry flowed influences of Pietism, Confessionalism, and the Inner Mission. In addition, he was caught up in the movement to foster missions among American Indians and German immigrants in both America and Australia. The little village of Neuendettelsau, Bavaria, to which he had been banished because of conflict with the authorities, became under his leadership a center from which liturgical, pastoral, and evangelistic impulses radiated into several parts of the world. He wrote prolifically, founded institutions and, above all, was an inspiring pastoral model. Multitudes flocked to his worship services and sought out his pastoral care. Missionaries sent by Loehe to Michigan and Indiana joined Walther and the Saxons of Perry County to form the Missouri Synod in 1847.[5]

British Christianity

While churches on the continent of Europe were losing ground, at least numerically, in Great Britain the trend during the 19th century was essentially the opposite. The secularizing forces of industrialization, urbanization, historicism, and scientism were also at work here. However, the spiritual energies released in the Evangelical Revival of the previous century were sufficient not only to stem the tide of de-Christianization but, combined with some new factors, to bring Christianity here to its highest level of vitality and influence.

During this period the Church of England recovered from a serious slump in pastoral care and outreach, and demonstrated more life and commitment to missions than ever before. Non-conformist churches continued to grow numerically and in terms of respectability. Voluntary societies devoted to various kinds of evangelistic effort multiplied. With their diverse appeals and opportunities, they captured the imagination and harnessed the energies of many spiritually awakened lay people. By the early years of the 20th century, church attendance was declining, signaling the drastic reversal that was to come. However, the general condition of the churches during the course of the 19th century was one of improved health and burgeoning growth. While these introductory comments refer most directly to England, they also apply largely to Scotland and Wales.

The need for improvement in the Church of England during the early part of this period was urgent. Only a small part of its constituency had been involved in the Evangelical Revival. The quality of pastoral care had plummeted. Many parish priests and even bishops were absentee incumbents who carried out their duties through underpaid, ill-prepared, weakly-motivated substitutes. Pluralism—the practice of holding several positions simultaneously—resulted in neglect of parishioners' needs. The rationalistic theology of many clergy exerted a suffocating effect upon their flocks. Worldliness, uninspired and perfunctory worship leadership, and indifference toward the mission of the church were all too common. Even church facilities were a serious problem. Many buildings were in woeful disrepair. Badly needed new structures in areas of rapid population growth remained unbuilt. Teeming multitudes of the poor and working classes in large urban centers were without churches and pastoral care. The sad fact is that the church was so out of touch with these segments of the population and so spiritually moribund that it probably could not have reached them even if it had been in a position to try.

After about 1830 things began to turn for the better. Administrative changes enacted by Parliament eliminated much absenteeism and pluralism. Measures were taken to improve the supervision of clergy and also to fund the construction of new churches. Although these actions were taken by political bodies for largely political reasons, they did have a salutary effect upon the church.

In addition, the Evangelical party, the element that had absorbed some of the emphases and practices of Methodism, grew in size and influence. They were active and versatile both in evangelistic outreach and in the cultivation of earnest Christian living. They focused much of their evangelism on the urban areas among those who were spiritually neglected and alienated. They produced a wealth of hymns and devotional literature, were deeply committed to humanitarian service and social reform, and became extensively involved in Christian education and missions. By the mid-19th century they were the dominant element in the Church of England. Numerous bishops identified with them. Lay involvement was strong. Numerous conference centers for the stimulation of spiritual life were established, the most prominent of which was at Keswick.

Throughout the first half of the 19th century this complex of renewal forces in the Evangelical party was combined with evangelistic elements. People who are warmed and deepened in their faith almost always are inclined to share it with others. Much of this went on at both the individual and parish level. Mass revivalism broke out during the last half of the century under American evangelists. Dwight L. Moody was their leading representative. Although the nonconformist churches were the chief beneficiaries, the Evangelicals of the Church of England also experienced some gains.

Quite a different element in the Church of England, a "high church" party, also contributed to revitalization. In its early stage it was known as the Tractarian or Oxford Movement, and it emphasized primarily the pre-Reformation heritage and commonalities with Roman Catholicism. At mid-century the movement was largely discredited when a number of leaders defected to the Roman church. Those who remained gave it a new direction, stressing particularly the enrichment of public worship and the corporateness of the church. In connection with this, many new hymns were composed and conferences of bishops were inaugurated. Known as the Anglo-Catholic Movement, this element also devoted itself to the evangelization of the urban poor as well as to their material betterment.

No group of Christians in Europe exhibited more vigor during the 19th century than the nonconformist churches of England—those which existed outside the established or state church. The impetus of the Evangelical Revival of the previous century continued and even accelerated among the Methodists. The Congregationalists and the Baptists also maintained their fervor and zeal and continued to increase numerically. The Plymouth Brethren and the Salvation Army, both evangelistically inclined, were born during this century. One factor that encouraged this expansion was the series of parliamentary actions removing the restrictions and disabilities under which these churches had previously existed.

In addition, the nonconformists received a substantial lift from evangelistic tours conducted by American revivalists. Charles G. Finney (1792—1875) conducted two preaching missions in the British Isles, (1848—50 and 1859—60), and his published works on revivalism were widely read there. Over a period of 25 years (1867—92), Dwight L. Moody (1837—99) made no less than five trips, three of them extensive. His effectiveness was enhanced by the assistance of the remarkable singer, Ira David Sankey (1840—1908). Popular response and impact were comparable to those of Whitefield and Wesley. A difference was that instead of resulting in new denominations, the work of these evangelists brought new strength and growth to existing churches, especially the nonconformists.

A variety of other factors also spurred the growth of the nonconformist churches. Great preachers occupied the pulpits of some of their urban churches and drew many, not only to their services of worship, but also to living faith in Jesus Christ. Perhaps the most outstanding was Charles Hadden Spurgeon (1834—92), a Baptist, for whom the Metropolitan Tabernacle was built in London. This vast structure, seating more than 5,000, was required to accommodate the large numbers attracted to his preaching. In addition, many new chapels and mission centers were built, both in the growing parts of the cities and in the low income areas. Ordinary lay people increasingly practiced personal witnessing. The rapidly growing army of ordained ministers was augmented by lay preachers. Women were enlisted and prepared for deaconess ministry. Sunday Schools were increasingly utilized as evangelistic agencies. The Young Men's Christian Association was organized in 1844 by George Williams, primarily as an evangelistic and nurture agency for the youth. Social, educational, and recreational programs were originally subordinate to the spiritual goals of that association. The Young Women's Christian Association, the female counterpart, was founded in the following decade.

The cumulative effect of these efforts was the steady growth of the nonconformists until, at the end of this period, they were approximately equal in number to the membership of the Church of England. This is a remarkable record in view of the fact that the general population also increased dramatically during these years, and that strong, contemporary forces—intellectual, social, and economic—were very unfavorable to Christianity.

Developments in Scotland, although important, may be described more briefly. The process there began with division and ended with reinvigoration and growth in all parties. Thomas Chalmers (1780—1847), a leader of the Evangelical Revival in Scotland, became convinced that the church could carry out its mission properly only if it was free of government control. In 1843 one-third of the ministers of the Church of Scotland withdrew to form the Free Church of Scotland. Totally deprived of state financial support by this action, the members of the Free Church gave and worked most generously, not only to support their ministers, but also to erect buildings and establish missionary work. Remarkably, the established church survived the trauma and was stimulated to new effort and outreach of its own. In time animosity between the parties diminished, and by the end of this period they were well on the way to reunion. The testing and challenges related to this division sparked increased devotion, improved preaching, production of hymns and evangelistic literature, and growing involvement in social ministry.[6]

Ministry to Transplanted Europeans

One of the key factors in Christian expansion during the 19th century was the massive migration of Europeans, especially to North America. Political and economic problems at home together with apparently unlimited opportunities abroad spurred tens of millions to make the long and dangerous sea voyage and, often with minimal resources, to meet the challenge of establishing themselves in a new land. Most of those who migrated were nominal Christians affected by the secularizing forces in Europe. There were, of course, some earnest and practicing Christians among them, and a few were motivated to migrate by religious considerations. There was some indifference and spiritual neglect, and not a few were hostile to Christianity.

Remarkably, a great many of these European migrants in the process of transplantation were converted or renewed spiritually and gathered into churches. This happened in Australia and Canada as well as in the United States. However, since the greatest numbers arrived in the United States, and since evangelistic momentum was sustained there longer than in the other two areas, the focus of this discussion will center on the ministry to transplanted Europeans in the United States.

Immigration did not automatically result in further Christianization. Transplanted Europeans did not spontaneously become more earnest and active Christians. They needed to be evangelized. The American churches, small and weak as they were, with a considerable amount of assistance from European Christians, gathered in a great harvest. The immensity of the task is awesome to contemplate. The U.S. population grew from 3,172,444 in 1790 to 91,972,266 in 1910. Most of this increase consisted of immigrants and their descendants. At the beginning of this period the American churches appeared totally inadequate to the task of reaching this flood of immigrants. Church members represented only about 10 percent of the population. Those churches that were to gain most of the immigrants were new and tiny. The Roman Catholics numbered only 25,000 in 1790, and only a small fraction of these were practicing church members. There were probably 10 times as many Lutherans at this point, of whom perhaps 80,000 were practicing church members. Yet somehow both bodies, especially the former, met the challenge. By 1914, 43 percent of the U.S. population claimed church affiliation—a segment four times larger than in 1789 despite a huge population increase. On the basis of the available information, it appears that the percentage of active Christians among European immigrants and their descendants in the United States in 1914 was at least two or three times greater than among their relatives in the homeland. In this section we examine the processes by which transplanted Europeans were enlisted and activated in American churches, or how in some cases they brought their churches with them.

The religious environment here was very different from what they were accustomed to in Europe and did not appear very conducive to the spiritual life and growth of individuals or ecclesiastical success. Instead of one dominant church, there were many churches competing for the attention and involvement of people. Instead of being provided and controlled by the state, religion here was dependent upon the financial support and personal involvement of adherents. In addition to the usual distractions and secularizing forces they had confronted in Europe, immigrants in the United States were preoccupied with adjusting to a strange land, trying to make a living in an unfamiliar context, and coping with the prejudice and resentment of those whose ancestors had arrived here earlier. Many immigrants settled in the cities and had to struggle with the poverty, crime, and vice that inevitably arose in urban industrial America. Others soon moved to the frontiers, where they faced isolation, danger, and hardship. Even those who gathered in small settlements of their own kind often found mere survival to be extremely difficult. In the face of all this, the churches' prospects of winning and assimilating many of these immigrants appeared dim.

The following discussion concentrates on only two of the many important ministries to European immigrants in the United States during the 19th century—those of the Roman Catholics and the Missouri Synod Lutherans. The former is by far the largest, and the latter one of the most vigorous and successful Protestant efforts. Furthermore, rather than a detailed account of the outreach to immigrants of these two bodies, we will restrict ourselves to an analysis of motivation, methodology, message, and results, but not necessarily in that order.

Roman Catholic Ministry to Immigrants

The Roman Catholic ministry to transplanted Europeans in 19th-century America resulted in spectacular numerical increase and institutional development. In 1800 the Catholic population in the United States was only 50,000. In 1914 it was 16 million, of whom half were foreign-born and most of the rest descendants of recent immigrants. During that century it grew to be the largest religious body in the United States, with a well-organized leadership, a vast army of able and dedicated professional workers, an elaborate educational system at every level, and extensive social service agencies.

This phenomenal advance was made in the face of serious problems. Ethnic tensions was one. Immigrants came from various nations—Ireland and Germany primarily—but from 1890 to 1910 a great many also came from Italy and other countries of southern and central Europe. During the early part of the era the hierarchy was dominated by the French, and this was resented by those of other ethnic backgrounds. Suspicion and jealousy threatened to fragment the Roman church in America along ethnic lines, and unity was maintained only with difficulty. In addition, there was a long and bitter struggle over polity and control of church property. Advocates of "trusteeism" wanted laymen to have a voice in the selection of their clergy and in the administration of parishes. This was put down painfully and slowly. Anti-

Catholic sentiment and activities mounted with the rising tide of Catholic immigration. Prejudice, discrimination, and even violence were common Catholic experiences in the United States well into the 20th century. Shortages of clergy and other professional personnel as well as insufficient funds handicapped the Catholic effort during much of this period. Yet despite these and other problems, many millions of immigrants were reached and gathered in. How did this happen?[7]

As the immigrant population poured into the nation, the boundaries and leadership of the Roman church were adjusted to accommodate them. Existing dioceses in areas where population was growing were subdivided in the interest of better pastoral care. As new areas south and west were about to open up, new dioceses were created. Beginning in 1829 there were regional councils of bishops to deal with the problems and potential of the Catholic immigration. From 1860 plenary councils were held on a regular basis. Acknowledging the unique situation of Catholics in the United States, Rome granted the hierarchy an unusual degree of freedom. In general, they exercised their authority and freedom in ways that were both wise and creative. To a remarkable degree they unified, Americanized, and spiritualized their flock during a period of rapid and enormous growth.

The supply of clergy and other workers was expanded greatly in order to meet the challenge of the immigration. Despite the increase, there was a chronic shortage during most of the period under consideration in this chapter. An influx of French workers who were fleeing the ravages of the Revolution (after 1789) alleviated the problem temporarily. However, their prominence and dominance was resented by those of other ethnic origins. Belgium was an early and important source of workers, although the number of Belgian immigrants was small. Germany and especially Ireland sent large numbers of workers to minister to the spiritual needs of those who had emigrated from their lands. Without these European missionaries the Roman church would have gathered a much smaller harvest among the immigrants.

During the last half of the 19th century the proportion of American-trained workers mounted steadily and ultimately constituted a majority. Among the workers were not only numerous clergy both secular and religious, but also many females involved in teaching and social ministries. Several religious orders were particularly active in evangelization: the Redemptorists, the Jesuits, and the Paulists. The latter, founded in 1858 under the leadership of Isaac Hecker (1819—88), originally consisted largely of American converts to Catholicism. The outstanding success of Catholic outreach to transplanted Europeans would have been impossible without this huge and zealous force of workers recruited both in Europe and America.[8]

The evangelistic commitment and involvement of these people was both the product and the extension of the revitalized European Catholicism discussed above. At a time when conditions in Europe were increasingly unfavorable for the Roman church, unprecedented opportunities were opening up in North America. Paradoxically—or providentially—many Europeans who resisted or ignored the ministry of their church in the homeland proved to be more receptive after transplantation. Others who had been faithful in their church practice while in Europe would be in danger of drifting away if they were not supplied with spiritual care and leadership. Both possibilities excited the evangelistic fervor of revitalized Catholics and stimulated the increase of missionary societies that recruited and supported workers for the American field.

Another method by which Roman Catholics enfolded European immigrants was by establishing new parishes and missions, often along ethnic lines. During the century before 1914, 12,000 new Catholic churches were founded, many consisting primarily of a single immigrant group. Especially early in the 20th century there was great pressure to organize parishes along ethnic lines and to staff churches only with priests of the same nationality as their parishioners. Although the bishops generally preferred integrated "American" parishes, they usually succumbed to immigrant demands. However, the immigrants had to fund the projects themselves. Parishes with a clear ethnic identity were especially attractive to immigrants. For the fulfillment of social and cultural as well as religious needs immigrants gravitated toward the Catholic church of their compatriots. Not only familiar worship, but familiar customs and a familiar language were strong attractions.

In rural and frontier areas the place of worship was often only a rude log chapel visited occasionally by an itinerant priest; nevertheless, it became something of a focal point for the Catholic immigrant community. In urban areas Catholics often began in abandoned Protestant church buildings. As numbers and resources multiplied, structures were erected, frequently similar in design to those of the nation from which most of the parishioners originated. As the process of Americanization continued, the ethnic parish lost much of its significance. However, during the 19th century and well into the 20th, it was a definite aid to immigrant ministry.

The parochial school played a vital role in bonding the children of immigrants to "mother church." In addition to instruction in the usual academic subjects, the students were thoroughly indoctrinated and initiated into recommended Catholic practices—attendance at mass, participation in the sacraments, and obedience to the rule of the church. Their sense of Catholic identity and loyalty was carefully cultivated. Thousands of ethnic or national parishes also operated parochial schools, which transmitted the language and culture of the European homeland.

A very important agency of Catholic outreach to transplanted Europeans was the parish mission. This was a series of daily preaching and teaching activities conducted in a parish, usually for a period of one week, by members of one of the evangelistic orders. Held ordinarily only once every three or four years, the parish mission was designed to attract and convert marginal or inactive Catholics (most immigrants were in these categories) as well as to generate greater commitment among those already in the fold. The preachers were skillful and emotional orators. They concentrated primarily on sin and on the need for repentance and transformed living, but they also offered God's mercy in Christ.

Preaching services were held in the evening, and basic instruction in Catholic doctrine was offered in the morning. Extensive advertising and promotion prepared for the mission. Dramatic ceremony accompanied it. A specific goal was to prepare participants for private confession and Holy Communion. For support and maintenance of faith afterward they were referred, not only to the sacramental ministries of the parish, but also to devotional confraternities. The latter were societies devoted to the veneration of Mary, the Sacred Heart of Jesus, the Rosary and similar uniquely Catholic expressions of piety.

Comparatively few parish missions were held in the United States prior to 1825, but by the 1860s they were a prominent feature of Catholic life. Many of the early ones, especially in remote areas, were held out-of-doors, in barns, courthouses, or wherever people could gather. During the second half of the century, when Catholic churches were more numerous and larger, the missions were held in them. Many thousands of such missions were conducted in rural areas and small towns, as well as in cities. People traveled for miles to attend. The impact was substantial. Converts were made. Peripheral members became active and religious interest soared. In time, the effect diminished and the process was repeated. The parish mission was not a complete evangelism program. Like its Protestant counterpart, the revival, it was a shot in the arm that was most effective when combined with ongoing nurture and pastoral care.[9]

Missouri Synod Outreach to Immigrants[10]

Like the Roman Catholics, Missouri Synod Lutherans were

extremely active and successful in reaching immigrants in 19th-century America. When the synod organized in 1847, it consisted of only 22 pastors and less than 2,000 members. On its 75th anniversary in 1922 the synod numbered 1,564 pastors and more than one million members. Although natural increase from births accounted for some of this growth, the great bulk of it was the result of intensive work among immigrants.

In addition to their traditional differences in doctrine and practice, Missouri Lutherans and Roman Catholics were confronted with very different circumstances in 19th-century America. The Roman Catholics had arrived much earlier. By the time the Missourians were organizing at mid-century there were already 1,606,000 Roman Catholics here, and their rate of growth was accelerating. Furthermore, the Missouri Synod presence and effort was concentrated in rural parts of what is now called the upper midwest. Although Roman Catholics moved into many of the same areas with great strength during the period of Missouri Synod expansion, they were concentrated most heavily in the industrial urban sections of the northeast. Missouri Lutherans focused their attention almost exclusively upon German immigrants. (Other Lutheran immigrant churches served those of other ethnic backgrounds.) Roman Catholicism, on the other hand, was composed of diverse ethnic groups from the beginning, and its outreach reflected this.

There are also some significant similarities. Both the Missourians and the Roman Catholics were committed to retaining their religious distinctiveness and were determined to resist the theology and practices of American Protestantism. Both were also convinced of their own correctness. As a result, they regarded it as their responsibility not only to rescue their people from indifference and unbelief, but also to prevent them from drifting into other denominations. The Roman church's position on this point was very adamant, for it taught that there was no salvation outside its boundaries. Although the Missouri Lutherans made no such exclusivistic claim, they were so sensitive to the danger of theological error in the other churches that they were as zealous as Catholics in trying to keep Lutheran immigrants out of these churches. While both bodies accepted and even recruited professional workers from abroad, they also recognized the importance of educating their own and undertook this as soon as possible. By the end of the 19th century both were able to provide most of their own clergy. Finally, both groups were thoroughly committed to the parochial school as an agency of outreach as well as nurture.

The Missouri Synod style of ministry to immigrants was set by

Friedrich Conrad Dietrich Wyneken (1810—76). After completing his theological studies in Germany, Wyneken went through an experience of spiritual deepening. Some time later his conscience was touched by an account of the deplorable spiritual condition of German Lutheran immigrants in the United States. In 1838 he set out to minister to them, arriving in the village of Ft. Wayne, Indiana late in September of that year. There he accepted the pastorate of a congregation whose pastor had died.

From this base he made a series of missionary journeys in the surrounding area. His approach was to seek out settlements or scattered families of German Lutheran background. Although a few were eager for worship and pastoral care, the earnest young pastor found that most were indifferent, preoccupied, or even hostile. Undaunted, he served whoever would respond and did whatever he could to get through to those who would not. On horseback and on foot, in good weather and bad, he continued his missionary journeys. His greatest frustration was that when he did locate or awaken a group of interested Lutherans, it was virtually impossible to provide them with regular pastoral care. There was a great shortage of pastors. His own capacity for service was already seriously overextended.

In order to generate interest in this ministry and to enlist additional clergy, Wyneken returned to Germany. For more than a year he traveled through his homeland addressing groups, raising money, and challenging prospective workers to respond to this urgent need. He also published a pamphlet entitled *The Distress of German Lutherans in North America*. In graphic terms it describes these pastorless people falling victim to indifference and worldliness or being drawn into non-Lutheran churches. The most significant result of his tour was a personal contact with Wilhelm Loehe of Neuendettelsau. Moved by Wyneken and his appeal, Loehe further publicized the cause and personally enlisted and prepared more than 80 professional church workers for that American field. In addition, he gathered more than 100 dedicated lay people to establish Lutheran colonies in Michigan, which he hoped would be useful in the evangelization of nearby Indians.

This work in Indiana, Michigan, and Ohio, founded by Wyneken and extended with Loehe's support, was merged with that of the Saxon immigrants in Missouri in 1847 to form the Evangelical German Lutheran Synod of Missouri, Ohio and Other States. Although known as the Missouri Synod from the very beginning and dominated by the Saxons, the Loehe people were actually more numerous and were the chief source of the synod's evangelistic and missionary impetus. A key factor in bringing these and other like-minded German Lutherans together was *Der Lutheraner* (The Lutheran), a periodical edited by C. F. W. Walther, leader of the Saxon Lutherans in Missouri. Circulated widely throughout the United States and in Germany, this magazine was a call for faithfulness to Lutheran confessional theology and practice. Eventually it advocated the outward union of all who were thoroughly committed to their Lutheran heritage. This was based on the conviction that most of the older eastern Lutheran bodies had seriously deviated from authentic Lutheranism.

While the Missouri Synod was forming, the midwest was already experiencing an influx of immigrants, many of whom were German Lutherans. In the 1850s, 1860s, and 1870s this influx grew steadily and spread all the way to the Pacific coast. As pastors became available from Europe, and increasingly from the synod's own seminaries, many engaged in exploration of the newly settled areas. Some were missionaries at large sent by the synod or its regional units. Others were pastors of established congregations, who would periodically leave their parishes for long and often dangerous journeys into the ever-expanding frontier. Pastors were encouraged to view their responsibility as extending to all who were within reach of their care.

As these evangelistic pastors traveled, they would look for settlements or scattered families of German Lutherans. If they were not already under pastoral care, they would be invited to participate in preaching services and to bring their children for Baptism. Wherever even a handful seemed sufficiently responsive and responsible, they were encouraged to organize congregations and request regular pastoral service from the Synod. Initially, one pastor would serve a number of these tiny congregations and preaching stations. However, as they grew in numbers and the supply of pastors improved, more and more congregations enjoyed the advantage of full-time resident pastors. Occasionally groups of interested German Lutherans would form themselves into congregations and apply to the Synod for pastors. In other cases, concerned individuals would request the Synod to begin a ministry in a new area. Most often people were contacted and congregations founded through the efforts of missionary pastors. There was some witnessing outreach by lay people, but for the most part this was pastoral evangelism.

A unique feature of Missouri Synod church planting during this era was the attention given to the Christian education of children, even on the frontier. Missionary pastors on their occasional visits would gather children together in order to teach them reading and writing as well as to instruct them in the catechism. Resident pastors in many cases served as teachers in their parochial schools.

From the very beginning the Synod undertook to educate teachers for these schools. As their numbers and congregational resources increased, teachers replaced pastors in most of the classrooms. The primary purpose of the schools was to foster Lutheranism among the upcoming generations and to transmit German culture to them. However, they also served an evangelistic purpose. Some German Lutherans were attracted more by the schools than by the churches that sponsored them. Through the involvement of their children, in time, many of these parents were also drawn to worship and converted or were deepened spiritually.

Outreach to immigrants, in many cases, began almost immediately upon their arrival. In both New York City and Baltimore, the Eastern District of the Missouri Synod commissioned immigrant pastors, who met the ships and helped the immigrants locate temporary housing close to other German Lutherans, as well as near a church and a school. In addition, they advised those who were heading west about the most desirable locations in which to settle, and they helped them with travel arrangements. Spiritual and moral guidance was combined with social and even financial assistance. From 1870 to 1883, Pastor Stephanus Keyl in New York cared for 27,000 immigrants and wrote nearly 4,000 letters in their behalf. Many of those people and their descendants became members of the Missouri Synod as a result of these ministries.

Expansion of American Protestantism

In the Great Awakening many churches of colonial America experienced substantial numerical growth and spiritual invigoration during the half century before the War of Independence (1776—83). But, as war clouds gathered and the storm broke, the Awakening subsided, except in the south. The disruptive conflict distracted people from spiritual concerns. Afterward the challenge of organizing a new nation and rebuilding neglected families and properties absorbed the interest and energies of many who otherwise might have been involved in the churches. Great numbers pulled up stakes in order to settle new lands on the frontier. In addition, European Rationalism, with its contempt for institutionalized religion, was taking its toll, especially among the young. By the end of the 18th century, Christian conviction and participation had sunk to a point as low or even lower than it had been at the beginning of the century before the Great Awakening. Ten percent of the population of the new nation or even less were active church members in the 1790s.

Then, at the very close of the 18th century and throughout most of the 19th, new life and growth appeared in many denominations. In the previous section we reviewed the mushrooming of the Catholic and Lutheran churches as a result of their ministries to immigrants. In this section we trace the expansion of churches that ministered primarily to descendants of older American stock. The gains made by these churches were as spectacular as those made by churches that concentrated on immigrants. In 1789 the combined membership of the Baptists, Congregationalists, Methodists, and Presbyterians did not exceed 150,000. By 1910 their combined membership (including the Disciples of Christ, a new denomination that emerged from these churches) totaled more than 15 million.

This increase occurred during a period of diverse and momentous changes. There were massive population movements all the way to the southern and western shores of the continent. Sectionalism fuelled by the slavery issue erupted in the Civil War (1861—65), which also divided many of the churches. Population increased greatly from births as well as from the waves of European immigrants. After the war, industrialization and urbanization changed the face of American society. Secularization, which had so devastated European Christianity, was less evident in the United States, but was quietly settling in even as the churches began to flourish. Controversy over both theological and social issues caused tension and division. Despite all of the competition and complications resulting from these changes, despite their own weakness and discouragement at the beginning of this period, the churches mentioned above rose up with zeal and energy to meet the challenge of a new age.

Once again it is necessary to limit the discussion drastically. We will not go into the important work done by some of these churches among transplanted Europeans. Nor will we deal with the rise of some of the new denominations, such as the Mormons, the Jehovah's Witnesses, and the Seventh Day Adventists. Outreach to blacks and American Indians will be covered very briefly. Only three major aspects of American Protestant expansion in the 19th century are explored below: (1) the "Second Great Awakening" in New England; (2) evangelization on the frontier; and (3) urban revivalism.

Second Great Awakening in New England

Following the War of Independence the Calvinist churches of New England were confronted not only with loss of members and of zeal but also with continuing controversy over revivalism and division over Unitarianism. However, beginning in 1796 or 1797 and continuing until about 1830, a Second Great Awakening took place. In its first phase (1797—1801), this consisted in a series of revivals in churches from Connecticut to New Hampshire. These were generally in the tradition of Jonathan Edwards. The messages were typically Calvinistic in content: God's sovereignty, man's hopeless corruption, and Christ's atoning love were the standard themes. When revival happened it was regarded as the work of God, not of man. The speaker was usually the pastor, and the style of preaching was low-key. The response of the people was earnest but restrained. The results were noticeable and sustained. People in considerable numbers were converted from indifference and negligence to spiritual and moral seriousness. About 150 churches experienced refreshment and growth during this first wave of revivals.

Just as this wave began to recede a new one began to rise. Under the presidency of Timothy Dwight (1752—1817) many students at Yale College (later Yale University) were stirred to new levels of faith and commitment. Since a sizable portion of these entered the pastoral ministry, the results of the Yale revival were far-reaching. The Awakening and American revivalism in general took a new direction when Nathaniel Taylor (1786—1858), professor of theology at Yale Divinity School after 1822, significantly revised Calvinistic theology in order to conform to the realities of the revival experience. While professing to uphold the Westminster Confession and other Reformed doctrinal standards, he rejected the depravity and spiritual helplessness of natural man and affirmed that man is a free, rational, and moral creature who can make a decision for God out of his own resources. As Taylor's influence grew, revivals were increasingly viewed as accomplishments of gifted preachers who could persuade sinners to believe and be saved, rather than as mighty acts of God by which He turned and transformed people. This brought Calvinists and those of Wesleyan descent close together on this key theological point. These two traditions have dominated the revival movement and have been the source of much American evangelism leadership. This accounts for the prevalence of "decision theology" in much evangelism literature and methodology.

Two other aspects of the Second Great Awakening became permanent features of American revivalism. One was methodological. Asahel Nettleton (1783—1844) developed programs of home visitation, personal consultation, inquiry meetings, and follow-up procedures that added to the effectiveness of his powerful evangelistic preaching. The other was a strong emphasis on moral reform and theological conservatism. Lyman

Beecher (1775—1863) combined a vigorous evangelistic ministry with campaigns against dueling and advocacy of temperance. In addition, like so many later revivalists, he joined the crusades against liberalism and Unitarianism.

An extremely important product of this Second Great Awakening was the organization of numerous voluntary associations dedicated to specific aspects of the Christian mission. Many of these were devoted directly or indirectly to evangelistic-missionary purposes. Some recruited and supported workers. Others printed and distributed Bibles and other Christian literature. Still others supported Christian education, especially Sunday Schools. Humanitarian concerns were the focus of a number of societies. They worked for temperance, the abolition of slavery, and assistance to the homeless and handicapped. Since denominations did not yet accept these causes as integral to their own mission, it was most helpful for concerned individuals to unite their energies and resources to meet these needs. Furthermore, it was valuable to the lay people in these societies to have meaningful and rewarding ways to exercise their ministries. The activation of the laity was a vital and lasting result of this revival movement.[11]

Evangelization on the Frontier

Although the English government had prohibited it, a trickle of settlers had crossed the Allegheny Mountains into Kentucky and Tennessee even before the War of Independence. However, when the Treaty of Paris in 1783 established the Mississippi as the western boundary of the United States, that trickle became a sizable stream. Most pioneers originated from Maryland, Virginia, and the Carolinas. While some small cities sprouted up, most of the settlers were thinly scattered. Life was hard and lonely as they struggled to clear land for crops or to harvest meat and furs from wild animals of the forest. There was constant danger from Indians, who were made hostile by the relentless encroachment of white people. Equally dangerous were the violent and lawless elements among the settlers themselves. Manners were coarse and mores harsh. Earthly survival or even sensual escape were of greater concern to many than eternal salvation. Church connections broken by the process of relocation were not automatically reestablished. Churches and clergy were scarce.

Remarkably, this area soon became a center of Christian revival. Many thousands of settlers were converted or deeply moved spiritually and gathered into churches. So dramatic and impressive were these revivals that their influence spread back into the southeastern states and even into New England, where they fed the Second Great Awakening that was already underway. Three denominations dominated these revivals—the Presbyterians, Methodists, and Baptists. Especially the latter two were launched into patterns of outreach and growth that ultimately made them the largest and strongest Protestant denominations in America.

By 1785 all three had planted churches in this area. The Presbyterians sent missionary preachers from western Pennsylvania. They founded congregations, presbyteries, and by 1802 the Synod of Kentucky. Baptist farmer-preachers, who were among the settlers, replicated the success that they had enjoyed earlier in the southeastern states. Not only did they gather Baptist settlers into congregations and make new converts from among the unchurched, but they also motivated many in their flocks to respond to the call to preach, thus multiplying their ministries. Since no special education was required for Baptist preachers, these new recruits were ready for service almost immediately. However, most notable in this new field were the Methodists.

Methodism had made a small but promising start in America late in the colonial period. In 1771 John Wesley sent Francis Asbury, a lay preacher, to organize the scattered American Methodist evangelists. At the first American Methodist Conference held in Philadelphia in 1773, the total membership of the society was only 1,160. By 1781 there were 15,000 members served by 84 evangelists. Methodists were organized as an independent American church in 1784 with Asbury as bishop. Membership jumped to 57,631 by 1790. Although organized and active throughout the new nation, the frontier was the scene of Methodism's most spectacular success.

The organization and ministry style of Methodism were especially well suited to the frontier situation. Very early the entire nation was subdivided into districts, and districts into circuits. A circuit was a territory that a traveling preacher could cover in four to six weeks time. The hardy, dedicated, and courageous preachers who covered the frontier circuits were the key to Methodist growth on the frontier. These were young men, usually unmarried, with no special education, who out of deep commitment to their Lord expended themselves sacrificially to reach lost and leaderless settlers with the Gospel. They traveled on horseback, by canoe, or on foot in all kinds of weather, preaching to whomever would listen in groups small or large. People who responded to their preaching were gathered into classes for mutual spiritual support and maintenance. Eventually resident preachers took over the work. However, it was primarily through the zealous and effective work of these itinerants that planted Methodism widely on the frontier and set its roots deeply into these developing areas. Highly mobile, down-to-earth, carefully supervised, and of unquestioned sincerity, Methodist circuit riders followed settlers into the ever-shifting frontier, ministered to their spiritual needs, and "Methodized" them. An outstanding representative of this remarkable group of evangelists was Peter Cartwright (1785—1872). Converted in 1801 after an intense spiritual struggle, he was transformed from a wild and worldly youth to one of the most colorful and respected Methodist missionaries on the frontier.

The distinctive and perhaps most important agency of outreach on the western frontier (Kentucky and Tennessee) early in the 19th century was the camp meeting. This was an extended series of revival services lasting for as long as a week, to which people came in great numbers from miles around. Participants lived in their own tents or wagons that they brought with them. Preaching services were conducted throughout the day and far into the night with the grounds being illuminated by torchlight and campfires. The meetings were interdenominational in character, conducted cooperatively by Presbyterian, Baptist, and Methodist preachers, who usually kept their distinctive doctrines and practices from becoming disruptive. Sermons emphasized the terrors of hell and the glory of heaven along with the necessity of a conversion experience in order to avoid the former and to be assured of the latter. The source of divine pardon and of eternal hope was the sacrificial, substitutionary death of Jesus. In order to prepare for a conversion experience, hearers were urged to abandon and to lament their sins and to pray for the Spirit's action in their hearts. The climax of the camp meeting was a celebration of the Lord's Supper, which was otherwise unavailable to many settlers and not celebrated frequently in most frontier churches.

A conspicuous characteristic of the camp meetings was extravagant emotional and physical manifestations in those being converted. Not only sobbing, crying out, and swooning—which were common already during some of the 18th-century revivals—but rolling, jerking, barking, dancing, and running were experienced by many converts during the earliest camp meetings. Although critics ridiculed them as fanatical excesses and even some preachers tried to suppress them, these manifestations were widely regarded as evidence of the Holy Spirit's transforming presence and work, bringing the sinner to repentance and faith.

The outbreak of this form of revivalism in the summer of 1800 was preceded by a decade of spiritual apathy in Kentucky and in much of the south, during which time faithful and devout church members prayed, fasted, and waited for revival. During this same decade the population of Kentucky tripled, going from 73,677 to 220,955, far beyond what the recently established churches could reach and gather in by customary methods. The very first true camp meeting was held at Gasper River in Logan County, Kentucky, under the leadership of James McReady (1758—1817), a Presbyterian minister who had come to the area after a period of revival ministries in North Carolina and Virginia. His congregations had been praying and waiting for revival in their midst for several years. When signs of revival began to appear, the Gasper River meeting was scheduled and word of it spread far and wide. On the last weekend of July 1800, people began assembling from as far away as 100 miles. A number of other preachers from various denominations assisted. Response was dramatic, especially among the youth.

News of the revival camp meeting spread throughout Kentucky and beyond, stimulating many similar meetings. The largest and most famous was held in August 1801, under the leadership of Barton Stone (1772—1844) and dozens of other preachers at Cane Ridge near Paris, Kentucky. Attendance estimates vary from 12,000 to 25,000. Until 1805 camp meetings were held by the hundreds not only in Kentucky and Tennessee but throughout the south. In addition, numerous traditional church revivals were inspired by the camp meeting experience. Church membership multiplied several times over, especially among the Methodists and Baptists.

Through these camp meetings and what followed them, evangelistic, revivalistic Protestantism became dominant in the south, profoundly affecting both the religion and culture of that region.

Although in its first phase the camp meeting was frequently interdenominational and care was taken to avoid controversial topics, polemical denominationalism did eventually intrude. Furthermore, Methodists became the chief sponsors of camp meetings, as Baptists and Presbyterians withdrew into their more traditional evangelistic practices. As the frontier areas became more settled and civilized, camp meetings became less emotional and more institutionalized. Eventually, they were largely displaced by church revivals and other types of evangelism more suited to settled and urban environments. However, as the frontier moved west, north, and south the more primitive style of meeting appeared there and fulfilled its purposes as effectively in the new frontiers as it had in the old ones. Until well after mid-century, the camp meeting was a vital evangelistic agency in the developing areas of the new nation.

What was the appeal of the camp meeting? What were the cultural, emotional and social factors that joined the religious components to enable the camp meeting to have such impact?

Unquestionably, people were drawn to the meeting out of hunger for contact with other people. Isolation and loneliness were severe problems for scattered settlers. In addition, there was the magnetism of dramatic and emotional experience to counteract the boredom and drudgery of daily life. Camp meetings were exciting. Some, it is clear, came more to practice sin than to seek salvation. Opportunities for drunkenness and sexual immorality were present even at gatherings that were primarily spiritual in intent. Not only critics of camp meetings but also their advocates deplored the seamy side which inevitably appeared. However, the primary attraction for most participants was an awakened sense of spiritual need. This was stirred up not only by preachments heard occasionally by missionaries and pastors, but also by the hard and dangerous environment in which the people lived. The need for divine help and hope was underscored by tragic life experiences so common on the frontier—devastating illness with no effective means of treatment, death from accident and assault as well as from sickness, crop failure, and hunger. Guilt and self-disgust over their godless ways afflicted more than a few. In some, there remained a nostalgic memory of meaningful and active Christian faith from an earlier time. Stories of the first Great Awakening were sometimes recalled. Among the faithful, prayer for new revivals was continuously offered up.

Undoubtedly, the strongest immediate attraction was the testimonies and invitations of those who had participated in camp meetings. As they related their experiences to relatives, friends, and neighbors, interest was multiplied and magnified. News of a forthcoming meeting was carried by travelers and itinerant preachers. Enthusiasm was contagious, and as the appointed time drew near people converged from all directions and in great numbers. Many participated repeatedly in revivals, having found them to be a source of great spiritual help as well as socially and emotionally satisfying. Enthusiastic and satisfied participants brought others with them to subsequent meetings.[12]

Presbyterians and Congregationalists united in an effort to establish congregations and provide pastoral care for the settlers on the frontier of the old northwest. Their Plan of Union of 1801 was a unique arrangement by which they encouraged Presbyterian and Congregationalists in a given area to form a single congregation. The minister and polity could be of either denomination, as the majority of the members decided. "Presbygational" churches, as the hybrid was frequently called, were planted throughout this part of the frontier. Not only the religion but also the culture of New England was transmitted and perpetuated through these congregations. Because of their more centralized government, the Presbyterians attracted most of these congregations into their affiliation. However, many of the pastors were Congregationalists trained in the revivalist theology of Nathaniel Taylor. To a significant degree, the impulse to evangelize the settlers on the northwestern frontier was a product of the Second Great Awakening. By 1910, largely as a result of this outreach, Presbyterians had increased to 2 million members from about 500,000 in 1780. Congregationalists, who were about 170,000 in number in 1780, grew to about 750,000 by 1910.[13]

Ministry to Minorities

The Christianization of black Americans during the 19th century is comparable in some respects to some of the mass movements of northern Europeans into Christianity during the middle ages. It was the case of a subjugated people absorbing the religion of their oppressors. Through the hideous process of enslavement and forced relocation, Africans were deprived of their traditional cultures and religions. Consequently, they had little resistance to the culture and religion of their new land. In the American environment they were exposed to Christianity and invited into it by some of the same people who held them in bondage. However, it was by no means forced conversion. Rather, the blacks appropriated the faith quite voluntarily, made it their own, and disseminated it widely among themselves. Some whites opposed the conversion of black slaves on the grounds that it might be difficult to justify retaining fellow Christians in slavery. But most Christian leaders, even those who did not challenge the institution of slavery, did insist that slaves be evangelized. Some white masters actively provided Christian ministry to their slaves. Motives were not always admirable. Some viewed conversion as a means of keeping their slaves honest and docile. Others were genuinely interested in their spiritual welfare.

From the very beginning some Christian voices were raised against the practice of slavery. The early leadership of the abolitionist movement was largely Christian. Before the end of the 18th century especially the Quakers and some Methodists took a firm stand against the holding of slaves by their members. By mid century most major denominations had divided over the issue.

Numerous white missionaries devoted themselves to the evangelization of blacks. In 1860 there were 99 white Southern Methodist preachers working full-time among plantation slaves. Most white churches in the south permitted and even encouraged blacks to participate in their worship services. Yet, they were required to observe a segregated seating arrangement. In revival meetings of both Great Awakenings blacks were frequently involved and responded with great fervor. In the north, where most blacks were free, they were permitted to belong to some white congregations but were not often welcomed as equals. The most important contribution of white to black spiritual and social well-being was the provision of many education agencies, most under Christian auspices. However, even during the period up to 1860, when black religious life was largely controlled by whites, there were significant numerical gains. In 1797 there were only about 65,000 black Christians in the United States, which represented only seven percent of the black population. By 1860 there were 520,000 black Christians, amounting to 11 percent of the black population, despite a fivefold population increase during these decades.

Most of this increase was not, however, the result of evangelistic outreach by whites. Rather, it was the result of blacks preaching and witnessing to blacks. Almost from the beginning some black converts felt the call to exercise spiritual leadership. Some free blacks preached to slaves as well as to other free blacks and even to whites. There were black congregations in the south as well as the north before the end of the 18th century. By 1816 the first black denomination had been formed, the African Methodist Church, with Richard Allen (1760—1831) as bishop. The activity of black preachers and the freedom of blacks to conduct their own religious activities in the south was severely curtailed after the Nat Turner Rebellion of 1830. Since Turner was a black Baptist preacher, white authorities deemed it unsafe to permit black preachers to function, for fear that they would foment further insurrections. Despite these restrictions, black slaves turned increasingly to Christianity, drawn largely by the witness of their fellow blacks. Consolation for their hard and demeaning lives, dignity and self-esteem as God's beloved children, hope for complete freedom and joy hereafter, combined with the central theme of pardon and renewal through the suffering and death of Christ, constituted an appealing and relevant message to oppressed blacks. The content of their faith was not significantly different from that of the white Christians around them. As the abolitionist movement spread and the Civil War progressed, thoughts of freedom from slavery and a new and better life in this world often merged with concepts of spiritual freedom and eternal deliverance. Black singing and preaching appear to reflect elements of their African heritage and expressed in unique ways the pain and frustration of the slavery condition.

After the Civil War, blacks increasingly took charge of their religious activities and institutions. Black congregations and denominations multiplied. Virtually all were Baptists or Methodists of one kind or another. The styles of ministry and worship of these bodies were particularly attractive to blacks. In the difficult years of reconstruction and the institutionalized intimidation and discrimination that followed, the church was the only social institution in which they were in a position to express their feelings and potential and take charge of their own affairs. Undoubtedly, a major factor in the strength and spread of Christianity among black Americans was the fact that very soon it became indigenous—self-determining, self-supporting, and self-perpetuating. By 1916 there were 4,602,805 black Christians in the United States, which represented 44 percent of the total black population. This is a proportion slightly larger than the Christian segment of the white population (43 percent) at this time.[14]

The effort to evangelize the American Indians was less successful. Although by 1914 about 45 percent of this minority group were in some sense related to Christian churches, the attachment was often weak and the impact of Christianity minimal. Reasons for this are not difficult to discover. During the 19th century, even more than in previous centuries, Indians were repeatedly driven from their lands by mounting waves of white settlers. Whenever this happened, whatever Christian work may have been initiated among them was usually disrupted. With monotonous regularity treaties and other agreements between the United States government and Indians were violated. Even at its best, the government's style of trying to assist Indians was paternalistic and demeaning. Tragic legacies of alcoholism and disease were among the most conspicuous elements of white "civilization" to take hold among Indians. Hundreds of missionaries, both Catholic and Protestant, worked sacrificially among the Indians. They started missions and schools. During much of the 19th century churches administered most government aid to Indians and conducted most of the education, which was paid for by the government. Frequently Christian missionaries tried to combat the injustices to which the Indians were subjected. Some devout converts were made, and some vital congregations were formed. However, for reasons mentioned above and others more difficult to identify, Indian response to Christianity was largely passive. Except in the Protestant Episcopal Church, few Indian clergy were ordained. Little sense of ownership of Christianity or desire to share it was transmitted to the rank and file. There was much defection to traditional Indian religion and some attempts to combine Christianity with these religions. Given the circumstances of the Indian experience, the wonder is not that the impact of

Christianity was not greater, but rather that it succeeded as well as it did.[15]

Urban Revivalism

Revival came earlier and became more solidly established in the frontier and rural areas of the United States than in the large cities. Competition for the attention of urban people, as well as for their time and involvement, was intense. In the anonymity of the city it was difficult to locate and focus personal attention on those in need of conversion. Secularism and skepticism were deeply entrenched, vice and materialism prevalent, indifference and apostasy endemic. Attempts early in the 19th century to bring revival to New York City were notoriously ineffective.

Urban revivalism first began to flourish under the ministry of Charles Grandison Finney (1792—1875). A lawyer by profession, after his conversion in 1821 Finney became an evangelist. In a career spanning four decades, he first electrified revival audiences in the small towns of western New York and ultimately preached with great success in Philadelphia, New York, and Boston. In 1835 he became president of Oberlin College in Ohio. From this position he was able to prepare hundreds of young preachers who continued and extended his revival ministry. In this academic setting he also devoted himself to theologizing about revivalism in such a way as to make an extensive and lasting impression on much of American Protestantism. Even during his long tenure at Oberlin he was active on the revival circuit for six months out of the year, including several visits to England.

An important part of Finney's contribution to revivalistic evangelism was methodological. Most conspicuous were his "new measures," some of which were standard features of frontier evangelism adapted to the urban situation. These included "protracted meetings"—in the manner of camp meetings. In addition, he employed the "anxious bench," a place at the front of the room where those seeking conversion could come for special prayer and ministry—another import from camp meetings. More innovative were public invitations for people to come forward as an indication of their commitment or recommitment, and the utilization of an inquiry or counseling room staffed by ministers and others prepared to give personal ministry to those who desired it. More than any before him, Finney insisted on elaborate, well-organized promotional campaigns, patterned after those used by politicians, in order to create interest, excitement, and expectancy. Teams of visitors went from door to door extending invitations to the meetings. Posters and handbills blanketed the cities. Cottage prayer meetings were held for days and weeks in advance of the revival in order to petition for divine support and to sustain human interest in the event.

Finney's most influential contribution to revivalistic evangelism was theological. Although he lacked seminary education, he was ordained as a Presbyterian minister in 1824. However, the doctrines of classical Calvinism, especially those that denied the freedom of the sinner to choose salvation, seemed irrational and unjust to him, as well as discouraging of evangelistic effort. Far more even than Nathaniel Taylor before him, Finney emphasized that conversion, like sin and unbelief, is a human decision. The task of the evangelist is to preach for that decision. Sinners need to know that because of the redemptive work of Christ, they now have the option either to remain candidates for eternal condemnation or to choose pardon and eternal blessedness. Finney did not believe that the sinner could make this decision unaided. The Holy Spirit helped by releasing the sinner from bondage to sensualism—which was the result of repeated, self-chosen surrender to sin—and by restoring his reason to a position of control. Yet the Spirit did not make the saving decision for the sinner. Rather, He enabled the sinner to make it for himself.

In Finney's opinion, revivals, like conversion, were the work of man. Unlike most earlier revivalists, Finney did not view mass awakenings as miracles or expressions of divine sovereignty, which occurred periodically according to His plan and initiative. Rather, Finney believed that God had put the resources for revival at the disposal of His people and that they could precipitate revival by utilizing these resources. These resources, or agencies, as he termed them, are both divine and human. The divine agencies are Providence and the Spirit. Providence arranges the external factors in such a way as to bring sinners into contact with His truth. The Spirit gives power to that truth as it is applied to the sinner. Human agencies are the preacher and the sinner himself. The preacher acts persuasively and energetically to get the sinner to take the Word of truth seriously and personally. The sinner, influenced by the preacher and others, including the Spirit, acts to submit to the truth, to obey, or to refuse as the case may be. A revival, then, is a carefully designed and executed experience in which these agencies combine to effect the conversion of many.

Finney's revivalist methodologies and his theology provoked much controversy. It constituted a frontal assault on classical Calvinism and was recognized as such. Ultimately, he left the Presbyterian church and became a Congregationalist. The importance of Finney is that to a significant degree he shaped the theory and practices of American revivalistic evangelism. The impact of his thought and work are still very evident in much American Protestantism.[16]

Dwight Lyman Moody (1837—99) was by far the greatest of the urban revivalists of the period between the Civil War and World War I. Although thousands were moved to take up revivalistic ministries during this era, and many of these, like Moody, worked in the cities, none attained his stature or success. In some respects he followed the example of Finney. However, much in his style was unique, as was his personality. He was an extremely confident, resilient, aggressive extrovert, who at the same time was sensitive and remarkably humble. After a rather quiet conversion as a teenager he moved to Chicago in 1856, where he became very successful in the shoe business. Simultaneously he established a large independent Sunday School of students recruited from the poor of Chicago's north side. This became a model of urban child evangelism, one of the most successful methods for reaching the urban poor. In order to provide suitable and comparable nurture for his Sunday School students as they attained adulthood, Moody established the Illinois Street Church in 1864. It soon became a large, flourishing, and independent congregation. Incredibly, during this same period, Moody was a leading force in the Chicago Y.M.C.A., recruiting members, raising huge sums of money for new buildings, and serving as a lay evangelist to troops during the Civil War. His energy was as boundless as his zeal and vision.

In the course of his Chicago activities, while ministering primarily to the poor, Moody cultivated a large and loyal following among the wealthy members of the Christian community. They were profoundly impressed by the man and his causes and supported them most generously, not only with money, but also with their personal involvement. Throughout the remaining years of his life, Moody could count on this well-endowed support group for all of his evangelistic ventures as well as for his personal needs. As successful business people in an expansive era, they appreciated an approach to Christian work that incorporated attitudes and methods similar to their own.

In order to free more time for his evangelistic activities, Moody resigned his lucrative and promising position in the shoe business. For a time he lived in near poverty, but affluent Christian friends soon arranged for his support. This continued and grew to the point that he enjoyed a standard of living that was more than comfortable. It should be noted that Moody's income was from this source and from royalties rather than from funds raised in connection with his evangelistic work.

During the 1860s Moody developed rapidly as an evangelistic preacher. Through frequent practice at his own church and in Y.M.C.A. activities, as well as by carefully studying other preachers, he developed his uniquely effective style. Grammar and organization left room for improvement. Delivery was unpolished. However, sincerity, warmth, clarity, color, and concreteness more than compensated for these deficiencies. Tremendously significant for his content was the influence of an English lay preacher, Henry Moorhouse, who, in 1867 as a guest speaker at Moody's church, expounded John 3:16 in sermon after sermon. The effect of this was to turn Moody's preaching emphasis from God's law and judgment to His seeking and rescuing love. For the rest of his days this was Moody's pervasive theme. Still another appealing aspect of his preaching was its comparative brevity. At a time when the sermons of most other preachers went on for an hour and more, Moody packaged his powerful messages in units of 20, 30, or, at most, 45 minutes.

Two additional factors readied Moody for the spectacular evangelistic career that was about to unfold. One was his teaming up in 1870 with Ira D. Sankey (1840—1908), a musician of exceptional native ability, who, accompanied by a harmonium, moved audiences deeply with his songs and led them in highly inspirational group singing. The songs, many his own compositions, were simple, subjective, and highly singable. They carried messages of Christian hope and comfort straight to the heart. They generated enthusiasm and expressed joy. Without Sankey, Moody, by his own admission, would have been sorely handicapped.

The other factor was Moody's "second conversion" experience during the winter of 1871. After a period of emotional and spiritual distress and inner conflict, he had an overwhelming personal experience of the Spirit's presence and power. His pride was broken and his resolve to serve the Lord wherever and whenever he was led was reinforced. Overcome by a sense of God's love, he wept for joy and gave himself without restraint to the preaching of Christ. Thus renewed, he was prepared inwardly to touch the hearts of millions.

It was in the British Isles from 1872 to 1875 that Moody became an evangelistic sensation. Although the original sponsors of his revival tour died before he and Sankey arrived, they were able to find new support and opportunities through Y.M.C.A. contacts. After an inauspicious beginning in York they moved on to Scotland, where, aided by supportive articles in R. C. Morgan's *The Christian* magazine, they began to attract growing audiences and evoke enthusiastic response. In addition to the large meetings, the evangelists met with special groups often in outlying areas. Publicity and promotion methods were refined and support from clergy increased. They worked tirelessly, and during their five months in Scotland they became celebrities—although criticism from traditional churchmen was abundant. They moved on to Ireland for several months and even in predominately Roman Catholic areas were received surprisingly well. Then they moved back to England.

During this phase of the tour, Moody developed some of his basic campaign machinery. Well-known evangelical leaders were recruited to administer the campaigns in each area. When no building of sufficient size was available, a large, temporary tabernacle was constructed. Careful attention was given to acoustics, and the inquirers' room was designed to give an impression of intimacy. In preparation for the campaigns, prayer groups were formed, house to house canvasses were conducted, and circulars were widely distributed. Above all, support of local churches and clergy was enlisted—broad, interdenominational support. Financing was arranged by local leaders from local sources. All of this was followed closely and reported extensively by the public press, generating mounting curiosity and expectancy.

In the great cities of England where they conducted lengthy revivals, the evangelistic team attracted huge numbers. Estimates of their total attendance during the entire British tour ran as high as three million. To the disappointment of Moody and his supporters, however, most participants were already church-going Christians rather than the unchurched, and middle- or upper-class people rather than the disadvantaged urban masses whom they were especially eager to reach. Nevertheless, there were numerous instances of conversion and reconsecration. The evangelistic mission of the church was given high visibility. Multitudes experienced exciting, revivalistic worship, which at least in modified forms was replicated in many evangelical churches.

From the perspective of American urban revivalism, the most important aspect of Moody's British tour is that it added tremendously to his reputation as an evangelist and created strong and widespread interest in similar campaigns here. After his return to the United States in September 1875 and a brief period of recuperation at his hometown of Northfield, Massachusetts, Moody began a series of campaigns in large cities of the northeast. Methodology developed in Britain was refined and applied. His ground rules were that there must be: (1) united support from the evangelical churches; (2) adequate facilities; (3) no competitive activities from the churches during his scheduled meetings; and

(4) adequate financing. Local leaders were in charge of preparations. Much of the "leg-work" was done by members and staff of the Y.M.C.A.

The tour took Moody and Sankey to Brooklyn, Philadelphia, New York, Chicago, and Boston. They spent two to three months in each city and were not finished until late 1878. Riding a crest of popular interest, they enjoyed great numerical success. As in Britain, however, participants were largely already Christian and of middle and upper classes. The impact of the campaigns is difficult to assess. Although Moody did not press for conversions in the manner of many evangelists, there were thousands nevertheless. New life and vigor were injected into some of the cooperating churches; however, except where sustained by strong pastoral care and nurture, they soon faded. Several adjustments were made in the campaign approach in order to improve their outreach and impact, but with limited success. He conducted hundreds of evangelistic revivals in cities throughout the nation in later decades, but none attained the size and scope of this first great urban tour of the late 1870s.

Moody's message was simple and non-controversial. Although he was not theologically sophisticated, he was steeped in the Bible and communicated its central message with great power. Like virtually all revivalists his orientation was Arminian or synergistic, viewing conversion as the joint effort of divine grace and the human will. His approach to Christian social responsibility was simplistic: convert individuals and they will automatically be able to take care of their own material needs and be willing also to help others.

His appeal to the masses was, perhaps, in part that he expressed the simple faith and values reminiscent of their rural background. His generous support from the business community may have been motivated in part by the hope that converted workers would be more productive and that religious revival would quell social unrest and disorder. However, genuine concern for the spiritual well-being of others was clearly predominant. At a very fundamental level, the appeal of the urban revival was that of an exciting, inspiring mass gathering, as entertaining and interesting as it was uplifting. It held recreational as well as spiritual attractions.

Late in the 1870s, Moody began to turn to other agencies that he hoped would significantly aid the cause of urban evangelism. One persistent problem was a shortage of workers committed to and competent for urban evangelism. Consequently, he determined to found educational institutions to prepare such workers. In Northfield he established separate schools for male and female youth. Although they became quality schools, they did not produce workers zealous for urban evangelism ministry. About a decade later, in 1879, he founded what was eventually known as Moody Bible Institute in Chicago. After a difficult beginning it became a large and thriving institution which trained thousands of zealous workers. A significant number, as a result of their urban evangelistic education, have gone on to serve as urban evangelists.[17]

Others followed Moody into urban evangelism, but with increasing emphasis on sensationalism. The last of the major figures in this period was Billy (William Ashland) Sunday (1863—1935), a former baseball player whose uninhibited antics and jolting language turned revivalism into a crude kind of religious vaudeville. By high pressure methods he gained thousands of "converts," and became a master at extracting large sums of money out of audiences and supporters. His career reached its peak in 1917 and then plummeted as the war and the "roaring twenties" diverted the attention of the masses to even more sensational objects.

These carefully organized, well-financed, highly publicized urban revivals featuring famous and colorful evangelists were bold and sincere Protestant attempts to Christianize the swelling populations of urban America. Their success was limited. Although comparatively few lasting numerical gains can be documented as a result of these revivals, they did appear to engender increased interest and dedication in existing Christians. In addition, they enlisted the participation and leadership of many lay people. They exhibited and elevated awareness of evangelism and focused attention on the importance of trusting in Christ and sharing Him. They kept Christianity before the public e e, even though not always in a favorable light. They were mass demonstrations of Christian conviction and solidarity. However, the evangelists themselves sometimes expressed disappointment in the scanty harvest of souls that they gathered in.[18]

World Missions[19]

A great new surge of missionary activity accompanied the revivals of the 19th century. The impulse to carry the Gospel worldwide grew strong, especially among English-speaking Protestants. Nor was the impulse squelched or frustrated. During this period (1789—1914), Christianity spread farther and gained more adherents from people of non-Christian cultures than during any previous period. Unprecedented quantities of money and manpower were poured into the cause of missions, and unprecedented numbers of converts were gained.

The magnitude of these efforts as well as the limited scope of this study make it impossible to summarize progress in even the most important mission fields. We will instead confine the discussion to several major developments in goals, strategy, and methodology that had very broad significance.

Although motivation for world missions grew out of revivals, opportunity for world missions grew out of the vastly increased colonial expansion of western European nations, of which the most aggressive and successful was Great Britain. (However, there were also notable instances in which missionary exploration and expansion preceded colonial expansion, e.g., the work of David Livingstone [1813—73] in Africa.) It was during this century that Great Britain, financed by the wealth of its industrial preeminence and aided by vastly improved transportation—steamship and railroad—established an empire on which the sun never set. In India, southern Asia, and Africa, where previously she had been content to trade, Britain now was determined to rule. Along with other western European nations, she carved huge holdings out of the African continent. The great nations of the Orient—China and Japan—were compelled to open their doors to western traders and influences. The islands of the Pacific and the West Indies were seized by Britain, France, and the United States. Along with the global political and military dominance of western nations came powerful cultural influences and the greatest Christian missionary effort that the world had ever seen.

It was during the 19th century that Protestant foreign missions came into their own. Previously Protestants had done little compared with the Roman Catholics, whose world missions enterprise girdled the globe already in the 16th century. Subsequently there were serious setbacks in the Catholic mission fields because of the decline of the colonial powers on which they depended—Spain and Portugal—as well as foundational weaknesses in the earlier work. Not only were efforts made to pump new life into Latin American Catholicism, but French and Belgian missionaries in particular initiated work in the colonial territories of their nations. However, during the last half of the 19th century and the first decades of the 20th, Protestant missions surpassed those of the Catholics. From Britain and increasingly from the United States, people who had been converted or spiritually deepened by Protestant revivals directed their evangelistic attention and effort to the multitudes of non-Christians throughout the world who were now reachable.

A remarkable and highly significant aspect of most Protestant missionary work during this era is that it was supported and controlled by voluntary societies. Neither the churches nor the governments provided funds or direction for these vast outreach efforts. Rather, it was groups of committed individuals who, aware of the unfolding missionary opportunities, gave unsparingly in order to take advantage of them. The very first to be formed was the Baptist Society for Propagating the Gospel (London, 1792).

Other societies, both denominational and interdenominational in character, soon followed, not only in Britain but also in the United States and on the European continent. By the early part of the 20th century there were many dozens. Unique and inspiring was the Student Volunteer Movement organized in 1886 at Moody's Mt. Herman Bible Conference. During the next several decades the S.V.M. sent 20,000 college students on volunteer assignments overseas. They were supported by 80,000 members at home. These societies promoted awareness of missionary needs and opportunities, recruited and trained workers and supported them in the field, published literature, and raised large amounts of money with which to finance their diverse operations. Perhaps as important as the fruits of their labor was what happened to the society members themselves as they became interested and involved. By accepting responsibility for a vital part of the church's ministry, they gained spiritual leadership experience and a sense of ownership that eventually carried over into other aspects of church life. Missionary societies were an important factor in the mobilization of the laity.

William Carey (1761—1834) more than any other individual ignited the flame of missionary zeal among English-speaking people. A Baptist cobbler-preacher, he wrote a treatise that laid a historical and theological foundation for the Protestant mission enterprise: *An Enquiry into the Obligation of Christians to Use Means for the Conversion of the Heathen* (1792). Along with other promotional efforts, this led to the formation of the Baptist Missionary Society, and Carey himself became the first missionary. He arrived in India in 1793 and worked for six years in an area controlled by the British East India Company, which imposed restrictions on missionary work for fear that it would cause unrest among the natives. In 1799, along with several others, Carey moved to Serampore, under Danish control, where missionaries were welcome and could work unhindered by colonial officials. His strategies became an agenda for much of the 19th-century missionary movement: (1) preach the Gospel wherever possible; (2) translate and widely distribute Scripture; (3) start native churches; (4) become acquainted with the culture and history of the people; and (5) train an indigenous ministry. To a remarkable degree he and his colleagues were able to carry out these strategies. In addition, Carey and his colleagues worked for social reform—the abolition of *suttee* (widow burning), temple prostitution, and other dehumanizing customs. They also introduced modern journalism to India, both in English and the vernacular.

Carey's work provided not only a model but also powerful motivation for countless other missionaries. The basic goals of 19th century Protestant missions were individual conversion, church planting, and the transformation of society. During the last half of the century these goals were refined and restated in the famous "three-self" formula, which remained standard for more than a hundred years: the purpose of missionary work is to establish and cultivate churches that will be self-governing, self-supporting, and self-propagating.

These goals were implemented by three major methods: evangelism, education, and medicine. Missionaries and their native helpers preached and taught the Christian message. They translated and distributed Scriptures and other Christian literature. They established and conducted schools, not only to serve the children of those who were already Christians, but also in order to attract children of non-Christians with the hope of gaining them and their parents. Initially these schools were at the elementary and secondary levels. However, Alexander Duff (1806—78), during his period of service in Calcutta (1830—48), started a program of higher education that was widely imitated. He set out to create a Christian intellectual elite among the Indians, to convert and educate promising young men of the higher castes in every aspect of western science and culture. These individuals hopefully would be interested and able to influence others for Christ. Although the experiment was an educational success, the graduates lacked evangelistic zeal.

The earliest missionaries, often with little or no medical training, dispensed some medicines and administered simple treatments and remedies as the occasion required. A physician-missionary accompanied Carey to India, and others followed, During the 19th century Christian missionaries were the only source of western medicine in many parts of the non-western world. The missionary motive was very prominent in much of this early medical work. Missionary physicians healed in order to provide opportunity and support for a Christian witness. As the century wore on, the medical work was conducted increasingly as an end in itself, and its explicitly evangelistic aspects receded.

Women missionaries increased tremendously in number and importance during this period. There were missionaries' wives from the very beginning; however, they were not necessarily directly involved in outreach ministry. The absence of women missionaries was a great handicap in many areas, because social custom prohibited male missionaries from having personal contact with women. At mid-19th century both

Protestants and Catholics began to send out single female missionaries. They were very effective in ministering to native women and in gaining their children. By the end of the century female missionaries outnumbered males. They proved to be as capable as they were committed. They displayed great physical and emotional strength as they met the challenges of the foreign fields.

Virtually all Protestant work in this century utilized the mission station approach. Through the means described briefly above, converts were made one by one and drawn into the Christian community. That community consisted primarily of western missionaries and their families. Because converts were often ostracized by their families and friends for becoming Christians, they were provided with food and shelter at the mission, and trained and employed in some capacity in the mission school, hospital, or printing operation. The mission station became a refuge and total support system for converts. The station also isolated them from friends and family in the non-Christian society around them. Not only religiously but culturally, converts and their children became westerners. They were totally dependent upon and dominated by western missionaries. Although this was intended originally as a temporary and transitional measure, it became permanent. Even after native converts were educated and placed in positions of ministry leadership, they were psychologically and economically subordinate to the missionaries, who were reluctant to release control. In general, mission stations converted comparatively few from the outside; most growth was by natural increase. The churches that were the center of these stations did not become self-governing, self-supporting, and self-propagating.

There were some notable exceptions. In several instances entire tribes and peoples moved rapidly into the Christian faith and fold. The Karens of Burma, a rather backward tribe, were gathered in by whole families and villages through one of their own number, Kyo Tha Byu. After being converted from a life of crime and violence, he accompanied an American missionary, George Dana Boardman (1801—31), who served for a few years among these people. Despite the death of both the American and the Karen missionary, and even despite recurring persecution by the government, Christianity survived and flourished among the Karens. By 1914 there were 47,530 Christians, 192 ordained and 541 unordained preachers, and 883 teachers. They trained their own leaders. Their work was virtually self-supporting financially. They were active in winning others. Somewhat similar was the process by which the Churas of Pakistan were Christianized.

The Bataks of Sumatra turned toward Christianity in great numbers after the conversion of their chiefs in 1866. The Rhenish missionaries who served them wisely determined to keep the church among them Batak, rather than European, in character. Native clergy were trained and ordained and their culture was kept intact. By 1911 there were 103,525 Batak Christians. In a number of the Pacific Islands—Tahiti and the Fiji Islands, for example—whole peoples followed their chiefs into Christianity. In Samoa, New Guinea, and many small islands around Tahiti, significant Christian outreach was performed by native teachers and catechists.

A new era of missionary methodology was ushered in by James Hudson Taylor (1832—1905). During a disappointing experience as a missionary to China under the auspices of the Chinese Evangelization Society, he determined that the most serious hindrances to the work were control by an outside agency, failure of missionaries to identify with the people they were trying to reach, and confining the work to a few coastal stations, thus neglecting the interior. He returned to China in 1865 determined to correct these mistakes. He founded what became the largest mission in the world—the China Inland Mission. Although financial support came from abroad, direction of the mission was centered in China in the person of Taylor himself. Workers were accepted from various denominations and of limited education, as long as they demonstrated commitment to mission and to a simple evangelical doctrinal statement. Workers were expected to identify with the Chinese people by means of dress and in other ways. The emphasis of the mission was on widespread evangelism, especially in the unreached interior of China. Pastoral work and education were kept subordinate to outreach. The approach was controversial but also attractive and effective. By 1882 all provinces had been reached and missionaries were established in most. By 1895, 641 missionaries drawn from many lands were in the service of the China Inland Mission.

Paternalism, the domination of new Christians and churches by western missionaries, was a problem that received very little attention during the 19th century and is far from solved late in the 20th. Christianity has spread most rapidly and developed most vigorously where new Christians have assumed responsibility for the church's care and outreach. Several cases of this in the 19th century were cited above and others in earlier chapters. When Christianity is being introduced in an area and new churches are being planted, those who are first to be gained need to have the opportunity and the authority to carry out their mission.

Some western missionaries sensed this and tried to implement it.

John Livingston Nevius (1829—93) had such a vision and initiated a great work in Korea based upon it. Something of this spirit was incorporated in the Batak Church. John Williams (1796—1839), known as "the Apostle of Polynesia," operated on this principle with great success.

However, most Christian missions throughout this period—both Protestant and Catholic—were dominated by western missionaries. Those whom they converted, educated, and in many cases salaried, could not easily challenge their authority or seize the initiative for evangelization. Many missionaries lacked confidence in the national Christians' ability to lead and extend the church. As a matter of fact, because they were kept in a dependent relationship, many national Christians were unready and unwilling for these tasks. Attitudes of white and western superiority were prominent. Furthermore, as noted above, the mission station approach so cut off Christians from the rest of society that it would have been very difficult for them to reach out effectively, regardless of their attitudes or those of the western missionaries.

The Protestant world missionary movement attained something of a climax in Edinburgh, Scotland at the first World Missionary Conference (1910). It was attended by delegates of evangelical Protestant missionary societies working throughout the world. (Roman Catholics and Eastern Orthodox did not participate.) A measure of the paternalism discussed above is the fact that only 18 delegates out of the 1,200 in attendance were from the younger churches. The rest were western missionaries. Under the leadership of John Raleigh Mott (1865—1955), an American layman who had been active in various youth movements, the conference reviewed the progress of the past century and possibilities for the future. "The evangelization of the world in this generation," a slogan developed by Mott on an earlier occasion, was prominent at Edinburgh. Christianity had been planted virtually everywhere. Opposition to the faith seemed to be crumbling in many places. Medical progress had reduced the terrible toll disease had taken on western missionaries in earlier decades. Mastery of many new languages and Bible translation work had opened communication to multitudes of people who were previously unreachable. Support for missions in terms of money and manpower was strong. Younger churches were beginning to produce their own leadership. No people had been found who could not understand the Gospel, although some were more ready for it than others.

Turning to the future, Mott suggested that during the next 30 years western missionary forces could expect to increase threefold, and the Christian population worldwide would at least double. Two world wars and the forces of secularization interfered with that timetable. However, it was surprisingly realistic, as the next chapter will indicate.

If this were a history of missions, considerable space would be devoted also to Roman Catholic and Eastern Orthodox missions. Although it was shaken and demoralized at the beginning of this period, the Roman church, as has been noted, experienced significant internal renewal and revived devotion to the worldwide mission of the church. Missionary societies involved lay people in the cause of world evangelization. Monastic orders new and old maintained existing mission fields and entered new ones. There was much heroic and sacrificial service. Like the Protestants, Catholic missionaries were essentially paternalistic, although serious attempts were made to transcend this. However, for the most part evangelistic goals, strategies, methods, and motives of Catholic missions during this century were essentially in continuity with those of the previous era. Eastern Orthodoxy, especially the Russian church, engaged in limited but significant efforts. Missions were established in the far eastern part of that great nation and also in Alaska and Japan. However, nothing in the approach of Orthodox missionaries was so distinctive or successful as to require comment here.

*   *   *

The 19th century has been designated as "The Great Century" by Kenneth Scott Latourette in his monumental study of Christianity and its expansion. This is probably an understatement. From the perspective of evangelism it was truly an incredible century. During this period Christians were making Christians of others in more parts of the world and in greater numbers than at any previous period. Not only were multitudes of new converts being gained from traditionally non-Christian peoples, but many who had been de-Christianized were being regained. During this incredible century, while the world population increased 230 percent, the Christian population increased 352 percent to 699.2 million people.

The picture is by no means entirely favorable. Much of the evangelization was superficial. Among non-western peoples Christian missionaries were usually paternalistic and insensitive to the cultural heritages of those whom they reached. Although the laity were beginning to be mobilized and were increasingly active in sharing their faith, Christian outreach was still largely being done by professionals. Evangelism was at times combined with oppressive institutions such as slavery and colonialism. Inadequate theology and excessive emotion were common.

Some appear to have used evangelism as an instrument of personal aggrandizement and gain.

Nevertheless, a review of the contents of this long chapter reveals far more that is positive—astonishing dedication, sacrificial service, diverse and visionary evangelism, and a global harvest of great magnitude. Christian observers, confident of the power of the Spirit in the Word, will recognize these developments, for the most part, as His blessing upon efforts to carry out the Great Commission.

A powerful surge of renewal and growth is frequently followed by relaxation and decline. However, as will be seen in the next chapter, the opposite occurred. As the 20th century progressed, except in some parts of the western world, Christians evangelized more vigorously, widely, and successfully even than in the incredible 19th.

VI/Meeting the Modern World
(1914 to the Present)

Christians approached the evangelistic challenges and opportunities of the modern world with great imagination and energy, which resulted in a multitude of innovative methods. They theorized and theologized about the evangelistic mission of the church as never before. As contemporary Christians evaluated traditional approaches they made some radical revisions.

Evangelism became increasingly sophisticated as modern research methods and technology were geared to the task. As the century progressed, pragmatic and result-oriented philosophies became prominent. The goal of evangelism, many insisted, was not only to sow the seed, but to harvest the crop, not only to proclaim the Word but to produce tangible response. A series of major conferences on evangelism, some national and others international in scope, both reflected and fostered evangelistic awareness. Deep differences of opinion developed and controversies erupted over the theory and practice of evangelism. It is an era characterized by ferment.

In many respects circumstances in the 20th century were unfavorable for evangelism. Two world wars and dozens or more limited conflicts were exceedingly disruptive, destructive, and distracting. Waves of global economic recession and depression eroded financial support for evangelism. The collapse of western colonial empires complicated and in some cases terminated evangelistic efforts in non-western countries. The rise of governments hostile to Christianity inhibited evangelism in many areas that once were strongholds of the faith. No less than 42 percent of the Christians of the world must practice and share their faith hindered by political restriction and repression. While some ancient religions are declining, others, such as Islam, are experiencing resurgence, and new religions are gaining many adherents from Christian backgrounds. The non-religious or atheistic segment of the human race has grown 1,000 percent in this century. In Europe and North America the percentage of active Christians has declined significantly under the impact of secularizing forces. Undoubtedly, these ominous developments have stimulated some of the creative and aggressive evangelistic efforts mentioned above.

Other efforts were evoked by new evangelistic opportunities presented by the modern world. Radio and television provided access to millions who could be reached in no other way. Improved linguistic skills and tools greatly facilitated translation and literacy work. Leaders of many emerging nations were educated in mission schools. As a result, they either identify with or have been significantly influenced by Christianity and, in some cases, are supportive of Christian ministry. Although western colonialism collapsed, western culture continues to spread, including some elements that may prepare people for the Gospel. Furthermore, the growing interaction between Christian and non-Christian people throughout the world opens many doors for evangelism. Christian tourists, students, and business people at times give a personal witness in places where public Christian work is prohibited. Conversely, their counterparts from these anti-Christian environments may learn to know Christ through contacts with Christians abroad. In some cases the withdrawal or expulsion of western missionaries has spurred national Christians to assume responsibility and the initiative for the spread of the faith. New possibilities, sometimes growing out of problems and setbacks, have incited new and fruitful evangelistic responses.

A great explosion of evangelism ideas and enterprises followed World War II (1939—45). Massive European immigrations, which had been the source of much evangelism opportunity during the 19th century, nearly dried up already before World War I (1914—19). Revivalism, too, appeared to be largely spent by this time. Until the late 1930s controversy between theological liberals and conservatives consumed the energies of many Protestants that otherwise might have been devoted to outreach. Missions themselves became controversial. In some cases missionaries substituted social ministry for Gospel proclamation and practiced cooperation rather than competition with non-Christian religions. Despite these delimiting factors, some evangelistic experimentation was initated before 1945, as will be seen, and much conventional work was continued. However, it was not until after World War II that the most important developments took place.

How may we assess the progress of Christianity during the modern era? The statistics are revealing. Numerically, Christianity more than doubled from 699.2 million in 1914 to 1,433 million in 1980, an increase of 205 percent. Yet, the proportion of Christians in the world declined slightly, since the world population increased by 208 percent during this same period. Great losses have been sustained in the communist world as a result of repression and persecution. For example, in the Soviet Union in 1900, 83.6 percent of the population nominally was Christian, while in 1980 this had dropped to 36.1 percent. In Europe and North America during the 1980s defections from Christianity are exceeding conversions by 1,820,500 persons per year. In the third world, however, conversions exceed defections by 2,272,814 per year. Natural increase (number of births over deaths) accounts for a far greater portion of the numerical growth worldwide.

In this ninth decade of the 20th century Christianity is most vigorous and expansive in Africa and Asia, where it is relatively new and greatly outnumbered. Especially encouraging is the fact that outreach in these areas is being carried out increasingly by national Christians. Nor are western Christians leaving secularism unchallenged. Virtually everywhere diverse and determined efforts are being made to re-Christianize the lapsed and the indifferent multitudes.

Perhaps the most significant statistic about Christian outreach in the 20th century is the growing portion of the world's population that has been "evangelized." This term applies to those who have been made aware of the Gospel through Christian literature and broadcasting in their language and/or witnessing Christians in their midst. In 1900 Christians constituted 34.4 percent of the world's population, and their outreach extended beyond this to include 51.3 percent of the world's population. In 1980 the Christian portion of the global population diminished to 32.8 percent, but the evangelized portion of the population increased to 68.4 percent. This means that the average Christian in 1980 was reaching twice as many people with the Gospel as his counterpart in 1900. Christian influence has magnified even while the percentage of Christians has declined.

As this study moves into the present, problems of dealing adequately with the subject multiply. The immensity and complexity of the world Christian movement are overwhelming. The quantity of data available is vast. Selection and condensation are done at the risk of distortion. In the following discussion the material is arranged under three broad topics: (1) methodologies; (2) theories and theologies; and (3) Pentecostalism's exceptional evangelistic record. Hopefully, this approach will convey at least some sense of how Christians in this modern era have tried and are trying to make Christians of others.[1]

Methodologies[2]

As was mentioned above, evangelism methodologies and techniques have proliferated in the 20th century. Christians concerned about outreach have developed a large variety of approaches, some very creative and attractive, for bringing Christ to the attention of others and for drawing them toward the fellowship of His church. Interest in and involvement with methodology is not necessarily based on the assumption that conversion is a human work. Many who view conversion as the work of the Holy Spirit believe that He operates through means—the Word and human agents, such as preachers, witnesses, or evangelists. Through a variety of methods Christians try to stimulate awareness of and interest in the Gospel. Or they endeavor to establish relationships and environments conducive to the effective communication of the Gospel, or attempt to identify those who do not yet believe in Christ but may respond, if made aware of Him. Evangelism methods are not, in most cases, intended to manipulate either people or the Spirit but rather to establish contact between the Spirit and people, creating opportunities and making arrangements for the Spirit to bring Jesus Christ to those who need Him.

A vital ingredient of virtually all effective evangelism methods is committed and loving Christians. Few are converted apart from contact with such Christians. Throughout history, including the present, the conviction, compassion, and concern of Christian people lived out in daily life and their sincere testimony have been major factors in drawing people to Christ. The warmth of Christian fellowship, the joy of Christian worship, and the meaningfulness of Christian Bible study have exerted magnetic attraction. The best methods are those that maximize interaction between Christians and non-Christians.

The importance of methodologies should not be exaggerated. Although people are won for Christ by deliberate, carefully-planned evangelism efforts, the number is not large. Studies show that in the United States at least 75-80 percent of those who join churches do so because of the informal invitation or witness of people close to them, such as relatives and friends. Only 10 or 15 percent join as a result of applied evangelism methodologies. This does not necessarily mean that evangelism methods are ineffective. It may simply mean that they are not being utilized very extensively. The single largest source of new Christians is the birthrate. During 1981, 39.1 million children were born to Christians throughout the world, and 15.8 million Christians died. This resulted in an increase in the Christian population of 23.3 million by births alone. On the other hand, the net gain worldwide from evangelistic efforts (number of conversions minus defections) was only 200,000. In other words, it would appear that outreach accounts for less than one percent of the Christian increase. In reality, however, the actual number of conversions is far greater—10 to 20 times greater, at least. The problem is that the high dropout rate mentioned above offsets most of these gains.

Denominational involvement in evangelism is a key factor in 20th-century evangelism. Prior to this, Protestant evangelism was done primarily by voluntary societies. It was the concern of special interest groups both denominational and interdenominational in character. However, during the course of the present era, especially since World War II, virtually all Protestant church bodies in the western world have accepted evangelism as part of their responsibility. In order to exercise this responsibility many have added staff persons designated for service in this area. Working at both the national and regional levels, these evangelism specialists have cultivated awareness of evangelism opportunities and obligations, developed programs, and conducted training activities. Their basic role has been to motivate local congregations for evangelism and provide them with resources.

An extremely important contemporary evangelism method is the planting of new churches. This is not an innovation of this era. It was a widely used method already in the previous century. In fact, throughout Christian history the founding of a worshiping-serving Christian community in a non-Christian, unchurched, or under-churched environment has been an effective way of making new Christians as well as of activating marginal Christians. Throughout much of the world many new congregations are started with money and staff provided by denominations, although significant numbers are also established as "daughters" of existing congregations.

In some third world countries a special kind of church planting has become the preferred method of outreach. In a community where Christian work is being initiated, instead of converting individuals, missionary-evangelists attempt to gather in whole families, clans, villages, and tribes, or, in urban settings, a significant social or cultural unit. Individuals who respond to the personal witness or public proclamation of the evangelist are requested to introduce the evangelist to his or her people—especially the leaders (parents, chiefs, teachers, etc.)— and help persuade them to consider the Gospel. The objective is to bring people into Christianity by groups, in which the new Christians can support each other. Individual conversions, in many cultures, separate people from their social groups. This makes it difficult to sustain the converts spiritually, and virtually impossible for them to evangelize others. As soon as a viable group has been converted, the congregation is formed and leadership is transferred to those chosen by the group from their own midst. The missionary-evangelist and sponsoring agency provide in-service training for these new pastors. They and their congregations are commissioned to reach out to those around them and even to plant new churches in adjacent communities. In one part of northern Honduras over a 15-year period (1965—80), 80 congregations with a total of more than 3,000 baptized members were founded by one mission society that employed this approach.[3]

Systematic community visitation was developed and extensively used during the period under consideration in this chapter. Revivalists of the previous era had employed similar methods on a limited basis in order to build audiences for their meetings. However, in the 20th century this approach was utilized in a very thorough and systematic way by congregations and groups of congregations as part of their own outreach. Ordinarily there are two stages to the process. First, a door-to-door religious survey is made of an entire community, or part of one, in which unchurched persons are identified. This is followed up by trained callers who present a Gospel witness and an invitation to participate in the worship and Bible study of a local congregation. In some cases, the visitation is carried out by one congregation, in other cases by a group of cooperating congregations.

One of the early proponents of this method was Elmer T. Clark, who in 1914 described it in *The New Evangelism*. Later it was replicated by many others with numerous variations. Initially, advocates presented community visitation as a superior alternative to revivals. Ultimately, it became a standard element in the outreach program of many congregations carried out either periodically or on a continuous basis. The advantage of community visitation is that it involves thorough penetration of the community, contacting many who would never attend an evangelistic service or meeting. It is a personal rather than a general approach, lending itself to a witness designed to meet the needs of a specific individual. The limitation of this method is that those conducting the survey and doing the follow-up are often only minimally competent.[4]

Crusade evangelism is the contemporary counterpart of revivalism. Between the world wars, although revival meetings were conducted throughout much of Europe and North America, they did not attract the attention or make the impact that they had in the previous era. Many believed that revivals were relics of a bygone age and had no relevance to the modern world. However, in 1949 Billy Graham (1918—   ) launched an evangelistic career essentially revivalistic in character. Subsequently he has conducted hundreds of crusades in major cities throughout the world and attained international prominence as an evangelist. In addition to his crusade work he speaks frequently on radio and television and has published many books and articles with evangelistic themes.

Graham's support staff of organizers and musicians far exceeds those of Moody, for example, both in number and sophistication. He conducts his crusades only upon invitation of a large, interdenominational group of sponsors in the inviting community. He accepts no remuneration from crusade offerings, but is supported financially by the Billy Graham Evangelistic Association and royalties from his many publications. Preparation for his crusades begins two years in advance, as his staff members guide local crusade leaders in building an elaborate organization to stimulate interest in and awareness of the crusade, enlist prayer and financial support, arrange for mass choirs, train counselors, and promote attendance. A culmination of each meeting is the point at which participants are invited to come forward to express their "decision for Christ"—either conversion or reaffirmation of faith. In major crusades over a period of weeks, tens of thousands make such decisions. Those who do are directed to the counselors who are on hand for this ministry. In addition, their names are forwarded to local cooperating congregations of their denominational preference for follow-up. At the end of 1976, after 29 years of crusade evangelism, Graham had preached face to face to more than 50 million people resulting in 1.5 million decisions.

Graham is the most celebrated of many crusade evangelists. He has a number of assistants who conduct his style of crusade in smaller cities. Many others throughout the world are engaged in similar work. A crusade can be nationwide, city or area wide, or confined to the neighborhood of a specific congregation. It is an organized attempt to communicate Christ to large numbers of people in public gatherings so that they accept pardon and eternal life through His atoning sacrifice and, ultimately, become worshiping, witnessing, serving members of local churches. The vast majority of those who attend, crusades are committed and practicing Christians for whom it is an experience of spiritual uplift. However, some unchurched people and marginal Christians are also attracted by curiosity, by the reputation of the celebrity-evangelist, by the personal invitation of Christian participants, or by the opportunity to consider Christ in an anonymous context. Of those who attend, some are always moved to decision.

Critics of crusade evangelism observe that few active disciples emerge from the large numbers of those who register decisions. Very little growth, if any, can be measured in cooperating churches following a crusade. Studies of people who recently joined churches reveal that two percent or less cite participation in a crusade as a determining factor. Apparently crusades are far more effective in generating enthusiasm among Christians than in converting non-Christians.

Others criticize most crusade evangelists for ignoring social issues. In reply it must be said that Graham crusades in the south were among the first large racially integrated gatherings in that part of the United States. Still others take exception to the inclusive nature of local support groups, which frequently involve theologically liberal churches as well as evangelical churches. However, crusade evangelists do not apologize for this, but instead welcome the opportunity to join with Christians of various positions for the task of proclaiming the Gospel. Lutherans take issue with the "decision theology" of all crusade evangelists, which assumes that the unforgiven sinner can make a commitment to Christ out of his own resources. Some Lutherans also object to doing evangelism without reference to the sacraments, which they recognize as essential forms of the Gospel, as well as to the doctrinal compromise implicit in an interdenominational crusade. But despite its limitations, crusade evangelism appears a method that will continue to be widely practiced and well supported.

Saturation evangelism is an extremely ambitious approach that attempts to compensate for the deficiencies of crusade evangelism. Designed by Kenneth Strachen of the Latin American Mission in the 1960s, this method has been used not only in Latin America, but also in Africa and in the United States. The objective is to mobilize all Christians of a nation for a diverse, sustained, year-long effort to reach all unbelievers in that nation with the Gospel. It involves enlisting and preparing pastors, establishing prayer and training groups for laity, stimulating evangelism awareness and activities in local congregations, utilizing the media, conducting local, regional and national crusades and distributing Scriptures widely. Saturation evangelism utilizes every available means to permeate a nation with the Gospel. The United States version was called "Key '73." In Latin America it has gone by the name of "Evangelism in Depth," and in Nigeria by "New Life for All." Wherever undertaken, saturation evangelism has succeeded in involving large numbers of Christians in various outreach activities and in proclaiming the Gospel widely. However, in most places little measurable church growth followed, despite the fact that numerous decisions were registered. The Nigerian campaign was an exception. There significant increases in membership and church attendance were recorded. To a greater degree than other saturation evangelism efforts, "New Life for All" stressed renewal of Christians and congregations in preparation for outreach. It also incorporated some unique elements that the Nigerians themselves suggested. The most important of these was the development of a specific evangelistic message to be shared in presentations to both individuals and groups.[5]

The evangelistic importance of Bible translation becomes more evident with each passing year, as investigators uncover growing numbers of languages of which they were previously unaware. At the beginning of this century portions of the Bible had been translated into 537 languages. In 1980 portions of the Bible were available in more than 1,900 languages, and translation work was in progress on an additional 986, of which 390 are first translations. Most of this work is carried out either by the United Bible Societies, a cooperative agency of various national Bible societies, or by the Wycliffe Bible Translators.

The latter organization, founded by William Cameron Townsend (1897—1982), is committed especially to doing work among people who have neither a written language nor, obviously, a translation of the Bible in their language. In 1982 translators and support staff of the Wycliffe organization numbered 4,255. Translators prepare for their work by attending the Summer Institute of Linguistics, where they are equipped with the latest and best linguistic tools. Armed with these, they move among a Bibleless people, reduce their language to writing, and teach some of them to read and write. Then, with the assistance of some of their most able students, they begin the task of putting at least parts of Scripture into that language. This then becomes the medium through which missionaries can evangelize these people and through which the new Christians can be nurtured and prepare themselves for outreach.

What remains to be done is, in one respect, even more awesome than what has been accomplished. In 1980 there were 7,010 known languages, which leaves 5,200 with no translation. The portion of the global population that used these unwritten languages in 1980 was 4.2 percent, or about 185 million. It is estimated that translations are needed in about 3,300 of these remaining languages. Some of the linguistic groups requiring this translation work number only in the thousands or even the hundreds. Regardless of the group's size, the same prodigious effort must be expended in order to reduce their language to writing and to translate Scripture into it.[6]

Fellowship evangelism includes a variety of methods that operate in the context of small groups, either those which already exist or some which are created specifically for outreach purposes. In the company of people with common interests, in a comfortable and informal atmosphere, the Gospel is shared, usually in the form of Bible study and testimony. Non-Christians or weak Christians are invited to participate along with active believers. For many this type of evangelism has been the doorway to new or revitalized faith. As our earlier chapters have made clear, fellowship evangelism is not a modern invention. It was utilized in one form or another in most other eras. The pietistic and Methodist cell groups are examples.

Perhaps the most frequently used setting for fellowship evangelism is the home. In some cases the group consists of family members and friends, both Christian and non-Christian, coming together for the purpose of Bible study, sharing, prayer, and socializing. For the Christians these gatherings may be a supplement to worship and Bible study in their congregations. For non-Christians and non-church members they may become a bridge leading to Christ and to a local congregation. The Christians in such a group may be of the same denomination, or it may be an interfaith gathering. Large numbers of such home Bible study groups have sprung up throughout the world, many with an evangelistic purpose or impact. Many non-Christian or unchurched people will more readily accept an invitation to someone's home than to that person's church.

Of the many that might be mentioned, perhaps the most spectacular example of home evangelism in recent years is what has happened in mainland China since 1949. It is estimated that there were 5.1 million Christians in all of China. Under the pressure of state and society that number was eroded until by 1975 there were only 3.7 million, despite great population growth. However, during these years of oppression and persecution and the loss of contact with outside Christians, Christianity survived primarily in house churches. These were completely indigenous groups that gathered secretly for prayer, Bible study, and fellowship. They lacked trained clergy and even complete Bibles in many cases, but they sustained and spread the faith. After 1976, when restrictions were lifted, all Chinese churches experienced growth. However, the house churches virtually exploded with growth. On the basis of investigations in the People's Republic of China during 1982 by staff and friends of the Chinese Church Research Center of Hong Kong, it is estimated that there are now from 25 to 50 million believers in the house churches alone. In the province of Henan, where missionaries made little progress in the pre-communist era, there are 1.5 million Christians in only 15 of 111 counties. In one county where there were 4,000 believers in 1948 there are now 150,000.[7]

Other types of fellowship evangelism are designed for special age and interest groups, such as children, youth, college students, business, and professional people. Some of these groups also meet in homes. In addition, armed forces personnel are being reached through Christian Service Men's Centers. The common elements of all fellowship evangelism are Christian study, witness, and prayer in an intimate, informal setting, where non-Christian and unchurched people can experience the love and faith of Christians as well as hear their saving message.

Personal evangelism methods are those that approach people as individuals. While crusade evangelism addresses large groups and fellowship evangelism deals with people in small groups, personal evangelism meets them one at a time. Most contemporary forms are derived directly or indirectly from the work of Reubun Archer Torrey (1856—1928). The most elaborate and perhaps most effective is Evangelism Explosion developed by James Kennedy, pastor of Coral Ridge Presbyterian Church, Fort Lauderdale, Florida. It involves a carefully structured, 16-week training course, which includes intensive study and memorization plus on-the-job training wherein the learner makes evangelism visits with a thoroughly trained and experienced caller. The program expands in a congregation by multiplication as those who are trained, in turn, recruit and train others. Evangelism Explosion is enhanced by a full line of printed materials for trainers, trainees, and those on whom they call. There is an international organization to coordinate and promote the program. Since its inception in 1967, Evangelism Explosion has trained tens of thousands who have made hundreds of thousands of personal evangelism calls.

An essential feature of this form of personal evangelism is a carefully structured presentation centered in the Gospel, which is introduced by two provocative diagnostic questions. After a period of getting acquainted, the caller asks the callee, "Are you at that point in your spiritual life where you know for certain that if you were to die today you would go to heaven?" If the answer reflects uncertainty, which is usually the case, the caller moves on to a still more pointed question: "If you were to die tonight and stand before God, and He were to say to you, 'Why should I let you into my heaven?' What would you say?" If the answer reveals uncertainty or dependence upon works, the caller makes a Gospel presentation developed around the topics of grace, man, God, Christ, and faith, followed by an invitation to join in a prayer of commitment. Careful follow-up procedures are also built into the method to assure the assimilation and nurture of the new Christian.[8]

More than a few trained in the Kennedy method have made adaptations that are more compatible with their theology, practice, and style of communication. An example from the Lutheran perspective, which provides an alternative to the Reformed decision theology of Evangelism Explosion as well as a greater emphasis on listening, is W. Leroy Biesenthal's *Dialog Evangelism*.[9]

Of the many other methods of personal witnessing widely used in the modern world, only one other will be mentioned. William R. Bright and his organization, Campus Crusade for Christ International, has developed a simple Gospel presentation entitled *The Four Spiritual Laws.* More than a billion of these presentations have been published in tract form since the late 1950s. Although designed initially for evangelism on college and high school campuses, this presentation has been used effectively for people of all ages and stations in life throughout the world. The presentation is adapted to the culture and special needs of each ethno-linguistic group for which it is translated. In addition to printing the tract, Campus Crusade provides training sessions for personal witnessing that utilize the tract as a tool. Several million college and high school students have been trained in this way during the past quarter century, along with large numbers of non-students.

The four "laws" expounded and applied in the presentation are: (1) God loves you and offers a wonderful plan for your life; (2) man is sinful and separated from God, therefore he cannot know and experience God's love and plan for his life; (3) Jesus Christ is God's only provision for man's sin, through whom you can know and experience God's love and plan for your life; (4) we must individually receive Jesus Christ as Savior and Lord, whereupon we can know and experience God's love and plan for our lives. Christians from other than Reformed decision-oriented theological positions have difficulty especially with the fourth "law." In addition, some feel the term "law" is not appropriate for statements, three of which are actually Gospel affirmations.

In 1976 and 1977 Campus Crusade headed up the largest and most penetrating evangelistic campaign in American history—"Here's Life America." It reached 10 million homes through 14,000 involved churches and 30,000 trained persons and resulted in at least 87,000 recorded decisions.

An evangelistic method unique to the 20th century is Christian radio and television broadcasting. In 1980 there were 1,450 Christian radio and television stations throughout the world with audiences of 292 million. In addition, there were 834 million who heard or viewed Christian broadcasts over secular stations. The total world audience to Christian broadcasts, excluding overlap in the two totals given above, is 990 million. (A listener is a person who on the average heard or viewed at least one program per month.) The magnitude of this form of outreach is mind-boggling. It is primarily by the extensive use of the broadcast media that Christian influence is expanding at a time when the Christian percentage of the world population is declining. In areas where there is religious freedom and ready access to churches, converts made through radio and television evangelism frequently gravitate toward those churches. However, significant numbers appear content to restrict their contacts with Christianity to the "electric church."

In environments hostile to Christianity or where Christianity is sparsely represented, numerous individual radio Christians and even radio churches have been discovered. In the latter, one convert gathers others around the evangelistic broadcast on a regular basis and may even found a permanent congregation. Where Christianity is repressed, individuals may not dare to involve others but, while outwardly adhering to the state-required religion or atheism, may secretly believe and practice Christianity sustained by Christian broadcasts.

A method often related to Christian broadcasts is Bible correspondence courses, which further inform and nurture those who have been brought to faith by the broadcast Word. In more than a few cases the correspondence courses have themselves been instruments of conversion. In 1975, for example, 500,000 Muslim youth from the Middle East were enrolled in Bible correspondence courses of whom more than 20,000 wrote in professing their Christian faith.

A pioneer in evangelistic broadcasting in the United States was Walter A. Maier (1893—1950), professor of Old Testament at Concordia Seminary, St. Louis, an institution of The Lutheran Church-Missouri Synod. In 1930, sponsored by the Lutheran Laymen's League, he launched a 36 program series called "The Lutheran Hour," over a national network. The depression temporarily interrupted it, but in 1935 it was resumed and steadily expanded until by the time of his death in 1950 it was heard by many millions over 1,200 stations throughout the world. The program continues to be one of the most widely broadcast radio programs in the world. The speaker since 1955 has been Oswald C. J. Hoffmann. Many other American denominations followed suit with radio programs featuring evangelistic speakers. A number of independent evangelists also established themselves as prominent radio personalities. Charles E. Fuller (1887—1968) of the "Old Fashioned Revival Hour" is one of the latter. In addition, innumerable evangelistic broadcasts were confined to local stations.

For decades most Christian broadcasts followed a format of preaching, praying, and musical selection. More recently a wide variety of programming possibilities have emerged including use of drama, panel discussions, popular Christian music interspersed with low-key witness comments, interviews with Christian celebrities, and even comedy that includes a Christian witness.

Evangelistic telecasts originated in the 1950s. "This is the Life," sponsored by The Lutheran Church-Missouri Synod, incorporated a clear Gospel presentation in a drama featuring a Christian family. Later the series diversified, developing Gospel themes in a variety of life-situation dramas.

Fulton J. Sheen (1895—1979), the noted Roman Catholic speaker and writer, was sufficiently attractive and popular to be commercially sponsored on prime-time television. His presentations were basically lectures on a variety of religious and ethical topics from a Roman Catholic point of view. Although not often explicitly evangelistic, Sheen was a marvelous communicator and an inspiring representative of his church, who undoubtedly evoked interest in and respect for Roman Catholicism.

The 1970s saw the rise of American evangelical and Pentecostal television figures. Pat Robertson, Jim Bakker, and Rex Humbard are among those who specialize in what might be designated as religious variety shows, which include Christian celebrities, inspiring testimonies, Gospel musicians, and, in some cases, healing. Others, such as Jerry Falwell and Robert Schuller, follow a pattern more like a conventional worship service, but with music, lighting, staging, and other features typical of secular television entertainment. Virtually all of the major Christian television programs claim to be doing evangelism, and they pursue financial support from Christian audiences in the name of evangelism. Research reveals, however, that few in their audiences are unchurched. An inordinate amount of their broadcast time is devoted to appeals for funds. The content of the programs is designed almost entirely to encourage those who already believe, rather than to win non-Christians. It is estimated that in 1980 $1.5 billion was raised from viewers to support these television programs.

Critics of Christian broadcasting point out that much of it, especially in the western world, is heard primarily by those who are already Christians, that it is, in fact, primarily nurture rather than outreach.

However, given the enormous numbers of listeners, even a very small percentage of non-Christian listeners represents a significant number, and, of that number, some do come to faith through what they hear. Virtually all Christian broadcasters can produce letters in which people profess to have been brought to Christ through their programs. The charge of triumphalism is often leveled against these telecasts, noting that they stress the joy and success that Christianity brings, while rarely mentioning the struggles, failures, and social responsibilities that are also part of it. As mentioned above, the most valuable Christian broadcasts are those that awaken and sustain faith in environments hostile to Christianity.

Theories and Theologies

Sometimes evangelistic theorizing and theologizing precede practice. Those about to undertake an outreach venture may consider how their beliefs and assumptions ought to affect their strategies and methodologies. In other cases, theory follows practice. Evangelistic experimentation and experience stimulate reflection, evaluation, and conjecture. Theological implications of existing methods and programs are explored and explained. As a result, adjustments may be made either in theological interpretation, practical application, or both. In addition, the psychological, sociological, cultural, political, and even the economic significance of evangelistic practice are investigated. On the basis of such investigation revisions may be proposed. More than one theological trend of the 20th century has challenged the conventional wisdom of evangelism and proposed radically different definitions and priorities. Spreading social, political, and cultural revolutions have forced evangelologists (specialists in the study and practice of evangelism) and missiologists to rethink their goals, means, and motives in relation to them. World conferences on evangelism have evoked controversy as well as cooperation and clarification. In no previous age have Christians been more analytical, critical, contentious, and speculative about the evangelistic mission of the church.

Developments in Mission Theology

One perspective from which to view theological and theoretical development in evangelism is that of mission theology. In the period under consideration the concept of the church's mission has been deliberated at length and revised significantly by major coalitions of the Christian world community. In previous centuries the church's mission was usually understood in terms of sending representatives of the church to convert non-Christians in distant places. More recently, especially since World War II, instead of understanding mission as only one part of the church's task involving only a few of its numbers, mission has been reinterpreted to include the church's total task in the world involving all of its members.

The question most central to the subject of this study is the relation between evangelism and the church's mission. Very closely tied to this is the question about the nature of evangelism itself. Three major Christian coalitions have addressed these questions in their own forums, and there has been some discussion among the coalitions. Distinct and conflicting emphases have surfaced as well as some points of convergence. The coalitions referred to here are the ecumenicals (or conciliars), the evangelicals, and the Roman Catholics.

The people and position referred to here as "ecumenical" are those who belong to or could identify with the World Council of Churches (WCC) and its Commission on World Mission and Evangelism. This tradition is in a direct line of descent from the World Missionary Conference held at Edinburgh in 1910. The International Missionary Conference (IMC), the continuing expression of Edinburgh, was originally committed to evangelism through united or cooperative efforts of the churches. Until the merger of the WCC and the IMC in 1961, the attention of both was focused on the church and its struggle to understand and carry out its mission. After the merger, however, the focus shifted to the world and the struggle for humanization over against injustice, racism, loneliness, and poverty. Through dialog and involvement with people of the world, Christians should seek to bring the fullness of God's salvation to bear upon personal, social and physical as well as spiritual dimensions of life.

In the push to identify humanization as the mission of the church, some ecumenical leaders not only ignored evangelism but actually rejected it as even part of that mission. The churches' task, they contended, was not to proclaim Christ so much as to convert the world, to bring non-Christians to faith and gather them into churches, but rather to transform the world, to combat all dehumanizing forces and institutions and create an environment in which all people can attain their fullest potential and enjoy the exercise of their human rights. In order to accomplish this, Christians are to unite with all in the world who share these goals, regardless of their religious commitment.

Reactions against what was regarded as overemphasis on sociopolitical involvement and virtual elimination of evangelism in the concept of mission began to appear among ecumenicals late in 1968 and have increased somewhat in strength and influence. Statements from some recent conferences (Upsala, 1968; Nairobi, 1975) have made some mention of evangelistic dimensions to the church's mission. However, the major thrust continues to be humanization, as events of the most recent meeting of the Commission on World Mission and Evangelism of the WCC (Melbourne, 1980) reveal. In summary, ecumenicals have radically revised their concept of mission from evangelization to humanization. Only recently are they beginning to reintroduce evangelism as part of that mission.

Evangelical mission theology has moved somewhat in the opposite direction. The people here designated as "evangelicals" are conservative Protestants of various kinds who are not related to the WCC. Their concept of mission, although it may also be enlarged to include all that the church is to do in the world, recognizes evangelism as the chief element of that mission. Evangelism itself is viewed primarily as the proclamation of Christ with the intent to convert and incorporate into churches those who respond.

In a series of world congresses (Berlin, 1966; Lausanne, 1974; and Pattaya, 1980), evangelicals increasingly acknowledged the necessity of including social involvement as part of the church's mission. However, in contrast with ecumenicals, evangelicals continue to give evangelism priority. Some evangelicals regard any inclusion of socio-political involvement as a false and dangerous compromise. Others are impatient for more bold and specific evangelical entry into the struggle for world improvement.

The 1960s also saw significant movement in Roman Catholic mission theology. Prior to Vatican Council II (1962—65) major mission statements of the papacy emphasized the conversion of non-Christians by the preaching of the Gospel and the planting of the church throughout the world. Vatican II stressed that the missionary task belongs to the laity as well as the clergy. The whole church is to proclaim and establish the kingdom of Christ among all people and in this way to become a sacrament of salvation for the world. In addition, the council encouraged openness to the world and to other religions, both Christian and non-Christian.

A council of Latin American bishops in 1968 at Medellin pressed for the church's involvement in the transformation of society in the direction of peace, justice, and material equity. Liberation theology emerged from Latin America in the 1960s. It made economic, social, and political liberation as much a part of salvation as release from sin and communion with God. At the Third Synod of Bishops in 1974 it was concluded that although the essential mission of the church is evangelization of the world, this is a complex, comprehensive process including the renewal of humanity through liberation movements as well as the communication of the Gospel and the incorporation of people into the church. The Apostolic Exhortation of Pope Paul III on *Evangelization in the Modern World*, which embodies these conclusions, is regarded by many as one of the most important evangelism statements of the modern era.

Still another development in Roman Catholic mission theology is the acknowledgment of "anonymous Christians." Based on the traditional Roman doctrine of prevenient grace, the anonymous Christian theory is that many people who neither know nor identify with Christ or His church are, nevertheless, responding to His gracious and transforming influence unawares. The church's mission to these people consists of making them aware of what they already are and have and of leading them more fully into it.

Like that of both the ecumenicals and evangelical Protestants, Roman Catholic mission theology has undergone pronounced change since the 1960s. A common element in all is growing commitment to socio-political involvement, with evangelicals giving it least emphasis, ecumenicals most, and Roman Catholics occupying a centrist position. Another common element is recognition of verbal proclamation of the Gospel and church planting as belonging to the mission of the church. In this case evangelicals give it the greatest emphasis, ecumenicals least, and Roman Catholics again occupy a middle position. Not only among but also within each group debate rages about what constitutes appropriate Christian social involvement as well as what the specific content of the proclaimed message should be. All parties sense and affirm the value of Christian unity in the mission of the church. Both the will of the church's Lord and the favorable impact of His Gospel upon the world appear to require manifestations of unity among His followers. However, there is much disagreement about the nature of that unity as well as the form that it should take.[10]

An additional issue calling for comment under the topic of mission theology is the exclusiveness of Jesus Christ. The questions are: Is He the only way to God and to eternal salvation? Is it necessary to have an explicit knowledge of and trust in His redemptive work in order to be saved? Is there a blessed life and world to come prepared only for those who belong to Him by faith? Is eternal judgment awaiting all who live and die apart from Him? Are His revelation and redemption communicated only through the Scriptural Gospel? Evangelicals, with few exceptions, answer these questions affirmatively. Some leading ecumenicals and Roman Catholic theologians answer them negatively or uncertainly. The cleavage is clear and wide and the debate vigorous. Evangelicals regard their position as the heart of the Christian message and mission. Their opponents consider it to be a time- and culture-bound concept in need of radical revision, if it is to be relevant in the modern era. It would be difficult to exaggerate the importance of this issue and the outcome of the debate. Both the content and the practice of evangelism are mutilated beyond recognition if the evangelical position is rejected.

Church Growth Movement

One of the most influential and controversial approaches to evangelism in this century is the Church Growth movement. Developed by Donald McGavran in the 1950s for application to the mission fields, Church Growth principles began to be applied to American churches two decades later by C. Peter Wagner and others. Since then, Church Growth principles have been elaborated and expounded in numerous books and periodicals. They have been communicated in hundreds of workshops throughout the world. Courses on various aspects of Church Growth theory and practice are offered by growing numbers of seminaries and colleges. Denominational evangelism leaders have become informed about Church Growth principles and have, in many cases, attempted to implement them in the congregations under their care. Despite the misgivings and criticisms of many, the momentum of Church Growth appears to be mounting and its impact deepening in this ninth decade of the 20th century. Only a few of its basic characteristics are singled out for discussion here.

One key characteristic is a very specific and traditional definition of evangelism and the insistence that evangelism so understood is the chief mission of the church. Evangelism, in Church Growth theory, is proclaiming Christ and persuading people to become His disciples and responsible members of His church. Any definition that identifies evangelism with Christian nurture or social ministry is rejected. Valuable and necessary as Christian schools, hospitals, and agricultural services are, they are not evangelism but rather preparation for—or fruits of—evangelism.

Closely related to the definition of evangelism is the Church Growth emphasis on the multiplication of churches. While conversion is a personal event, it also has broad social implications. In many cultures people come to faith in Christ most readily along with members of their families, friends, or fellow workers. Instead of focusing merely on the conversion of individuals, Church Growth advocates the gathering of entire groups to Christ and establishing churches in their midst under their own leadership. Churches thus planted are in an advantageous position to reach out to those in their immediate social context. The most effective way to make new Christians is to plant new churches, according to Church Growth.

The principle of the homogeneous unit is integral to the church planting emphasis as well as to church growth. Sociology, history, and common sense reveal that people are most likely to be influenced toward faith in Christ by others like themselves. Every society is a mosaic of subcultures—distinct racial, ethnic, linguistic, vocational, or economic groups with barriers of various heights and strengths dividing them. Christian work takes root and grows best within these social units. Ideally, there should be a separate evangelistic effort to each major subculture, gathering those who respond to the Gospel into new churches and equipping them to penetrate evangelistically into the rest of that subculture. To insist from the outset that people cross cultural lines in order to come to Christ is to place unnecessary barriers in their way. Initially, the evangelist operates within existing social structures and parameters, confident that as new Christians grow spiritually, they will discover from Scripture that we are all one in Christ Jesus. In this way barriers between Christians will eventually disintegrate and the unity of the church will be manifest.

Church Growth theorists advocate directing evangelistic efforts to those segments of a population judged to be most receptive. "Win the winnable while they are winnable," is the recurring theme. This is based on the assumption that receptivity can be determined with reasonable probability by means of properly interpreted sociological, anthropological, and historical data. At a time of major social change or relocation, for example, or when their existing sources of identity or security are failing, people tend to be more open to the Gospel. Whatever the reasons, whether predictable or not, when people of a specific group begin to turn to Christ in significant numbers, evangelistic resources should be concentrated upon them in order to take fullest advantage of their receptivity. Send most of your harvesters where the crop is ripest. A Christian witness should be maintained wherever possible, however, even among those who are indifferent or resistant. Beginnings must be made among all kinds of people, not only to gain the few who will respond readily, but in order to prepare for a major ingathering, if and when widespread receptivity occurs. The point is not that evangelism is to be done only among those who are most receptive, but rather that it is only reasonable and responsible to invest a larger portion of human and financial resources where the prospects of conversions and church growth are most promising.

Pragmatism is a prominent feature of the Church Growth approach. It calls for careful analysis of progress and problems in the life and work of churches. Methods and programs that do not work, that do not bring people to Christ and into the church, should be replaced by those which have demonstrated their effectiveness elsewhere or which have been designed specifically for this situation. It is valid and necessary to evaluate evangelistic effectiveness statistically. The importance of statistics is based on the fact that the numbers stand for people. God wants to gain people and people can be counted. Numerical growth is not the only kind of growth. Internal growth, the building up of the believers by Christian nurture, is also vital. But unless new Christians are also being added to the church and becoming functional members, God's plan and purpose are being frustrated and the church's commission to disciple the nations is not being carried out.

Church Growth is not an evangelism method or program. Rather, it is an interdisciplinary study of the human factors that appear to aid or impede the growth of churches. Church Growth practitioners believe that the Holy Spirit is the only one who can make the church grow by creating faith and incorporating believers into the worshiping-serving community of Christians. However, since He works through human beings and human relationships, there is material that can be analyzed by the relevant social sciences and utilized in the practice of evangelism. Scripture and Christian theology give us insight into the Spirit and how He works to reach people. The social sciences tell us a great deal about how people interact and react. Imaginative use of insights and information from both sources are essential for making good decisions about how, when, and where to do evangelism. Although not a program or a method, Church Growth is a broad frame of reference and a useful analytical tool for those who make basic decisions about the church's outreach ministry.

Criticisms of the Church Growth movement are legion. Some, from the ecumenical camp, challenge its underlying assumptions. The purpose of the church, they argue, is not its own enlargement by making converts, but rather the humanization of the world by socio-political involvement. Others, from the evangelical camp, question the emphasis on harvesting. The results, they say, are entirely up to the Holy Spirit. Our responsibility is merely to be faithful in sowing the seed. Regardless of the size of the harvest in any given place, we should keep on sowing with equal diligence. European critics tend to write off Church Growth as the product of a typically American success-oriented mentality, which confuses more with better and relies on technique rather than theological substance. The principle of the homogeneous unit is widely challenged as a denial of the unity of the church and a compromise with non-Christian moral values. Some are offended by the attempt to integrate theology and the social sciences in the service of evangelism. Others condemn the attempt to identify and reach those who are most receptive as psychological and sociological manipulation. Still others claim that to concentrate on the receptive is to neglect those whose need is greatest—the indifferent and obdurate.

No attempt will be made here to present the replies of Church Growth advocates. Suffice it to say that they attempt to consider the criticisms carefully and to respond cogently and respectfully. A tremendous amount of discussion and experimentation has been sparked by this fresh and stimulating movement.[11]

Cultural Awareness

Especially since the 1970s theoreticians of evangelism have become conscious of the part that culture plays in the process of making Christians. In previous eras missionaries and evangelists were frequently insensitive to or even destructive of the cultures of those whom they won, although significant exceptions to this have been noted in earlier chapters. However, as missionaries and evangelists became more knowledgeable in anthropology, sociology, and communications, they realized the importance of understanding and identifying with the cultures of those whom they were evangelizing. Not only in the case of foreign missions but also in outreach to some within one's own nation and community formidable cultural barriers must be crossed. Growing awareness of these cultural factors and strategies for responding to them constructively is a prominent feature of much contemporary evangelism.

A concept which has emerged from this rising cultural awareness is "contextualization." This term designates doing evangelism in a manner that is truly culturally relevant. It involves thoroughly understanding the world view of those to be evangelized, making every effort to empathize and identify with them and to acknowledge whatever is good and valid in their world view. It requires addressing their questions, concerns, and felt needs. In addition, it involves expressing the Gospel message in terms meaningful to people of that culture and world view in the context of a personal life-style appropriate to the content of the message. Contextualization calls for adaptation of the Christian message to a new culture without compromising or distorting the content.

It also seeks responses to the Gospel which are a natural part of that culture—in music, art, dance, and literary style integral to that culture. It specifically forbids the unnecessary intrusion of foreign cultural elements or the displacement of anything in the native culture that is not contrary to Christian teaching and values. Contextualization assumes that a culture will be changed once it is penetrated by Christianity. However, this should be a positive and conservative process of change, enhancing the best elements of that culture, adapting others, and eliminating only those that are intrinsically evil. While Christianity affirms much in all cultures, it also stands in judgment over all, calling into question whatever violates the will of God and the welfare of people.

The danger accompanying all attempts at contextualization is syncretism—adjusting not only the form but also the substance of Christianity in order to accommodate a culture. This would include the incorporation of views and values of non-Christian religions into Christian teaching, worship, and ethics, thus creating a synthesis of Christianity and other religions. Not only in third world countries where the presence and influence of pagan religions is still strong, but also in the western world the corruption of Christianity by culture is frequently evident. However, this danger does not justify the refusal to contextualize, for the only alternative to contextualization would appear to be irrelevance.

A significant contribution to culturally aware evangelism is Ralph D. Winter's typology. He identifies three kinds of evangelism. E-1 is sharing the Gospel with a person from your own cultural unit, someone of your own ethno-linguistic group. E-2 is evangelizing a neighboring people or group with a related language. E-3 is reaching out to someone of a totally different language and culture. Eventually Winter added a fourth type, E-0, evangelizing those already within your community of faith, although perhaps in need of renewal. E-1 is within one's own culture, E-2 within a cognate culture, and E-3 requires crossing into a strange culture. Evangelism is more challenging and requires greater sensitivity and skill as one moves from E-0 to E-3. Winter's contention is that the world's greatest need at this point in history is a massive increase in E-2 and E-3 evangelism.[12]

Ministry of the Laity

A theological insight rediscovered and increasingly used in contemporary churches is the "priesthood of all believers." This is the teaching that not only the clergy but all Christians are called into the service of Christ and His church. The laity are to regard themselves not merely as clients of the clergy, but also as fellow-workers, not only as consumers of salvation, but also as dispensers. This doctrine is presented clearly in Scripture and affirmed by virtually all Christian denominations, Catholic as well as Protestant. However, in practice, from the very early Christian centuries until the present, it has been largely neglected.

Renewed interest in this doctrine and its implications for evangelism began to surface in the late 1940s. It has increased steadily into the 1980s with no sign of diminishing. Essentially it is the conviction that the privilege and responsibility of bringing other people to Christ belongs not only to the professional leadership of the church but to all the members. Among the authors who reintroduced this theme and created a new wave of interest in it are Elton Trueblood, James Smart, and Hendrick Kraemer.

Initially this doctrine was interpreted to mean that every Christian is to be an evangelist, one who boldly and convincingly confronts those whom he meets with the Good News of Jesus and the invitation to believe. More recently it has been proposed that the gift of being an evangelist in this sense is given to only some Christians, perhaps 10 to 15 percent. Nevertheless, all Christians are called and equipped to be witnesses, to share simply and personally what Jesus and His redemptive work mean to them. In addition to verbal witness, every Christian has the opportunity to point others to God and His love by a life which reflects His presence and influence. The point is that lay people have a right and a duty to be involved in the very heart of the church's spiritual ministry. Their efforts and energies should not be directed only to the budget or the physical plant of the church. They should be enlisted and equipped for this high privilege of sharing Jesus Christ with one another and with the world.

The affirmation and clarification of the ministry of the laity has important implications for the understanding of pastoral ministry and other church leadership roles. Guidance for this is provided by Ephesians 4:11-16, which describes church leaders as Christ's gifts to His people, whose function is to equip them for their ministry. In other words, church leaders are not to do the ministry for the people, but rather to assist and prepare them to exercise that ministry themselves. The heart of that ministry is speaking the truth of the Gospel in love. When spoken to those who already belong to Christ, that Gospel aids their maturation. When spoken to non-Christians, it effects conversion. Leaders of the church, then, are there to help the members become more proficient and effective in communicating the Gospel. Rather than demeaning the role of church leaders, the ministry of the laity elevates their importance.

me.

The recovery of the ministry of the laity has been an important factor in the renewal of many churches. In preparing to share Christ with others, many Christians have grown spiritually themselves. The experience of bringing others to Christ has brought many witnessing Christians a joy and sense of purpose in life they had never previously known. Stagnating and declining congregations have become vibrant and appealing, as members informally and in programmed efforts have become serious about their outreach ministry. The ministry of the laity refers to nurture as well as outreach, and these aspects, too, have been productive of renewal. However, because of the nature of this study, the discussion above is restricted to aspects of outreach.[13]

Pentecostalism's Exceptional Evangelistic Record

Perhaps few Christians of the modern era can match the evangelistic activity and effectiveness of the Pentecostals. What began as a search for an outpouring of the Spirit by students of Bethel Bible College of Topeka, Kansas in 1900 soon developed into an international renewal movement. By 1911 independent Pentecostal congregations were springing up in numerous cities, and not long after that pentecostal denominations began to form. Despite ridicule and criticism from other Christians and a considerable amount of internal dissension, Pentecostalism has grown rapidly and steadily in many parts of the world. By 1980 it was the largest Protestant denominational family in the world with 51.2 million members, more than half of whom are in the third world. This puts them nine million ahead of the next largest group, the Lutherans, who numbered 42.2 million in that year. Only if those united churches consisting of both Lutherans and Reformed are included does the total number of Lutherans (63.3 million) exceed that of the Pentecostals. The impact of Pentecostalism is considerably greater even than the 51.2 million figure would indicate. An additional 11 million in other denominations have been significantly affected by pentecostal teaching, practice, and experience. This phenomenon is known as "Neo-Pentecostalism" or the "Charismatic Movement." It is fitting to conclude this chapter on evangelism in the modern world with a brief review of the record of these, the most evangelistic of all contemporary Christians.

The purpose here is not to summarize the history of world Pentecostalism nor to examine and evaluate its theology. Rather, it is to explore those factors that appear to account for its phenomenal ability to win and to keep new members. Studies of Pentecostalism suggest that not its distinctive doctrines or practices, but rather its evangelistic attitudes and style are the key to its remarkable growth. What follows is based particularly on the experience of Latin American Pentecostalism. However, it is characteristic of much Pentecostalism elsewhere in the world.

Evangelism is their top priority. Lay people as well as leaders, new as well as experienced members, are led to realize that bringing others to Christ is their highest privilege and duty. Not all exercise that privilege or are successful at winning others, but those who do are the object of special recognition. Their church activities reflect this central and pervasive purpose. In some places worship services are preceded by street meetings in which the members fan out into the city, gathering crowds by singing and preaching, and then endeavor to bring their audiences along to their church service. In other places they rely heavily on radio ministries to invite people to Christ and their churches. Some conduct crusades. Most churches stress aggressive personal evangelism on the part of individual members. Many churches seek and seize opportunities to establish daughter churches. Teams of lay evangelists explore adjacent neighborhoods and communites, witnessing to individuals and establishing small Bible study groups. These frequently grow into preaching stations and, ultimately, into congregations. They do not seem to be locked into any specific evangelism method, but innovate and adapt as the situation requires. For the most part this commitment to evangelism appears to be regarded as a joyful privilege rather than as a grim duty.

They have evangelistic pastors. In many parts of the world one does not become a Pentecostal pastor by attending a seminary. Instead, one attains that office by demonstrating his ability to win people to Christ, incorporate them into a church, minister to their needs, and maintain their respect and cooperation. In other words, they come up through the ranks as Bible class leaders, lay evangelists, and apprentices to become experienced pastors. In many cases they obtain a charge of their own by founding a new church. If a church of an aspiring pastor grows and thrives to the point that it needs his services full-time and can pay for them, he becomes a full-time pastor. Otherwise, he remains a part-time or spare-time pastor. Even many pastors of very large Latin American pentecostal churches have entered their position in this manner. Although they may be short on education, they are long on practical experience. Furthermore, they possess evangelistic zeal and aptitude that they can transmit to their members. By personal study and various kinds of in-service education, many eventually acquire some theological competence.

Another factor undoubtedly accounting for much of the success of Pentecostal evangelism is that it is almost immediately and completely

indigenous. When new work begins, those who are converted and gathered into little churches are very soon given responsibility for the care,
control, and expansion of their churches. Because they have ownership
and freedom they are able to express the Gospel and their response to it
in forms familiar and meaningful in that culture. Furthermore, this
sense of ownership engenders pride in their church and a desire to
involve others in its worship. The leadership of the church is from their
own midst or, at least, of their own kind, and is accountable to them.
They are not inhibited about seizing the initiative because of depen-
dency upon outsiders. For better or for worse, the church is theirs, or,
rather, they are the church in that place. Guided by the Spirit and the
Word and their own common sense, they usually keep it going and
growing.

A serious danger that accompanies rapid and extensive indigenization is deviation from authentic Christianity. Pentecostalism has suffered
much of this throughout the third world, especially in Africa. New and
inexperienced Christians trying to adapt the faith to their culture may
and do frequently distort it, mix it with elements of paganism, or are
misled by strong and ambitious leaders into cultism. Many of the African independent churches, which have been multiplying so profusely
since mid-century, have fallen prey to these evils. Having separated from
Pentecostal mission churches, they have gone their own ways. Although
many appear to have retained their Christian character and seek recognition from and fellowship with more conventional churches, others
have clearly drifted into syncretism or even back into paganism.

Much of Pentecostalism's magnetism is unquestionably related to its
emphasis on tangible experiences of divine power. This is also one of its
most controversial features—condemned and feared by many other
Christians, not without reason. Many Pentecostal authorities themselves
readily admit that this aspect of their practice has been susceptible to
serious abuse—fanaticism, extremism, even exploitation. However, all
Pentecostals insist on the validity and necessity of experienced divine
power. This is, indeed, part of the essence of Pentecostalism. Holy Spirit
baptism, healing and other miracles, tongues, prophecy, exorcism,
visions, and revelations—to Pentecostals these are important evidences of
the presence and power of God in their lives. They are tangible signs
that the victory accomplished by Jesus Christ is a reality in their lives
and world. They are a source of confidence, encouragement, and liberation from the corrupt and enslaving forces of this world. Some Pentecostals virtually make these evidences of divine power the basis of their
faith, a substitute for the Gospel of Christ's atoning work. Others see

them as a result of faith in the Gospel and signs pointing to Jesus and the validity of His saving work.

The purpose here is not to evaluate theologically Pentecostal teaching and practice concerning these "sign gifts," as they are called. The author has some serious reservations about them, as the note on this section indicates. However, even a critic of Pentecostalism can appreciate the interest and excitement evoked in Christians and non-Christians alike by experiences perceived as evidences of God's power at work in their midst. People are often attracted initially to a Pentecostal gathering because they have heard reports of miraculous healings, deliverance from addiction, the mending of broken lives—all by direct applications and experiences of divine power. Many who come out of curiosity, as well as those who come out of a deep sense of personal need, discover to their satisfaction that the reports are true and that the power is real. Pentecostals are convinced that God is present and powerfully active in their midst and through their ministries. They seriously and regularly expect Him to do strange and wonderful things in their behalf. Countless testimonies appear to confirm that this does, in fact, happen. Attracted by the wonder of God's power, many who come to Pentecostalism also discover the greater wonder of His love in Christ. Pentecostals do not regard expressions of God's power as substitutes for or distractions from His saving love in Christ, but rather as further evidences of it. The Savior from sin is also the Savior from sickness and other human trouble, according to these evangelistic Christians.

Pentecostalism is a varied and complicated movement. The comments above are by no means an adequate characterization of it or even of those aspects that account for its evangelistic effectiveness. The above paragraphs merely highlight a few of the most obvious and important factors that help to explain why it grows and spreads so rapidly. Pentecostal observers will be dissatisfied with this discussion. They are not content to explain their growth in terms of evangelistic attitudes and ministry styles. Their explanation would rather emphasize the direction and participation of the Holy Spirit in their work as the single most critical factor.[14]

*　　　*　　　*

It is, of course, too soon to write a definitive analysis of 20th century evangelism. We are too close to the events even to tell whether or not we are drawing to the end of another historical era. There are indications that evangelism awareness and interest are rising even in church bodies which have ignored it for decades. Truly spectacular evangelistic activities are underway in Africa, Asia, and some parts of South America. Some of the most able, committed, and visionary Christian people in the world are devoting their lives to stimulating and improving the church's evangelistic performance. Lay people in growing numbers are discovering their evangelism opportunities and obligations. The profusion of evangelistic methods and theories, of which this chapter offers only a small sample, are promising resources for the future, as well as an impressive tribute to the evangelistic devotion of Christians in the recent past.

Notes

Chapter I

1. Kenneth Scott Latourette, *The First Five Centuries, A History of the Expansion of Christianity* (New York and London: Harper & Brothers Publishers, 1937), I:369. Recent estimates of the population of the Roman Empire are 33 million in A.D. 27, increasing to 46 million in A.D. 200, and falling to 23 million by A.D. 550. See *World Christian Encyclopedia: A Comparative Study of Churches and Religions in the Modern World, A.D. 1900—2000*, ed. David B. Barrett (Nairobi, Oxford, New York: Oxford University Press, 1982), p. 796. An interesting and informative study addressing some of the topics discussed in this chapter from a history of religions perspective is A. D. Nock, *Conversion: The Old and New in Religion from Alexander the Great to Augustine of Hippo* (London: Oxford University Press, 1933). A significant work covering this era published after this chapter was prepared is E. Glenn Hinson, *The Evangelization of the Roman Empire: Identity and Adaptability* (Macon, Georgia: Mercer University Press, 1981).
2. W. H. C. Frend, *Martyrdom and Persecution in the Early Church: A Study of Conflict from the Maccabees to Donatus* (Garden City, New York: Anchor Books, Doubleday & Company, Inc., 1967), pp. 119, 125, 187, 195, 201, 241, 252.
3. Ibid., Chapter Seven.
4. Latourette, p. 133.
5. *2 Clement 13.*
6. Origen, *Against Celsus*, Books III and XII.
7. Adolph Harnack, *The Mission and Expansion of Christianity in the First Three Centuries*, trans. and ed. James Moffatt (New York: Harper & Brothers, 1961), pp. 9—10.
8. Michael Green, *Evangelism in the Early Church* (Grand Rapids: William B. Eerdmans Publishing Company, 1970), pp. 172—75. This interesting section is based in part upon Origen, *Against Celsus*, 3:55.
9. A revealing collection of excerpts from the early fathers demonstrating this attitude is Eberhard Arnold, *The Early Christians: A Sourcebook on the Witness of the Early Church*, trans. Douglas A. Moody (Grand Rapids: Baker Book House, 1970, 1972). See the section, "Christian Self-Portraits," especially selections 9 (Justin, *Dialogue with Trypho*, 110:3-4), 11 (Justin, *First Apology*, 16), 16 (Ibid., 14), 23 (*Letter to Diognetus*, 10), 40 (Theophilus of Antioch, *To Autolycus*, Book III:15), and 43 (Minucius Felix, *Octavius*, 37:1-5).
10. *Dialogue with Trypho*, Chapter 142, in *The Ante-Nicene Fathers*, ed. Alexander Roberts and James Donaldson (Grand Rapids: William B. Eerdmans Publishing Company, 1951—56), I:270. The Eerdmans set is the American reprint of the Edinburgh edition.
11. More detailed analysis of motivation for early Christian evangelism generally congruent with this section is Green, Chapter 9. See also William C. Weinrich, "Evangelism in the Early Church," *Concordia Theological Quarterly*, XLV (January—April 1981), 62—65.

12. See Green, especially Chapters 3, 4, and 5.
13. Numerous typical examples may be found in Henry Bettenson, trans. and ed., *The Early Christian Fathers: A Selection from the Writings of the Fathers from St. Clement of Rome to St. Athanasius* (London: Oxford University Press, 1956).
14. See the excellent modern translation and introduction in *Early Christian Fathers*, trans. and ed. Cyril C. Richardson (New York: Macmillan Publishing Company, Inc., 1978), pp. 205—24.
15. For example, *The Martyrdom of Potamiaena and Basilides* and *The Acts of Phileas.*
16. S. D. F. Salmond, "Introductory Note to Gregory Thaumaturgus," *The Ante-Nicene Fathers*, VI, p. 6.
17. Green, p. 219.
18. Eusebius, *The History of the Church from Christ to Constantine*, trans. and intro. J. A. Williamson (Baltimore: Penguin Books, 1965), Book 6, 3.

Chapter II

1. Kenneth Scott Latourette, *The Thousand Years of Uncertainty A.D. 500—A.D. 1500, A History of the Expansion of Christianity* (New York and London: Harper & Brothers Publishers, 1938), II:3.
2. James Thayer Addison, *The Medieval Missionary: A Study of the Conversion of Northern Europe A.D. 500—1300* (Philadelphia: Porcupine Press, 1936), pp. 71—74.
3. *Western Asceticism*, vol. VII in The Library of Christian Classics. Selected translations with intro. and notes by Owen Chadwick (Philadelphia: The Westminster Press, 1958), pp. 13—17.
4. Gen. 1-2; Deut. 6:10-11; 10:8-12; note especially 14:22-26; Pss. 104; 127; 128; Is. 65:17-25; Mal. 3:10-12; Matt. 5:25-33; 14:13-21; 15:32-38; Luke 7:18-23, 33-34; John 2:1-11; Rom. 8:18-23; 14; 1 Cor. 9:3-14; 10:23-31; Col. 2:20-23.
5. A classical example of the elitist appeal of asceticism from the fourth century is Basil of Caesarea, *An Introduction to the Ascetical Life*, trans. Sister M. Monica Wagner, C.S.C., in *St. Basil's Ascetical Works, The Fathers of the Church* (Washington: The Catholic University of America Press, 1962), 9:9-13.
6. See Phillip Rousseau, *Ascetics, Authority, and the Church in the Age of Jerome and Cassian* (Oxford: Oxford University Press, 1978).
7. Herbert B. Workman, *The Evolution of the Monastic Ideal from the Earliest Times Down to the Coming of the Friars: A Second Chapter in the History of Christian Renunciation* (Boston: Beacon Press, 1913), Chapter 1.
8. Helpful discussions of the definition of mysticism and of the basic literature are found in *Late Medieval Mysticism*, vol. XXIII in The Library of Christian Classics, ed. Ray C. Petry (Philadelphia: The Westminster Press, 1957), pp. 17—22; William Fairweather, *Among the Mystics* (Edinburgh: T. and T. Clark, 1936), pp. 1—4; and Dom. M. Cuthbert Butler, *Western Mysticism: The Teaching of Augustine, Gregory and Bernard on Contemplation and the Contemplative Life, Second Edition with Afterthoughts* (New York: Harper & Row, 1922, 1966), pp. xiii—lxii, 3—15.
9. Adolph Koeberle, *The Quest for Holiness: A Biblical, Historical and Systematic Investigation*, trans. John C. Mattes (Minneapolis: Augsburg Publishing House, 1936), Chapters I and II.
10. Hilda Graef, *The Story of Mysticism* (London: Peter Davies, 1966), pp. 135, 138, 158, 167, 171, 195.
11. *Late Medieval Mysticism*, pp. 293, 297, 298.
12. Anna Groh Seesholtz, *Friends of God: Practical Mystics of the Fourteenth Century* (New York: Columbia University Press, 1936), especially Chapter V.
13. Ibid., Chapter IX.
14. J. N. Hillgarth, ed., *The Conversion of Western Europe 350-750* (Englewood Cliffs, New Jersey: Prentice Hall, Inc., 1969), p. 2. See also Carl A. Volz, *The Church of the Middle Ages: Growth and Change from 600 to 1400* (St. Louis: Concordia Publishing

House, 1970), Chapter 1.
15. Latourette, pp. 227—28.
16. Addison, pp. 50—52.
17. William R. Cannon, *History of Christianity in the Middle Ages: From the Fall of Rome to the Fall of Constantinople* (New York and Nashville: Abingdon Press, 1960), pp. 88—90. See also Addison, pp. 47—50.
18. Latourette, pp. 179—93; Addison, pp. 52—56.
19. Addison, pp. 56—71; Latourette, pp. 186—91.
20. Cannon, pp. 16—21; Latourette, pp. 22—36; Hillgrath, pp. 71—82.
21. Latourette, pp. 107—10; Addison, p. 31.
22. Latourette, pp. 161, 236—39.
23. Stephen Neill, *Christian Missions*, The Pelican History of the Church, vol. VI, gen. ed. Owen Chadwick (Middlesex, England: Penguin Books, 1964), pp. 53—55.
24. Neill, pp. 58—59.
25. Addison, pp. 22—28.
26. Latourette, pp. 115—22.
27. Addison, pp. 30—31.
28. Ibid., pp. 28—39.
29. Latourette, Chapters III and IV.
30. Ibid., pp. 212—21, 261—62.
31. Addison, pp. 3—8, 75—89; Latourette, pp. 36—45.
32. Bede, *The Ecclesiastical History of the English Nation*, intro. by Vida D. Scudder (New York: E. P. Dutton and Company, 1910), Book I:XXIII-XXXIV, pp. 32—58; Neill, pp. 66—69; Latourette, pp. 63—72; Addison, pp. 81—82.
33. Willibald, *The Life of St. Boniface*, in *The Anglo-Saxon Missionaries in Germany: Being the Lives of S. S. Willibrord, Boniface, Sturm, Leoba and Leubin, Together with the Hoedeporicon of St. Willibald and a Selection from the Correspondence of St. Boniface*, trans. and ed. C. H. Talbot (London and New York: Sheed and Ward, 1954), pp. 25—62; Richard E. Sullivan, "The Carolingian Missionary and the Pagan," *Speculum*, XXVIII, 4 (October 1953), 705—40; Addison, pp. 9—15, 42—47, 89—98, 119—29; Latourette, pp. 85—102.
34. Latourette, pp. 327—34; Neill, pp. 116—37.
35. Alexander Schmemann, *The Historical Road of Eastern Orthodoxy*, trans. Lydia W. Kesich (Chicago: Henry Regnery Company, 1963), pp. 302—08; Latourette, pp. 258—59.
36. Hillgrath, pp. 12, 13, 59, 123.
37. Bede, Book II, 10, pp. 83—84.
38. *The Life of Otto, Apostle of Pomerania*, by Ebo and Herbordus, trans. C. H. Robinson (London, 1920), quoted in Addison, p. 154.

Chapter III

1. Steven Ozment, *The Age of Reform 1250-1550: An Intellectual and Religious History of Late Medieval and Reformation Europe* (New Haven and London: Yale University Press, 1980), pp. 22—42; and, by the same author, *The Reformation in the Cities: The Appeal of Protestantism to Sixteenth-Century Germany and Switzerland* (New Haven and London: Yale University Press, 1975), pp. 22—32.
2. Roland H. Bainton, *Here I Stand: A Life of Martin Luther* (New York and Nashville: Abingdon Press, 1950), Chapters I—III.
3. E. G. Schwiebert, *Luther and His Times: The Reformation from a New Perspective* (St. Louis: Concordia Publishing House, 1950), pp. 293—302, 603—12.
4. Ibid., pp. 631—36.
5. Hans J. Hillerbrand, *The World of the Reformation* (New York: Charles Scribner's Sons, 1973), pp. 40—41.
6. Elizabeth L. Eisenstein, *The Printing Press as an Agent of Change: Communications and Cultural Transformations in Early-Modern Europe* (Cambridge: Cambridge Uni-

versity Press, 1979), I:303—10; Hillerbrand, pp. 31—37.

7. Owen Chadwick, *The Reformation*, The Pelican History of the Church, vol. III, gen. ed. Owen Chadwick (Middlesex, England: Penguin Books, 1964), Chapter 1.

8. A. G. Dickens, *Reformation and Society in Sixteenth Century Europe* (New York: Harcourt, Brace & World, Inc., 1966), pp. 74—77; Harold J. Grimm, *The Reformation Era 1500—1650* (New York: The Macmillan Company, 1954), pp. 155—58; Bainton, Chapter 18.

9. Ozment, *Reformation in the Cities*, pp. 121—31; Dickens, pp. 77—79.

10. Grimm, pp. 233—53.

11. Hillerbrand, Chapters 5 and 8. For a more complete discussion see John T. McNeill, *The History and Character of Calvinism* (New York: Oxford University Press, 1954).

12. The discussion in this section largely follows A. G. Dickens, *The English Reformation* (New York: Schocken Books, 1964), especially Chapters 2, 4, 13, 14. See also Chadwick, Chapters 4 and 6.

13. Franklin H. Littel, *The Origins of Sectarian Protestantism: A Study of the Anabaptist View of the Church* (New York: The Macmillan Company, 1952), pp. 109—13.

14. Claus-Peter Clasen, *Anabaptism: A Social History, 1525-618, Switzerland, Austria, Moravia, South and Central Germany* (Ithaca and London: Cornell University Press, 1972), Chapter 2.

15. Chadwick, Chapters 8 and 9, offers a helpful interpretive discussion of the developments summarized in this section.

16. This section is based on Kenneth Scott Latourette, *Three Centuries of Advance, A.D. 1500—A.D. 1800, A History of the Expansion of Christianity* (New York and London: Harper & Brothers Publishers, 1939), III: Chapters III, IV, VIII, XII, XIII, XIV. See also Stephen Neill, *Christian Missions*, The Pelican History of the Church, vol. VI, gen. ed. Owen Chadwick (Middlesex, England: Penguin Books, 1964), Chapters 6 and 7.

Chapter IV

1. These dates mark the ascendancy of Pietism to its greatest prominence and influence. Although it subsided after this period, Pietism has survived in various forms into the present and has periodically experienced resurgence.

2. Chief resources consulted up to this point are Dale Brown, *Understanding Pietism* (Grand Rapids: William B. Eerdmans Publishing Company, 1978); Theodore G. Tappert, "Orthodoxism, Pietism, and Rationalism," *The Lutheran Heritage, Christian Social Responsibility*, a symposium in three volumes, ed. Harold C. Letts (Philadelphia: Muhlenberg Press, 1957), II: Chapter 2; Philip Jacob Spener, *Pia Desideria*, trans. and ed. with intro. by Theodore G. Tappert (Philadelphia: Fortress Press, 1964); Philip Jacob Spener, *On the Spiritual Priesthood of Believers*, trans. in Henry Eyster Jacobs, *A Summary of the Christian Faith* (Philadelphia: The United Lutheran Publication House, 1905); F. Ernest Stoeffler, *The Rise of Evangelical Pietism, Studies in the History of Religions* (Leiden: E. J. Brill, 1971), IX: Chapter IV.

3. F. Ernest Stoeffler, *German Pietism During the Eighteenth Century, Studies in the History of Religions* (Leiden: E. J. Brill, 1973), XXIV:Chapters I—III; Thomas Coates, "Were the Reformers Mission Minded?" *Concordia Theological Monthly*, XL (October 1969), 600—11.

4. Stoeffler, *German Pietism During the Eighteenth Century*, Chapter IV; Clifford W. Towlson, *Moravian and Methodist: Relationships and Influences in the Eighteenth Century* (London: The Epworth Press, 1957), Chapter II.

5. The term "Great Awakening" is used here in its broadest sense. It refers not only to the New England revivals beginning in 1734 and ending quite abruptly in 1742, but also to a series of revivals beginning in the middle colonies already in the mid 1720s and continuing especially in the southern colonies until the outbreak of the Revolution and beyond.

6. William G. McLoughlin, *Revivals, Awakenings, and Social Reform: An Essay on Religion and Social Change in America, 1607-1977* (Chicago and London: University of

Chicago Press, 1978), pp. 1—97.

7. Edwin Scott Gaustad, *The Great Awakening in New England* (New York: Harper & Brothers Publishers, 1957); Alan Heimart and Perry Miller, eds., *The Great Awakening: Documents Illustrating the Crisis and its Consequences* (Indianapolis and New York: The Bobbs-Merrill Company, 1967).

8. Sydney E. Ahlstrom, *A Religious History of the American People* (New Haven and London: Yale University Press, 1972), Chapters 15—20; Abdel Ross Wentz, *A Basic History of Lutheranism in America*, rev. ed. (Philadelphia: Fortress Press, 1964), Chapters VII—VIII; F. Ernest Stoeffler, ed., *Continental Pietism and Early American Christianity* (Grand Rapids: William B. Eerdmans Publishing Company, 1976).

9. Kenneth Scott Latourette, *Three Centuries of Advance: 1500 A.D.—1800, A History of the Expansion of Christianity* (New York and London: Harper & Brothers Publishers, 1939), III:216—224.

10. See Arnold A. Dallimore, *George Whitefield: The Life and Time of the Great Evangelist of the Eighteenth Century Revival*, volume I (London: The Banner of Truth Trust, 1970); Robert G. Tuttle, Jr., *John Wesley: His Life and Theology* (Grand Rapids: Zondervan Publishing House, 1978); Martin Schmidt, *John Wesley: A Theological Biography*, volume II, John Wesley's Life Mission, Part I, trans. Norman P. Goldhawk (New York and Nashville: Abingdon Press, 1966); Towlson, *op. cit.*

11. Stephen Neill, *Christian Missions*, The Pelican History of the Church, vol. VI, gen. ed. Owen Chadwick (Middlesex, England: Penguin Books, 1964), Chapter 6; Latourette, Chapters V, VIII, X, XI, XIV.

12. Neill, pp. 200—35.

Chapter V

1. Kenneth Scott Latourette, *The Great Century in Europe and the United States of America 1800—1914, A History of the Expansion of Christianity* (New York and London: Harper & Brothers Publishers, 1941), IV:Chapters I—III. Less sanguine in his assessment of this period is Joseph L. Altholtz, *The Churches of the Nineteenth Century* (Indianapolis and New York: The Bobbs-Merrill Company, Inc., 1967). See also James Hastings Nichols, *History of Christianity 1650-1950: Secularization of the West* (New York: The Ronald Press, 1956), Chapter 1.

2. Henri Daniel-Rops, *The Church in an Age of Revolution*, History of the Church of Christ, 2 volumes, trans. John Warrington (Garden City, New York: Image Books, Doubleday & Company, Inc., 1967), especially Chapters VI and VIII; also Kenneth Scott Latourette, *The Nineteenth Century in Europe: Background and the Roman Catholic Phase*, in *Christianity in a Revolutionary Age: A History of Christianity in the Nineteenth and Twentieth Centuries*, volume I (New York: Harper & Brothers Publishers, 1958).

3. Nichols, Chapter 8; Walter O. Forster, *Zion on the Mississippi: The Settlement of the Saxon Lutherans in Missouri 1839—1841* (St. Louis: Concordia Publishing House, 1953), pp. 10—14.

4. Alec R. Vidler, *The Church in an Age of Revolution, 1789 to the Present Day*, The Pelican History of the Church, vol. V., gen. ed. Owen Chadwick (Baltimore: Penguin Books, 1961), Chapter 2; Kenneth Scott Latourette, *The Nineteenth Century in Europe: The Protestant and Eastern Churches*, in *Christianity in a Revolutionary Age: A History of Christianity in the Nineteenth and Twentieth Centuries*, volume II (New York: Harper & Brothers Publishers, 1959), Chapter III.

5. Latourette, *The Nineteenth Century in Europe: The Protestant and Eastern Churches*, Chapter V. For the background and early experience of the Missouri Synod, see Forster, as well as Carl S. Mundinger, *Government in the Missouri Synod: The Genesis of Decentralized Government in the Missouri Synod* (St. Louis: Concordia Publishing House, 1947), and Carl S. Meyer, ed., *Moving Frontiers: Readings in the History of the Lutheran Church—Missouri Synod* (St. Louis: Concordia Publishing House, 1964), Chapters I—IV.

6. Vidler, Chapters 3, 4, 5, 12; Nichols, Chapters 14, 20; Latourette, *The Nineteenth Century in Europe: The Protestant and Eastern Churches*, Chs. XXVI—XXVIII, XXXII.

7. Edwin Scott Gaustad, *Historical Atlas of Religion in America* (New York and Evanston: Harper & Row, Publishers, 1962), pp. 29—36, 101—11.

8. Latourette, *The Great Century in Europe and the United States of America*, pp. 229—55; John Tracy Ellis, *American Catholicism* (Garden City, New York: Image Books, Doubleday & Company, Inc., 1956), Chapters II and III; Richard M. Linkh, *American Catholicism and European Immigrants (1900—1924)* (New York: Center for Migration Studies, 1975).

9. Jay P. Dolan, *Catholic Revivalism: The American Experience 1830—1900* (Notre Dame, Indiana, and London: University of Notre Dame Press, 1978).

10. Meyer, Chapters III, IV, and V; W. H. T. Dau, ed. *Ebenezer: Reviews the Work of the Missouri Synod during Three Quarters of a Century*, augmented ed. (St. Louis: Concordia Publishing House, 1922); Walter A. Baepler, *A Century of Grace: A History of the Missouri Synod 1847—1947* (St. Louis: Concordia Publishing House, 1947); F. Dean Lueking, *Mission in the Making: The Missionary Enterprise Among Missouri Synod Lutherans 1846—1963* (St. Louis: Concordia Publishing House, 1964), Chapters 1—3.

11. Sydney E. Ahlstrom, *A Religious History of the American People* (New Haven and London: Yale University Press, 1972), Chapter 26; William G. McLoughlin, *Revivals, Awakenings, and Reform: An Essay on Religion and Social Change in America, 1607—1977* (Chicago and London: The University of Chicago Press, 1978), pp. 98—122.

12. John B. Boles, *The Great Revival 1787-1805* (Lexington, Kentucky: The University of Kentucky Press, 1972); Charles A. Johnson, *The Frontier Camp Meeting: Religion's Harvest Time* (Dallas: Southern Methodist University Press, 1955); Ahlstrom, pp. 429—45; Gaustad, pp. 55—58, 74—81, 87—91.

13. Ahlstrom, Chapter 28.

14. George C. Bedell, Leo Sandon, Jr., and Charles T. Wellborn, *Religion in America*, second ed. (New York: Macmillan Publishing Company, Inc., 1982), Chapter 7; Ahlstrom, Chapter 42; Latourette, *The Great Century in Europe and the United States of America 1800 A.D.—1914*, Chapter IX.

15. Latourette, *The Great Century in Europe and the United States of America 1800 A.D.—1914*, Chapter VIII.

16. John Stanley Matteson, "Charles Grandison Finney and the Emerging Tradition of 'New Measure Revivalism,' " unpublished Ph.D. dissertation, University of North Carolina at Chapel Hill, 1970; Bernard A. Weisberger, *They Gathered at the River: The Story of the Great American Revivalists and Their Impact upon Religion in America* (Boston and Toronto: Little, Brown & Company, 1958), Chapters IV and V; McLoughlin, pp. 122—31; Bedell, Sandon, and Wellborn, pp. 166—71.

17. James F. Findlay, Jr., *Dwight L. Moody: American Evangelist 1837-1899* (Chicago and London: The University of Chicago Press, 1969); McLoughlin, pp. 141—45; Ahlstrom, pp. 740—46; Weisberger, Chapter VII.

18. Ahlstrom, Chapter VIII.

19. Material for this section is based primarily on Stephen Neill, *Christian Missions*, The Pelican History of the Church, vol. VI, gen. ed. Owen Chadwick (Middlesex, England: Penguin Books, 1964), Chapters 8—11; Latourette, *A History of the Expansion of Christianity*, volumes IV—VI (New York and London: Harper & Brothers Publishers, 1941, 1943, 1944); and Ralph D. Winter and Steven C. Hawthorne, eds., *Perspectives on the World Christian Movement: A Reader* (Pasadena, California: William Carey Library, 1981), Chapters 16—23.

Chapter VI

1. Statistics and some interpretation in these introductory comments and throughout this chapter are based on David Barrett, ed., *World Christian Encyclopedia, A Compara-*

tive Study of Churches and Religions in the Modern World A.D. 1900-2000 (Nairobi, Oxford, New York: Oxford University Press, 1982), especially pp. 1—20. An additional helpful resource is James A. Berquist, "Evangelism in Current Ferment and Discussion: A Bibliographical Survery," *Word and World: Theology for Christian Ministry*, I, 1 (Winter 1981), 59—70.

2. See J. D. Douglas, ed., *Let the Earth Hear His Voice: International Congress on World Evangelism, Lausanne, Switzerland, Official Reference Volume, Papers and Responses* (Minneapolis: World Wide Publications, 1975), especially "Contemporary Evangelism Practices," by George W. Peters, pp. 181—207.

3. Ralph D. Winter and Steven C. Hawthorne, eds., *Perspectives on the World Christian Movement: A Reader* (Pasadena, California: William Carey Library, 1981), readings 62—71 (especially 62, George Patterson, "The Spontaneous Multiplication of Churches," pp. 601—16).

4. Kenneth L. Chafin, "Evangelism Since World War I in the United States," in Paulus Scharpff, *History of Evangelism: Three Hundred Years of Evangelism in Germany, Great Britain and the United States of America*, trans. Helga Bender Henry (Grand Rapids: William B. Eerdmans Publishing Company, 1966), pp. 312—33.

5. George W. Peters, *Saturation Evangelism* (Grand Rapids: Zondervan Publishing House, 1970).

6. *World Christian Encyclopedia*, p. 13; William Cameron Townsend, "Tribes, Tongues and Translators," *Perspectives on the World Christian Movement*, pp. 250—52; Philip Yancey, "Cam Townsend's Mission: Let God Do the Talking." *Christianity Today*, XXVI, 11 (June 18, 1982), 14—18.

7. Jonathan Chao, "Churches in China: Flourishing from House to House," *Christianity Today*, XXVI, 11 (June 18, 1982), 24—26. The *World Christian Encyclopedia* in its discussion of China (pp. 230—34) gives no indication of this remarkable spurt of growth. The present author is not in a position to confirm or reject Chao's estimate, but even if his total figure is very high, it is evident that house churches have experienced spectacular growth in at least some parts of the People's Republic.

8. D. James Kennedy, *Evangelism Explosion*, rev. ed. (Wheaton, Illinois: Tyndale House Publishers, 1977).

9. Published by the Board for Evangelism, The Lutheran Church—Missouri Synod, St. Louis, Missouri, n.d.

10. Rodger C. Bassham, "Mission Theology: 1948-1975," *Occasional Bulletin*, IV, 2 (April 1980), 52—58; James A. Scherer, "Prospects and Problems in Global Evangelization," *Word and World: Theology for Christian Ministry*, pp. 9—19. For a review of contemporary Roman Catholic thought, see *Evangelization in the World Today*, ed. Norbert Greinacher and Alois Muller (New York: The Seabury Press, 1979). *The Conciliar-Evangelical Debate: The Crucial Documents*, ed. Donald McGavran (Pasadena, California: William Carey Library, 1977), displays the tension between ecumenicals and evangelicals, along with extensive evangelical commentary by the editor. An important historical study of the changes in mission theology from a conservative evangelical position is Arthur P. Johnston, *The Battle for World Evangelism* (Wheaton, Illinois: Tyndale House Publishers, 1978).

11. Donald A. McGavran, *Understanding Church Growth* (Grand Rapids: William B. Eerdmans Publishing Company, 1970); C. Peter Wagner, *Your Church Can Grow* (Glendale, California: Regal Books, 1971). A recent and representative critique is Ralph H. Elliot, *Church Growth that Counts* (Valley Forge, Pennsylvania: Judson Press, 1982).

12. *Perspectives on the World Christian Movement*, Part III: The Cultural Perspective, especially reading 41, David J. Hesselgrave, "World-View and Contextualization," pp. 398—410; *Let the Earth Hear His Voice*, Part VII, Theology of Evangelization Papers and Reports, sections S—Y, also Ralph D. Winter, "The Highest Priority: Cross-Cultural Evangelism,'" pp. 213—58; Leslie Newbigin, "Mission in the 1980s," *Occasional Bulletin*, IV, 4 (October 1980), 154—55.

13. See Oscar E. Feucht, *Everyone a Minister: A Guide to Churchmanship for Laity and Clergy* (St. Louis: Concordia Publishing House, 1974).
14. C. Peter Wagner, *Look Out! The Pentecostals Are Coming* (Carol Stream, Illinois: Creation House, 1973), is an analysis of Latin American Pentecostalism from a Church Growth perspective. Standard histories of the movement are W. J. Hollenweger, *The Pentecostals: The Charismatic Movement in the Churches*, trans. R. A. Wilson (Minneapolis: Augsburg Publishing House, 1972), and John Thomas Nichol, *Pentecostalism* (New York, Evanston, and London: Harper & Row, Publishers, 1966). An excellent critique of Pentecostalism is Frederick Dale Brunner, *A Theology of the Holy Spirit: The Pentecostal Experience and the New Testament Witness* (Grand Rapids: William B. Eerdmans Publishing Company, 1970).